MICHAEL MANDIAK
131 MEADOWBROOK DRIVE
LACKAWANNA NY 14218-2034

W9-AVB-521

THOSE MAGNIFICENT FLYING MACHINES

First solo: Avro 548, Brooklands,
August 1928

Sports flying:
D.R.R., Tipsy and Richard Muspratt,
Lympne, 1946

Supermarine test pilot: Sea Otter, 1942

THOSE MAGNIFICENT FLYING MACHINES

A Pilot's Autobiography

DON ROBERTSON

Supermarine test pilot: Spitfire Mk XXI and XII prototypes, 1942

Naval fighter pilot: Fulmar, 1940–42

Naval pilot: D.R.R. and Sea Gladiator, 1941

BLANDFORD PRESS
POOLE · DORSET

First published in the UK 1984 by Blandford Press,
Link House, West Street, Poole, Dorset, BH15 1LL

Copyright © 1984 Blandford Press Ltd

Distributed in the United States by
Sterling Publishing Co., Inc.,
2 Park Avenue, New York, NY 10016

British Library Cataloguing in Publication Data

Robertson, Donald R.
   Those magnificent flying machines.
   1. Robertson, Donald R.   2. Air pilots
   —England—Biography
   I. Title
   629.13′892′4   T.540.R/

ISBN 0 7137 1402 6

Typeset by Asco Trade Typesetting Ltd., Hong Kong
Printed in U.K.

Contents

Acknowledgements

I should like to thank all those friends who have helped me with this book, especially Richard Riding who lent me a large number of photographs, Jeffrey Quill for checking the Spitfire portion for accuracy, Simon Young for his advice on layout, Bee MacKinnon (P. V. MacKinnon) for help on technical details of many wartime aircraft, Buster Hallett (Captain Nigel Hallett RN DSC) for advice on Naval background, and Richard Muspratt (Squadron Leader) for reminiscences of test work together at Boscombe Down.

In Canada recently, after a period of 50 years, I met Stan McMillan, my Senior pilot, and Tim Sims, with whom I shared many experiences and was able to refresh my memories of flying in the North.

My thanks, too, to others who have helped by suggestions and advice, and particularly to my wife, without whose encouragement I would never have finished these memoirs.

DEDICATED TO MY WIFE ELLA

Foreword

Only 80 years after the Wright brothers made the first controlled, powered flight at Kitty Hawk, non-stop flights between London and California by aeroplanes carrying more than 300 passengers are a commonplace. Military aeroplanes fly regularly at twice the speed of sound and Concorde provides a daily and luxurious passenger service across the Atlantic at this speed.

The aeroplane has introduced a completely new dimension into transport and hence into modern life and international affairs. Journeys which once took weeks or months are now completed in a day or little more. People have become mobile to an extent undreamed of at the turn of this century and, amazingly, this has all been achieved in little more than the natural lifetime of a man.

Yet there were times when, to those involved in aviation, progress often seemed slow and laborious; every inch of the way seemed a struggle against all manner of problems and frustrations, technical, operational, financial, political and human. Particularly did this apply during the early part of Don Robertson's flying life.

He learned to fly privately in 1928 and then went to Canada where he found employment in a company operating aeroplanes into the far North. It was the aeroplane which opened up those vast inhospitable snow-bound regions, carrying supplies and mail to areas hitherto accessible only by sledge and dog team. Northern Canada was, of all places, a 'natural' for aviation, and this account of early pioneering commercial flights makes a fascinating and unusual tale.

Technically and operationally, World War II provided a massive stimulus to aviation. The acute urgency and background of prolonged crisis meant that problems had to be solved more or less regardless of expense and human effort. The second part of the book describes Robertson's activities as a Fleet Air Arm pilot at sea, and then as a test pilot, first at Vickers-Supermarine, where he was a most valued colleague of mine, and later at the Aeroplane & Armament Experimental Establishment at Boscombe Down. Here he was engaged in the testing of new and high performance fighter aircraft for the Royal Air Force and Royal Navy as well as armament testing. This culminated in the testing of some of the very early jet fighters, so his extensive flying experience took him from the 'stick and string' days of the twenties to the dawn of the jet age.

Don Robertson was particularly well fitted both by training and temperament to be a test pilot and to be closely involved in the often abstruse and frustrating problems which beset the development of new aircraft. He was a practical engineer who loved engines and all things mechanical and who instinctively knew that before you can presume to test something you must first thoroughly understand what it has to do, how it does it, and why.

The book will awake many memories with those who flew, as Don Robertson did, during the great formative years of aviation and it cannot fail to be of great interest to those who study the amazing history of the aeroplane.

Jeffrey K. Quill, OBE, AFC, FRAeS

First solo: Avro 548, Brooklands, August 1928

Sports flying: D.R.R., Tipsy and Richard Muspratt, Lympne, 1946

Supermarine test pilot: Sea Otter, 1942

"TiPSY"

G-EBVE

PART I

BUSH FLYING

Supermarine test pilot:
Spitfire Mk XXI and XII prototypes, 1942

Naval fighter pilot: Fulmar, 1940 – 42

Naval pilot:
D.R.R. and Sea Gladiator, 1941

1 *A Camel on the beach*

To a small boy the coast at Hunstanton in Norfolk seems to stretch to the ends of the earth. In a way you might say that for me it was true, for there in the summer of 1917 I saw my first aeroplane. I was playing on the broad flat beach when I heard an odd noise approaching from the sea, the sound of an engine spluttering and eventually stopping altogether. To my intense excitement, a few moments later an aeroplane appeared through the broken cloud and glided towards us with its propeller stopped and no sound but the wind whistling in the flying-wires; it made a perfect landing, splashing through the pools of water left by the receding tide and coming to a stop only a hundred yards away. I dropped everything and ran over to see, arriving first but hesitant about going too close.

It was a single-seater biplane, very rakish and with a big propeller. The pilot jumped down from the cockpit and walked round to the front to look at his engine, which was dripping oil. His face and goggles were spotted with black oil; his leather helmet had a patch of fur on the forehead and rolls of leather protecting each ear; a long double-breasted brown leather overcoat came down below his knees and gave him an air of authority. In my eyes he was a real hero to be able to fly such a thrilling machine.

By now a small crowd had gathered and with a man on either side lifting the tail we all pushed on the wings, wheeling the aeroplane backwards up the beach above the high-tide mark to the safety of dry sand. I remember the power-ful-looking engine, partly enclosed under a shining metal cowling; above all I remember the thrill of actually touching it and noticing how lightly built were the silver wings. Before the local policeman arrived to guard it, I peered into the cockpit with its small hinged windscreen and saw the two cocking handles and oiled breaches of guns gleaming in the sun. There was a strange smell about: not only the dope but something sickly and sweet, and I plucked up courage to ask the pilot what it was. That was how I first learned that the rotary engine of the Sopwith Camel used castor oil. Next morning when I hurried down to the beach before breakfast, it had already gone, but mixed with the disappointment was the beginning of my determination to be a pilot.

That summer in Hunstanton we were staying in a large Victorian boarding-house and several times in the middle of the night Zeppelins came over: we were dragged out of bed to crouch in a cupboard under the stairs. There was plenty of warning as they were slow fliers and their engines could be heard some way off as they came in from the direction of the North Sea. In fact, no bombs were ever dropped on us and they must have been using the Wash as a good navigational fix on the way to London. The very thought of having the enemy over our small country town was at the time considered well beyond the accepted rules of warfare.

A Sopwith Camel — the first aeroplane which the author saw.

The author made his first solo in this Avro 548, powered by an 80 hp Renault V-8 air-cooled engine, at Brooklands in August 1928.

Our real home was in Buckinghamshire at Beaconsfield. One evening while I was doing my homework my mother called me outside to watch an air-raid on London: the sky was lit up by searchlights and anti-aircraft gun-flashes and, as we stood watching, one searchlight beam swinging to and fro suddenly picked up a reflection from the hull of a Zeppelin. Immediately, the other searchlights coned in, picking it out brilliantly against the night as a perfect target. Shortly afterwards, I saw a burst of flame from the top which very quickly spread forward. The nose dipped and as the craft gathered speed in a dive the flames enveloped the whole nose. The bare skeleton framework of the hull could clearly be seen as the Zeppelin disappeared behind the trees in the distance. It seemed unbelievable that such an enormous craft could disintegrate totally in a few seconds.

A few years later in 1924 I was waiting to hear the result of my exams and went to Hendaye in the South of France to stay with my parents. Seeing a flying display advertised at Biarritz, about twenty miles away, I persuaded my father to drive me over. The grass airfield was narrow and flat with tall trees at each end; a celebrated French army pilot, Captain Robin, was to give an exhibition of stunt flying in a parasol monoplane with strut-braced wings. In taking off he kept the wheels on the ground until just short of the line of trees, when he pulled up into a vertical climb. At the top he did a neat stalled turn, diving vertically and flattening out only just

in time to roll his wheels along the ground to the opposite end of the field, when again he pulled up vertically and followed with a stall turn and dive. This he repeated for the third time, having ended each climb with a little more height in hand.

He then went on to give a very polished display of more conventional manoeuvres such as loops, rolls and a spin, finishing with a circuit of the airfield in a continuous series of rolls, a feat I now know to be particularly difficult. As he passed over our heads in a final dive and zoom about five feet of the starboard wing broke off and fell away. He had enough speed to be able to continue for some distance with only two-thirds of the wing, but as his speed decreased so the wing went down and he disappeared behind some trees in a righthand turn. Like a fool, with many others I ran over to see what had happened, only to be met in a gate-way by a group of men carrying the very badly injured Robin on a short length of wooden fencing.

One lesson I did learn from seeing this accident was never to be curious and go and gape at a crash. Nevertheless, I was determined to make flying my career. On returning home, although under age, I applied for a short service commission in the Royal Air Force. On attending the medical examination board at Hampstead I was turned down as my eye-sight did not meet the required standard, much to the relief of my parents but my own disappointment. As an alternative, and very much a second choice, my father persuaded me to take a three-year apprenticeship course in engineering with Armstrong Siddeley Motors at Coventry.

2 A training of sorts

Armstrong Siddeley made cars, aeroplane engines, tanks, torpedoes and, at the subsidiary company of Armstrong Whitworth, aircraft. It was a progressive company in many fields of engineering. It pioneered the self-changing gearbox, the supercharging of aeroplane engines and all metal construction of aircraft. After some months in the various machine shops, I found myself in the aircraft engine experimental shop where we stripped down Sir Alan Cobham's Jaguar engine with which he had just flown in his seaplane to Singapore and Australia. The two fitters were 'Alf' and 'Charlie' who in their youth had built by hand some of the early cars. A skilled man in those days made the whole car, frame, petrol tank, radiator and of course the engine; he even filed the cams for the engine's valves before keying them to the camshaft. These men were really born mechanics with great practical knowledge, the backbone of our engineering industry before mass-production took over.

The first superchargers were high-speed centrifugal fans driven by three equally spaced step-up gears from the crankshaft. These gears incorporated slipping clutches to cushion the loads during acceleration. The wedge-shaped friction pads frequently melted from slipping, and molten metal, like bronze wire, filled the casing. I know, because my job was to rub the new clutch pads in with grinding paste. However, the Jaguar was the first supercharged high-altitude engine to achieve regular production, thus giving the RAF's Siskin superior climb performance over any rival fighter.

In the experimental shop, we built an entirely new and bigger air-cooled radial called the Leopard. It was rated at 800 hp, a tremendous power at that time. After working until late one night servicing the engine on the test bed, I was bicycling in to work next morning and was about a mile

The Armstrong Whitworth Siskin IIIA, with supercharged Jaguar engine, was the RAF's first all-metal high altitude fighter, 1926. (Flight)

The Armstrong Whitworth Atlas was the first Army co-operation aircraft. Note the trailing pick-up arm. (Flight)

away when I heard it start up. The noise was shattering and could be heard over a large part of Coventry, but on arrival we were called up by the chief tester to be told that it had seized up and we had to saw it apart to find the cause. It was obvious what had happened, as there was no oil in the pipes; evidently someone had forgotten to turn on the main oil cock. It was finally accepted by the authorities as being due to an air leak through a fine hair crack in an induction pipe causing a weak mixture and, consequently, a burnt piston. This episode was my first disillusionment with the workings of authority, and when, shortly afterwards, the General Strike took place I made up my mind that, on completing my apprenticeship, I would go abroad.

Armstrong Siddeley employed about 8,000 men in all when the General Strike took place. As an apprentice, I was not directly concerned, but when the time came to walk out, the older men, in spite of urging by hot-heads, were reluctant to go, spending a lot of time cleaning their machines, looking over their shoulders for reassurance from their immediate neighbour. They were fully aware of the danger to their jobs, but it takes a lot of moral courage to stand up among one's fellow men and raise objections—most of us do not have that sort of courage. Finally, at about 11 o'clock, Mr J. D. Siddeley, the Chairman, with the Works Manager and

Secretary, came round to every department and he made a brief speech. He said that the company could not carry on with a partial labour force, and that they all had to go. Tragically, only about half the men ever got their jobs back, and the slump continued until the start of rearmament in the middle thirties.

My last year in the aircraft drawing office was interesting. The Atlas, an all-metal day bomber for the Royal Air Force, and the Argosy, a three-engined air liner for Imperial Airways, were being designed and built. Apart from some indifferent draughtsmanship, my only contribution was to design the fuel filter for the Atlas. Bovril at that time used a circular clamp to hold the lid on the top of the bottle and I pinched this idea to fasten the filter element to the base; hardly original, but it did go into production.

The normal working week was forty-seven hours including Saturday mornings, but the apprentices were allowed a half day once a week to study at the Coventry Technical College. There the standard of education was appallingly low with teachers who no doubt had qualifications but were indifferent to the imparting of information to their students. My previous formal education at Rugby had ended abruptly when my father was invalided out of the army, but even there the application of mathematics and science to engineering was not explained to me, and it was very many years before I realised what a lot I had missed.

At that time, 300 or 400 Armstrong Siddeley cars were being produced a week. These were still made on a batch

Evocatively photographed in flight over the City of London, the Armstrong Whitworth Argosy 'Giant' airliner for Imperial Airways, with a 12-passenger cabin, made its maiden flight in 1927.

production method in very large machine shops. All the lathes, milling machines, grinders and so on were driven by belts from overhead shafting making it impossible to see the far side for the forest of belting, just like any scene of the dark satanic mills of the industrial revolution. Yet in spite of the age of the machinery, parts for the aeroplane engines and aircraft were being made alongside parts of cars. The ad-

vances in machine tools made since then have transformed the engineering world by introducing automatic and electrically controlled tools. The Americans, whose early labour force was largely made up of unskilled immigrants, were necessarily, and still are, the producers of these new mass-production tools, whereas we have tended to rely on our very skilled artisans.

Another fundamental change which has taken place since then has been in the elimination of a separate chassis. In 1925, Coventry's streets were full of skeleton car chassis being driven by testers sitting perched up on makeshift soap boxes. Armstrong Siddeley, however, were the exception to the rule, as they made their own bodies. These were built using a wooden frame over which was stretched a tough fabric. The salesmen must have stressed the elimination of squeaks and rattles but played down the durability factor.

My own interest had originally been focused on cars, which seemed to me to have a very big future, but the glamour of working on aeroplane engines and aircraft was too strong. It was fortunate as the motor industry soon proved to be unreliable with slump following boom, as one manufacturer or another caught the mood of a fickle market, leaving its competitors without orders. In the case of Armstrong Siddeley, the time from which they had been unable to produce enough cars to meet the demand until they could virtually sell none was only a couple of months.

Armstrong Siddeley were well placed to benefit from the spin-off from research and development expenditure on aeroplane engines. Aluminium pistons and white-metal bearings were just coming into use for car engines, improving efficiency and relieving the new car buyer of a large part of the irksome job of running in. All cars fitted with the new-fangled front wheel brakes carried a red triangle warning plate on the back, a kind of status symbol. As the production of cars increased so did the percentage of unskilled drivers, with the consequence that the shortcomings of the crash type gearboxes and jerky clutches of the day became very evident. Although the company had pioneered the installation of fluid flywheels and self-changing epicyclic gearboxes with some success, these features had to be shelved under the pressure of increased costs. Ultimately, it was the Americans who came up with the practical and cheap answer, a synchronising device which prevented the driver clashing the gear teeth. The Englishman who invented it could find no manufacturer in this country interested, so he took it to Detroit and sold an exclusive licence to General Motors, who still use it to this day.

My last year was spent in the aeroplane drawing office, making frequent visits to the aerodrome at Baginton, where the Atlas and the Argosy were being built. There had been relatively few developments in aerodynamics since World War I, and design was focused on improving the structure. Wood gave way to metal, and rubber shock-absorbing cord to coil springs in the undercarriage. Looking back, it is interesting to see how the design of new vehicles is influenced by the old: as instances, the first cars were called horseless carriages, and they looked it; the carriages of early trains copied the stage coach; and aeroplanes were at this time still under the influence of the original stick-and-string conception. Specially shaped sheet steel and tube construction merely replaced the wooden spars, frames and longerons. The biplane layout was relatively efficient up to about 100 mph, but any suggestion of reducing drag by building a monoplane was taboo; some scientist had ordained that no

The Argosy's passenger cabin — in 1927, aeroplane designers had the final say, not interior decorators.

monoplane structure could be made strong enough, and the Air Ministry were therefore not in the market for them.

The only effort made to improve aerodynamic efficiency was the building of a special experimental aircraft incorporating a biplane wing with adjustable root fittings. These allowed the same wing to be re-rigged with a bigger gap, and more stagger and sweepback. It was quite the most awful-looking monstrosity, but was one way of measuring the effects on drag before the days of full-scale wind tunnels.

For those of my generation it is hard to accept the new words used in aviation today. Aileron, fuselage and nacelle all reflect the early French influence. In the thirties, the newly formed Air Registration Board, as advisers on Civil Aviation to the Air Ministry, laid down that a propeller should become an airscrew, a fuselage an airframe. Much later, in deference to our American allies, an aerodrome became an airfield. Inevitably, the language of the industry gradually changed, but even now I wince on hearing the word 'plane', or worse still 'airplane', although I sometimes use the word aeroplane instead of aircraft myself. Developments in the field of propulsion have by stages gone from propeller through pure jet, turbojet, bypass jet, turboprop, ducted propellers — we are almost back to where we started — but the latest term to be coined, namely the RB. 211, is, in my opinion, a poor effort to describe this great Rolls-Royce high technology engine with its huge inbuilt ducted impeller.

In the summer of 1928, with some knowledge of aircraft engineering behind me, I went with all my savings to the Brooklands motor-racing circuit to learn to fly privately. The year 1928 was still in the aftermath of the Great War, and anyone connected with civil aviation was considered either scatter-brained or a playboy. On my first flight Colonel Henderson, who owned the school of flying, took off and then at 100 feet handed the Avro 504 over to me with the remark, 'Keep her straight.' Later, after telling me to make a turn, he allowed me to get into a tighter and tighter spiral dive until I found, purely by chance in a panic, that by putting on top or opposite rudder I was able to get myself out of a frightening situation. It was a crude lesson, but one I never forgot.

A bungalow near the Byfleet banking close to the old Hawker sheds was living quarters for a mixed crowd of aviators, racing drivers, actors and rich sportsmen. Drinking started early and finished long after the pubs closed. There were no regular hours but life moved fast.

Among the older experienced pilots there was still an atmosphere of devil-may-care left over from the war. The average life expectancy in France had been only a matter of weeks, and the first flush of excitement must soon have paled, leaving unbearable tensions. Drinking habits acquired then had left their mark.

While in Coventry I had not been interested in the usual pub crawl beer drinking, simply because it was too expensive and every penny counted. At Brooklands, however, to be in the swing and keep up with one's friends, one had to drink spirits. Certainly, flying in an open cockpit with the wind in one's face, and the cold, noise and anxieties of it all did produce a fierce thirst. Always in the back of one's mind was the thought of danger; even during the three-week course one of the students, a Miss Welby, spun in and was killed, while both Colonel Henderson and an instructor called Davenport had fatal accidents shortly afterwards. We were only one generation after the Wright brothers; it was too short a time for man to have absorbed and overcome all the thousands of new problems presented by actually flying. Nevertheless, even with the then current knowledge, the whole approach was far too casual.

At weekends we used to fly over to a field by the river at Runnymede, and take up joyriders at five bob a head. My job was to sell tickets, but it was well worth it, as I got two cross-country flights free.

The Avro 504 was a good trainer. It was relatively safe and

The only Avro 504 Anzani-powered built, G-EBWO, A 10-cylinder double-row radial of 100 hp, the Anzani was a predecessor of the type of engine which powered the following generation of civil aircraft which finally linked the continents. (via Richard Riding)

yet its controls accentuated such effects as a sensitive rudder and aileron drag; not having any fixed fin area, it had a lack of directional stability and made correct use of the rudder vital. Our motley collection had various engines including two V-8s, the RAF 90 and the Renault 80 driving a large four-bladed propeller through reduction gears, and also a 10-cylinder Anzani radial. This Anzani engine must have been one of the first air-cooled radials to be built, a classic conception to be followed by a very long line of highly successful engines. The Anzani, however, was very weak in detail design, with automatic inlet valve, single ignition and an exhaust manifold which looked like a plumber's dream. The worst feature was the inadequate length of the cooling fins, obvious to the pilot soon after leaving the ground when the power gradually faded as the engine began to overheat. It is interesting to visit the aeronautical section of the Science Museum in South Kensington to study and compare the Anzani with a Bristol Centaurus. I think you will wonder at what man can achieve in a period of twenty-five years if he puts his shoulder to it.

Duncan Davis sent me off solo after five and a half hours dual in five flying days, an important consideration with flying costing £4. 10s. an hour and a wage of thirty bob a week. The wind happened to be from the northwest that day which meant a short landing run across the aerodrome. Just to make matters more difficult, the approach from the direction of St George's Hill was over the River Wey, while an overshoot meant finishing up in the sewage farm. By tradition, a first solo called for a round of drinks and it was with acute embarrassment that I found myself standing a round at the British Automobile Racing Club bar in their club house near the paddock on the finishing straight, being shy and out of my depth in such company.

Nevertheless, I felt honoured to be surrounded by the high

The staff of the Henderson Flying School, Brooklands, 1928. (via Richard Riding)

and mighty of the motor-racing world, my schoolboy heroes. Two years before, I had seen the first British Grand Prix Motor Race when a chicane was introduced into the finishing straight. It had attracted the cream of the drivers from the European circuit. Divo with a new Talbot was an exhibitionist and, aided by the very open cockpits of the racing cars of the day, he drove spectacularly, his check cap back to front, arms waving, skidding through the artificial corners, then accelerating away with the new supercharged engine making a noise like a stuck pig. Benoit, on the other hand, in the very latest supercharged Delage, had much more finesse, although he was probably equally fast, but his exhaust blew a gasket and orange flames could be seen through the louvres of the bonnet as he opened the throttle. Every few laps he had to pull into the pits, where he jumped out and put his feet into a basin of water. Parry Thomas, a world speed record holder, had designed his own road racing car, the Thomas Special, known locally as the 'flat iron'. Its main

feature was that it was very low with the driver sitting practically on the ground, but it did not seem to handle too well. Segrave, true to form, stuck to his Sunbeam, which, if I remember correctly, was not supercharged and could not compete on performance.

On completing the required three hours solo I was ready to take the tests to obtain an aviator's certificate. This was issued under the authority of the Royal Aero Club who were solely responsible for the conduct of private flying. A member of the club, in my case one of the instructors, had to certify that the required tests had been satisfactorily completed; they really amounted to little more than a demonstration that the pilot could handle an aeroplane. Three take-offs and landings, one of the latter without using the engine, a figure of eight at 1500 ft and the ability to recover from a spin was all that was called for. Armed with the aviator's certificate and a letter from my doctor I applied for my private pilot's licence. A few weeks later a manilla envelope came through the post, and inside was Private Pilot's Licence No. 1560 issued by the Air Ministry, signed by the Director of Civil Aviation himself, Sefton Brancker.

3 Hungry beginnings

During May 1927, Charles Lindbergh made his epic flight from Long Island to Paris. This was an inspiration to me and really decided my future but, of far greater importance, it led to a flood of money from both the US Government and private sources becoming available for civil aviation in the boom days before the Wall Street crash. A number of small companies were started in the United States both to manufacture and to operate aircraft. These spilled over into Canada where, before the War, my family had lived for three years when my father was seconded to the Canadian Army as an instructor at the Royal Military College, Kingston, Ontario.

Shortly after obtaining my pilot's licence, I was offered a job with International Airways of Canada at their head office in Hamilton, Ontario with the princely salary of $100 a month. For a young man in England it was a real break. With two million unemployed and after years of depression at home it was an incredible change to arrive in the New World. It certainly was a New World, with confidence, optimism and money everywhere but it was not to last.

International Airways was a grouping together of all the odd aircraft companies operating in Eastern Canada under the chairmanship of General J. H. MacBrien, who had been head of the Canadian Expeditionary Forces. Looking back, it is clear that the financiers had hoped to make a killing by unloading the shares on the gullible public, but the financial crash on Wall Street forestalled this. At that time it was not realised that the operation of aircraft in the civil role was almost entirely dependent on assistance, or finance, from the Government. The company's main source of revenue was an airmail-cum-passenger daily service from Montreal to Toronto using Fairchild FC2s.

Shortly after my arrival in Hamilton, Ontario, I was sent to Ottawa in charge of the office of the photographic division. Our company was engaged on a government contract for aerial mapping and making a survey or assessment of the quantities of timber in Northern Ontario by taking oblique photographs of the forests. The timber, used as pulp in papermaking, was one of the main sources of wealth in the vast northern area.

The Ottawa social scene was not really my line but, while in Hamilton, I had bought a new Model A Ford for $500 which was an asset, especially as there were plenty of parties at the Country Club on the far side of the river and good skiing in the Laurentian mountains. It was a good life for young people, much freer than at home in England, and I greatly enjoyed finding my own way in this new society.

That winter at Ottawa there were no opportunities for flying, but I became involved in someone else's incident. The company owned a three-seater open cockpit biplane called a Swallow which was used for joy-riding. One week it was at a town 25 miles down the Ottawa River and I received a telephone call from the head office to say that the aircraft had had an accident and I was to go there and report back. The aircraft was on skis with a tail skid of extra large area. Where the tail skid arm entered the fuselage there was a gap through which snow had entered and become packed tight into a solid lump. The additional weight in the tail, together with the two passengers in the side-by-side rear seat had moved the centre of gravity aft and the pilot had evidently got into a flat spin during a turn. The aircraft hit the snow-covered ice on the river in a horizontal attitude very hard indeed with the result that the pilot's seat had collapsed across the legs of his two passengers who both had broken legs. They were in hospital feeling angry, very sorry for themselves and wanting to know how much compensation they were going to get from the company. Both of them were French Canadians which stretched my schoolboy French to the limit and I fear my explanations and apologies were hardly satisfactory.

By the spring of 1929, MacBrien, realising that the promoters had merely used his name, had resigned and, with a financial squeeze taking place, our Ottawa office was closed. My next move was to the Fairchild Aerial Surveys Division at Grand Mère, Quebec, as an engineer and aerial photographer. Here I found a number of English pilots and a well organised undertaking financed by the big pulp and paper company at Grand Mère. It is interesting that just ten years after the war there were only about 170 Canadian licensed pilots out of the 10,000 or so trained pilots demobilised in 1918. Among the experienced pilots who had recently retired from the Royal Air Force were Wardle, Bythell, Troup and Lumsden.

The company was an agent for the American Fairchild Aircraft Company and had a number of Fairchild FC2s, some fitted with the 400 hp Pratt & Whitney Wasp and others with Wright Whirlwind J5s of 220 hp. The FC2 was a rugged, highwing monoplane, strut-braced with a welded tube fuselage, and could carry about 1,000 lb. We had a contract to support an exploration and gold mining company prospecting in an area north of the transcontinental railway in northern Quebec. A shuttle service from Oskalaneo to the camp ferried in supplies daily. I had hoped to get some flying but found instead that my full time was taken gassing up and keeping the aircraft serviceable (it took me some time to get used to 'gas' instead of 'petrol'). As there was no road from the station, getting the 45-gallon drums of fuel to the base was quite a problem. Rolling the drums off the railway trucks down a slope into the lake, we would lash them together and tow them to our operating base behind a small outboard-engined boat. Petrol or gas being lighter than water, the drums floated satisfactorily.

At the base was a pet bear. It had been captured when its mother was shot. It used to play about round the camp just like a puppy but it very quickly grew up and we tethered it to a cable stretched between two trees to give it a chance to move around. However, from being playful it became quite fierce and the friendly pat of its claws became a vicious swipe, specially if one was not looking. Eventually, lifting it by its collar, a leather bootlace, we lowered it into a sack and took it to the other side of the lake. On freeing it, after cocking its leg, it scuttled off into the bush.

Back at Grand Mère there was a Liberty-engined HS2L flying boat, a salvaged relic from the war. Its flying speed was around 70 mph and it was the only aircraft to my knowledge in which it was possible for the off-duty crew member to climb out of the open cockpit and sit on the wing with his back to the flying wires, enjoying the sun. The engine, a 400-hp V12, was a nightmare to keep serviceable as each cylinder had a separate water-jacket with flexible connections: I think the Jubilee hose-clip must have been invented around about this time.

The Fairchild FC2-W2 was a pioneer workhorse of the Canadian Northland. (RCAF)

One of our main activities was aerial survey. We flew backwards and forwards in the HS2L over the centre of Montreal while I took photographs for city planning purposes. Later, when a big extension of the electrical power lines was in progress, we flew over the proposed routes for new lines. This had the advantage that a close study could be made of the various properties and farms which would be affected without the owners knowledge of the survey. Not perhaps quite ethical but arguments could be advanced both for and against the practice and I have little doubt it still goes on.

It was a carefree, casual life. Taxiing in our Vickers Vedette, a small flying-boat, to the small landing stage on the lake near Grand Mère one evening, Lumsden cut the engine a bit late and I could see we were clearly going to hit a wooden post at the end. Seeing a figure running down to ward off the blow, Lumsden, with his service background and in his inimitable style called out, just before the crunch, 'It's all right, there are lots more where this came from.' Unfortunately, it was the President of the company; he was not amused.

A bombshell came in October 1929, when it was announced that the company was closing down and we were all given the sack. The Wall Street crash was already beginning to bite in Canada and signs of the coming depression appeared. Although England had had a depression for years, the social structure was still intact. I had not realised that Canada had no such stability and was quite shocked when some old family friends in Toronto who had a large house in the best residential area with two cars and a steady business in tobacco broking suddenly went bankrupt. Thousands of other fam-

Crews and passengers at Edmonton's new Municipal Air Harbour before departure for Fort McMurray on 8 December 1929 in CF-AJQ, CF-AJR and CF-AAL. Rear row, left to right: I. Glyn Roberts, pilot (ex-RAF); Cy Becker, pilot and company managing director; John Melvin, Hudson Bay Co. Inspector; R. W. Hale, Post Office Inspector; Maurice Burbridge, CFI, Edmonton Flying School; Ted Watt, reporter; Front row, left to right: Don Robertson, air engineer, 'A' licence pilot; Reg Jackson, office manager; 'Boom' Lumsden, pilot (ex-RAF); A. R. C. McMullen, pilot; Stan Green, air engineer.

ilies also were literally penniless overnight. It was impossible to raise cash for anything. Even cars became unsaleable.

All the English employees moved to Montreal where Lumsden, Bill Wardle and I shared some rooms in Peel Street. To start with, we all had some savings and Peter Troup even moved into the Windsor Hotel for a time. Alcohol flowed very freely and I acquired a taste for whisky, even being able to distinguish one brand from another. During a party in Troup's room one night the manager of the hotel rang up and said, 'It is very late for entertaining a lady in your room, sir.' To which Troup made the apt reply, 'Oh no, you are quite wrong; she is entertaining me!'

As our savings ebbed away and the cold weather arrived we began to get worried. There seemed little hope of getting any flying job.

Montreal was the Paris of North America and with prohibition in New York the weekend Friday-night train used to run in up to fifteen sections, bringing in the visitors that flooded the place. It was exciting but expensive. We used to get up about midday to save energy and have only one meal a day. I got to know where one could get the maximum volume for the minimum price. To this day I remember what it was to be hungry, without the money to buy adequate food. The word hungry is used in a very loose sense in ordinary everyday conversation; the reality is quite different. Canada was no Welfare State and to be unemployed in the cold winter weather was no joke.

By early December 1929 my funds had run down to the point where I had just enough left to buy a steerage passage home when I received a telegram from Edmonton, Alberta. This was from an American whom I had briefly met in Montreal, a strange character who had tried to interest us in piloting flying boats between Nassau and somewhere vaguely off the Florida coast but out of sight of the US Coast Guard! He was now a consultant to a new aviation company in Alberta which was offering me a job as an engineer. In triumph, I stepped onto the next train, buying the ticket for the four-day journey with the last of my dollars.

4 *Airmail to the Arctic*

Commercial Airways of Edmonton was formed on the strength of a Government contract to take the mail to all the trading posts on the Mackenzie River. Mail carried was not subject to a surcharge but any letter, say one posted in the United Kingdom, went automatically by air. Up to the start of the scheduled weekly air service all mail had been carried by dog team in the winter, and an old steam stern-wheeler owned by the Hudson's Bay Co., called the *Northland Echo*, in the summer, two deliveries a year. Our aircraft were painted red and carried the Royal Mail cypher on each side, and the operational staff were officially sworn in as authorised to carry mail. We also carried printed cards to enable us to swear in temporary postmen to take over the post in the event of failure to reach our destination. The carriage of mail is not to be treated lightly, and its safety is paramount. Although other claims have been made to being the first airmail service, to the best of my knowledge these were subject to a surcharge and not at ordinary rates.

It has now been largely forgotten but the bait offered to the railway promoters to build railways from coast to coast across Canada was a strip of land ten miles either side of the tracks. Both the Canadian Pacific and the Grand Trunk companies raised their finances in London, but after Herculean efforts to complete the first transcontinental route it was quickly found that the traffic did not justify the two railways and the Grand Trunk went bankrupt. The Canadian Government took it over (without compensation) and called it the Canadian National. Edmonton, a railway town, became the capital of Alberta and the natural departure point for all forms of exploration and prospecting for minerals in the North. It was also the headquarters of Commercial Airways which was formed with the intention of improving transportation in the vast, potentially rich area of the Mackenzie River and Northwest Territories. It is difficult to build railways in those marshy treeless areas. The ground is frozen to a depth of several feet and any steel structure such as a railway track or radio mast attracts the sun's heat, causing the foundation to melt and become unstable. Rivers all flow north or north-easterly into the Arctic Ocean which, for all practical purposes, is not navigable by sea-going ships. The advent of aircraft was therefore the start of a new era with Edmonton becoming the hub of a worldwide network of air routes.

The managing director of the new company was Cy Becker, one of Canada's great aces of World War I with 28 enemy aircraft to his credit; he was still an active pilot. He ran the Company from the Edmonton office, which was convenient as a centre of communications, allowing him to keep in contact with the Alberta Government and also with the administrative headquarters of the Northwest Territories at Fort Smith, one of the weekly ports of call on our route north.

The company's base for operations was Fort McMurray, situated on the Athabasca River at the end of the railway 200 miles north of Edmonton. The weekly train brought the mail and from there we flew it down north to the various fur-trading posts, a distance of about 1600 miles to Aklavik on the delta of the Mackenzie River. We also carried passengers when space was available, Hudson's Bay officials, prospectors, trappers, and Roman Catholic priests. There were isolated Roman Catholic, as well as Anglican, missions at three or

The author, wearing fancy mukluks, with the Lockheed Vega at Fort McMurray in January 1930. The Vega was the first aerodynamically 'clean' aeroplane, except for the undercarriage. It had a monocoque structure and a cantilever wing.

Mail for the North being loaded into a Bellanca Pacemaker (300 hp Wright Whirlwind J6 engine) on 11 December 1929 by 'Wop' May (right) and the author (centre).

four of the trading posts teaching the Indian and Eskimo natives; once a year we would fly Bishop Breynant of the Northwest Territories on his rounds, our arrival being greeted by a turnout of the entire settlement. He gave me a Bible suitably inscribed as a momento of one of these tours which survived until it was burnt in the London Blitz.

The fleet consisted of five aircraft, two Bellanca Pacemakers, two Bellanca CH300s and a Lockheed Vega. The Vega was a beautifully streamlined highwing monoplane of wooden monocoque construction, quite unsuitable for the North, and it was quickly withdrawn. The Bellancas, which differed only in their undercarriage design, were strut-braced highwing monoplanes, the main feature being that the wing struts and the whole fuselage were of a lifting section. With a 300 hp Wright Whirlwind J6, it would cruise at about 100 mph with a useful payload of 1,000 lb.

'Wop' May, another World War I Canadian fighter pilot, was chief pilot. He had had considerable experience of flying in cold weather and our aircraft had been modified locally to incorporate his ideas. Skis were of ash and hickory with laminated pedestals. The oil pipes had been lagged with asbestos string and the oil tanks enclosed in a felt and canvas jacket to retain the heat. With a similar object, every aperture in the engine cowling was blanked off. Very large hand-operated draincocks were fitted to the oil tanks to drain the hot oil on stopping the engine. Special containers were made up to collect the oil and used for reheating it over a campfire or blowtorch before start up in the morning. The danger of the oil freezing in the aircraft's oil tank was a constant worry and the engine could never be idled for more than a minute or two as slow circulation would lead to the oil congealing in the pipelines and a build-up of pressure in the system.

Overnight an engine would freeze rigid and before it could be turned it was necessary to apply heat. We carried heavy canvas and felt covers with an asbestos trunk into which was placed a plumber's blowtorch. On an average winter's day the engine would come free after about one and a half hours and the propeller could then be turned. An alternative type of cover consisted of a heavy tent over the engine, which had the advantage of warming up the engineer as well. Engine starting was by a hand-cranked inertia starter which gave us independence from any outside source of power.

Having taken so much time and trouble to warm up the engine and the lubricating oil before take-off, we found on reaching cruising altitude that the oil would sometimes over-heat. An air-cooled engine relies heavily on its circulation of oil for internal cooling and this over-heating was a serious matter. It was only when we fitted external air thermometers

A handbill of Commercial Airways' mail route to the Arctic, issued in 1929.

MACKENZIE RIVER DISTRICT

RATES

From Fort McMurray To—

To—	Passenger	Express Per Lb.
Fort Chipewyan	$ 35.00	$ .20
Fort Fitzgerald	65.00	.35
Fort Smith	65.00	.35
Fort Resolution	100 00	.70
Hay River	135.00	.75
Fort Providence	160.00	.85
Fort Simpson	205 00	1.00
Fort Wrigley	240 00	1.35
Fort Norman	280.00	1.65
Good Hope	325 00	2.15
Arctic Red River	375 00	2.50
Fort McPherson	390 00	2.60
Aklavik	410.00	2 70

The above are the rates for ordinary schedule flights on the route mentioned.

Special flights may be arranged for.

Each passenger is entitled to carry 25 lbs. of baggage free, all in excess of that weight charged accordingly.

All traffic rates listed above are subject to change without notice.

MAP OF
Air Lines to the Arctic
OPERATED BY
Commercial Airways
LIMITED

POINTS of CALL
AGENCIES
AIR BASES

PACIFIC OCEAN

SCALE OF MILES

WINTER SCHEDULE 1929 - 1930

NORTH-BOUND
Leave Fort McMurray
For Fort Resolution :
Nov. 27; Dec. 4, 11, 18, 25;
Jan. 1, 8, 15, 22, 29;
Feb. 5, 12, 19, 26;
Mar. 5, 12, 19, 26; Apr. 2, 9.

For Fort Simpson :
Nov. 27; Dec. 25; Jan. 22;
Feb. 12; Mar. 5, 26.

For Aklavik :
Nov. 27; Jan. 22; Mar. 26.

SOUTH-BOUND
Leave Aklavik :
Dec. 3; Feb. 28; Apr. 1.

Leave Fort Simpson :
Dec. 5, 28; Jan. 28; Feb. 15;
Mar. 8; Apr. 3.

Leave Fort Resolution :
Nov. 29; Dec. 6, 13, 20, 28;
Jan. 3, 10, 17, 24;
Feb. 1, 7, 15, 21, 28;
Mar. 8, 14, 21, 28; Apr. 4, 11.

On the above flights, the aircraft will stop at intermediate posts.

The schedule is tentative, and rigid adherence to it will depend upon weather.

SHIPPING INSTRUCTIONS:

Mark North-bound Parcels care of "COMMERCIAL AIRWAYS LIMITED, FORT McMURRAY, Alberta", via Northern Alberta Railways' Express—"Air charges COLLECT" or "PREPAID".

Shippers are required to prepay Railway Express Charges to Fort McMurray on North Bound Traffic.

EXAMPLE :

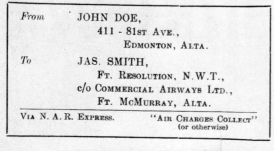

From	JOHN DOE, 411 - 81ST AVE., EDMONTON, ALTA.
To	JAS. SMITH, FT. RESOLUTION, N.W.T., c/o COMMERCIAL AIRWAYS LTD., FT. McMURRAY, ALTA.
VIA N. A. R. EXPRESS.	"AIR CHARGES COLLECT" (or otherwise)

Pack parcels securely. Parcels must be kept within the following limit (outside measurements)
12-in. x 20-in. x 60-in.

Add 2-in. to width for each decrease of 12-in. in length.

C. BECKER, General Manager.

that we discovered that in the cold of the North there is often a big temperature inversion. Normally the air gets colder with height by about 3°F per 1,000 feet but not infrequently we found a 30°F temperature *rise* in the first 1,000 feet. A suitable modification to the engine installation overcame the difficulty.

A forced landing in the North can be dangerous. Our survival kit weighed about 160 lbs and tended to get bigger with experience. An axe, tent, snowshoes, rifle, fishing gear and collapsible stove and food were all stowed in the rear fuselage while our personal sleeping bags and clothing went into the main cabin. A campfire is extremely inefficient and burns a lot of wood. We quickly decided to carry collapsible stoves which could be used inside a tent thus providing warmth and cooking facilities with much less effort, an important consideration when the conservation of body energy was vital. We carried matches separately in a corked bottle in a convenient pocket. It would hardly be possible to survive one night during the winter in the far North without a source of heat.

McMurray was on the junction of the Athabasca River with the Clearwater River. Fortunately, at some time a channel had been gouged out between the two rivers by the ice break-up causing a flood. This snye, as it is called, provided a perfect base for maintenance purposes with smooth ice in winter and little current in summer. A shed on skids called a nose hangar, with on one side a canvas curtain capable of being drawn tight round the back of the engine bay, provided with a stove, gave good facilities for engine maintenance while parked on the ice. There was an hotel of sorts owned by a Mr O'Coffee; understandably, living conditions were somewhat elementary with the sole provision for washing being a barrel of water in the kitchen and an outside privy. However, the single living-cum-dining room had a large and effective wood stove which warmed the whole building, including the bedrooms which opened on to an inside gallery. Outside the front door was a thermometer which I have seen indicate 50° below zero in winter and 90° above in summer.

Cold in the North is relative. Zero weather, that is to say 32°F of frost, is cold and 50°F below zero is very cold. Fortunately, very cold weather tends to be still and calm but any wind at any temperature makes life difficult, and one is forced to seek shelter for protection. Even a deep breath catches in one's throat as the frost tries to freeze one's lungs. One learned not to grasp any metal door handle with the bare hand. Even the inside of a front door handle would freeze to the skin, and required the protection of gripping it through one's coat pocket.

Suitable clothing was a problem. The local general store had rough shirts, mackinaws and breeches. Most of us wore leather flying helmets, the airman's equivalent to the city gent's bowler, and we gradually acquired all the desirable extras: Royal Canadian Mounted Police uniform breeches, fur mittens, Eskimo parkas and sealskin mukluks. The latter items were only to be obtained on a barter basis, there not being much use for bits of paper on the Arctic coast. Parkas were made of untanned caribou skin with trimming of different markings to denote the particular tribe. A very special one would have the hood part trimmed with wolverine, the only fur which has the unusual property of not freezing to your face from condensation of your breath. Extremities such as hands and feet were particularly vulnerable to the cold; we wore woollen gloves and we normally kept our gloved hands tucked into huge fur mittens slung from a cord round the neck. No shoes, particularly if leather or rubber soled, can ever be worn, only a kind of boot made of sealskin called a mukluk which becomes soft and pliable after being well chewed by Eskimo women. Spare socks are important and it became routine practice to hang up one's socks by a fire every night so as to ensure absolute dryness. One of the main secrets of keeping warm is never to get hot from over exertion; sweating is not only a loss of energy but will cause condensation and one's outer clothing then acts as a form of refrigerator.

Of all the pilots and engineers based at McMurray, there was only one who really knew the North. Jack Bowen had lived there most of his life, and for eight years had driven his dog team taking the mail from Fort Smith to McMurray, as well as being driver for the Royal Canadian Mounted Police.

Breaking a trail on the first trip of the winter or after a snowstorm was very tough going, and other travellers would wait for Jack to leave, then follow quickly behind. The distance covered in any one day varied greatly according to the weather and surface conditions. A frozen lake is easy going, whereas fresh snow means that the lead dog has to make progress in a series of leaps, hardly conducive to fast travel. A good time for the journey from McMurray to Chipewyan would be about five days for the 160-odd miles.

Jack Bowen once made the journey from Fort Norman to Cambridge Bay (about 700 miles) without a map, but just on hearsay — 'Turn right at Bear River, follow along the north shore of the lake, follow a river draining from the north east corner, cross two lakes, etc., etc.' Dark growth on the tree trunks gave the direction of north, the sun at midday (if out) gave south. For food, he carried flour, sugar and tea, supplemented by rotten fish from Eskimo caches near the Arctic coast. An incredible journey through totally uninhabited wastes. His only comment was to wonder how the dogs survived on half a frozen fish a day! Compared with Jack, the rest of us were a lot of greenhorns so far as survival in the real North was concerned, but I think he must have learned a thing or two from us about aeroplanes. During World War II, he became engineer in charge of maintenance at the

The first scheduled mail arrives at Fort Resolution on the Great Slave Lake in three Bellancas in December 1929.

Edmonton flying school, which produced thousands of pilots and navigators for service in Europe.

My own arrival at McMurray was not auspicious. In early December 1929 I flew up as a passenger in the Vega with Cy Becker, and without any heat in the cabin I got thoroughly chilled. On landing Cy Becker got stuck in the snow and could not get the aircraft moving again. I got out and by pushing the tail sideways managed to free the skis, and he taxied on to park. On joining the others after a struggle to make my way through 200 yards of deep snow, I was greeted with the news that my nose was frozen. Tim Sims, who had come up to McMurray as a representative of the Wright engine company, acted very promptly and rubbed it with snow and a fur glove, which saved my nose, but it was covered with water blisters, and to lose a layer of skin at the beginning of winter was unfortunate. It does not take long to freeze anything in the propeller slipstream when the temperature is 30° below zero. Twenty-five years later at a party in London given by Jack Davis, who was working for Canadair, a comparative stranger came up to me and said: 'I once saved your nose.' He had recognised me after all that time, and I was indeed grateful to him.

I was detailed off to fly with 'Loopey' Lumsden, an ex-service officer whose uncle was Lord Trenchard, the 'father' of the Royal Air Force. He was a first-class, very polished pilot who liked his comforts, and we got on well together. In many ways flying in the North is like sailing with a companion on a passage in a small yacht: mutual respect and the ability to work together under adverse conditions without a clash of personality are very important.

Although I was employed as an engineer, my pilot's licence was current and I usually did a lot of the routine flying. There was no training like flying with experienced men in the days before radio, weather reports and air traffic control. The pilot was in supreme charge and made all the decisions.

Knowledge of the route and the weather conditions likely to be encountered were important but above all airmanship and knowing when to turn back can only be acquired by experience and by building up hours in the air. In flying with experienced men I was indeed lucky.

After two months' flying with Lumsden I was transferred to 'Wop' May. In the previous year, he made an emergency flight to the Peace River district where there had been an outbreak of diphtheria. He and his friend Vic Horner set out from Edmonton with the anti-toxin in an open cockpit de Havilland Moth in sub zero temperature. This episode together with his wartime experience of being under attack by the famous Baron von Richthofen at the very moment when this, the greatest German ace, was himself shot down by Roy Brown VC, another Canadian, had made him famous. He had kept part of one of the splintered propeller blades of the red Fokker Triplane as a relic and reminder of his luck.

'Wop' had, by the time I got to know him, become a tough hardworking serious person with a bent for engineering. From the moment of leaving McMurray with the mail until our return in a fortnight or so, we were together constantly and got to know each other well. He was always very conscious of the degree of cold and, of course, being a Canadian, had the right clothes for the job, but I could never understand his habit of opening his side quarter window, taking off his glove and putting his fingers outside in the airstream to feel the temperature. One good tip of his, was to put a fur rug over our knees and the controls to retain the heat from a rather inadequate so-called heater, rather like a couple of old women out for a drive in their carriage in the park.

It was company policy to allocate specific aircraft to the various pilots and so we naturally took over the latest Bellanca to be delivered, the Pacemaker. The new type of undercarriage, replacing the old shock cord, became very hard in the extreme cold, and I replaced the hydraulic fluid with paraffin. Some of the landing areas were of soft snow where it was like landing on a feather bed. Others, in particular Fort Resolution on the Great Slave Lake, were fully

25

Bellanca Pacemaker on skis with a team of huskies and 'carry-all' arriving to collect mail. Note the canvas engine cover with an asbestos trunk.

exposed and rough. The wind would blow the snow over the smooth ice into waves which would freeze into hard ridges 18 inches to two feet high. Take-off and landing in these conditions imposed very heavy strains. A further hazard was that the snow horizon would sometimes merge into an overcast sky, making the judgement of height in the approach and hold-off very difficult. Arrangements were made with the local trading posts to lay out a line of spruce boughs to indicate the smoothest runway, and these also eased the landing problem as they gave a good definition of height. A further problem was the lack of any indication of wind direction or speed, although sometimes it was possible to pick out against the snow background a wisp of smoke from a log cabin.

On our first flight to the Arctic we were diverted to take a prospector from Fort Norman to Fort Franklin on the Great Bear Lake, which had once been the most westerly of Franklin's winter quarters when searching for the North West Passage. Prospectors were understandably secretive in their searches for minerals and did not encourage questions. But about this time, 1930, a French Canadian prospector called Labine discovered pitchblend or uranium ore at what was later to be called Eldorado. Flying along the east side of Great Bear Lake in a Fokker piloted by Punch Dickins of Western Canada Airways, a rival company, he noticed that on an outcrop of rock a certain area was bare of snow, and deduced this was due to some radioactivity. Up to that time the only known source of pitchblend ore was the Belgian Congo; with such a monopoly of the supply, the price of radium was in the region of £30,000 an ounce, and it was mainly used in the treatment of cancer. The Canadian source was, I believe, used for the first atom bomb. Uranium's

peacetime use in power stations in taking over from oil may well prove to be the biggest source of energy the world has ever known.

The North West Territories, an enormous area uninhabited except for a few Eskimos, Indians and isolated trappers, was administered by the Federal Government in Ottawa. There was a small establishment at Fort Smith on the Slave River just over the border from Alberta. All travellers either from or to the North had to pass this way as there was, until the day of aeroplanes, no alternative route. It had a small hospital, the only one in the whole area, and we were often called upon to pick up injured and sick people, not to mention a number of expectant mothers. The latter were a menace to us as the journey was often left until the last moment and in the event of bad weather there was a tendency to press on to our destination incurring risks we would not otherwise have taken. On one such flight en route from McMurray to Edmonton we were forced to turn back after completing most of the journey and landed after a bumpy three-hour flight just in the nick of time.

There were three radio and weather reporting stations on our route, one at Fort Resolution on the Great Slave Lake, one at Fort Simpson and the most northerly one at Aklavik on the Mackenzie Delta. Advance weather conditions were not available and in any case blind-flying instruments had not been heard of, but our time of departure was radioed ahead and in the event of non arrival the authorities would be notified. The Mackenzie River itself had been surveyed and mapped but the tributaries and outlying lakes were only shown dotted; presumably the information had been supplied by odd trappers and prospectors. The settlements along the river were at intervals of about 200 miles; these fur trading posts had been established by the Hudson's Bay Company but were then being challenged by Northern Traders who were cutting in on the old HBC territory and were regarded by HBC as upstarts. The sign 'H.B.C.' over the store was usually referred to by their rivals as 'here before Christ'. As postmen, we were made very welcome by them all, but one was aware of the competition even at these lonely outposts.

The relatively frequent deliveries of mail which we made were not regarded by all with favour. Instead of one annual return of trading to the head office, they were pestered with form filling, fur market prices, statistics, and all the paper work of bureaucracy. In compensation, our aircraft were never 'dry' and many was the Scotsman, manning these HBC posts, who appreciated a nip or two. It was absolutely forbidden to give or sell alcohol to the Indians, whose stomachs were not accustomed to it, but every white man was allowed one case of spirits a year. This arrived in midsummer on the annual visit of the *Northland Echo* and was disposed of usually within a week.

5 *Aklavik run*

The last flight to Aklavik that winter was in the latter half of March 1930. In addition to a lot of mail we also had two Norwegian passengers, neither of whom could speak any English. From the first it was a tough trip with bad visibility, snow and heavy winds. We left Fort Simpson on the morning of 18 March and were scheduled to land at Wrigley, but the river there flows fast and the ice had broken into huge and jagged chunks leaving only a narrow smooth strip near the bank. 'Wop' decided that landing was too risky and so, having thrown out a bag of mail, we pressed on towards Fort Norman. The weather started to close in with heavy snow and a 50 mph headwind. Looking down from about 200 ft one could see that the wind was blowing the snow over the ice in a blizzard and I have never before or since flown in such bumpy air. The gusts were so fierce that the airspeed indicator was jumping between about 70 and

110 mph and Wop was using more or less the full movement of the stick and heavy bursts of power to maintain control of the heavily-laden aircraft. There was no question of being able to make a turn at that height and we could only keep on following the west bank of the river ahead, with me following every turn and landmark with my finger on the map rather like a rally driver's navigator. Fort Norman, on the east bank, was very exposed and our only possible landing place was a cutting parallel to the river which had been gouged out by the floods in the annual break-up of the ice. It was vital to land straight ahead and not overshoot.

The author with the Bellanca at McMurray in winter 1929–30. The canvas-ended nose hangar in the right background was for engine maintenance.

The author inspects the Bellanca Pacemaker's tail for damage at Fort Norman, Makenzie River, March 1930. Note the drift caused by the drum holding down the port ski.

After three hours and twenty minutes in the air I told Wop that I thought we were nearly there. We landed blind in deep driving snow. There was no sign of our cache of fuel drums and we taxied slowly ahead. Every now and then an extra gust would lift the aircraft six feet into the air and using the engine we landed again and again. After about half a mile I spotted a drum and while the aircraft was held stationary on the throttle I managed to get a rope round the drum and attach it to a wing strut. The others then helped and we rolled the other drums on top of the skis. Drifts formed immediately behind these, effectively holding the skis down. I attempted to dump the oil but it froze in the draincock.

Our passengers were fortunately accustomed to winter conditions but they had both been very airsick and were frightened. Although safely down we were still in considerable danger of exposure. The settlement was two miles away across the river, and with visibility in the blizzard down to twenty yards there was no possibility of reaching shelter. An aircraft's cabin can get very cold, and normally one would always set up a tent and build a fire, but this was impossible as we dared not go out of sight of the aircraft. Fine

snow was drifting into every nook and cranny through ill-fitting windows and doors but by shifting the mailbags on to the front seats and hanging one sleeping bag across the front of the cabin we made it as sheltered as possible. Meanwhile, the aircraft was lurching about on its undercarriage and every now and then the tail would lift off the snow and drop back with a bump. I dared not attempt to light the blowtorch to get some heat; in any case my hands were too cold.

It was a miserable night. We huddled together two to a sleeping bag, head to foot, to preserve what warmth we could, eating slabs of frozen chocolate and taking nips of rum. There was not much sleep that night. At about six next morning there was a lull in the storm and we immediately set off on foot, single file across the river. Progress was slow, climbing over jagged pieces of ice six feet high, but we finally reached the opposite bank. The locals were astonished to see us and could hardly believe that we had flown in the previous day. We had been fortunate in making the most of the lull because the blizzard closed in again, and it was three days before we were able to make an expedition across the river to see if the aircraft was still safe.

It took me a day's work to thaw out the oil trapped in the

29

tank and to brush out the drifted snow. The space between every cylinder fin was packed solid, as was the back of the engine, including the magnetos. The rear of the fuselage was also full; fine snow seems to get through the tiniest hole. But nothing had been damaged and after four days we were able to continue the journey in glorious sunshine. There was no radio station at Fort Norman and we knew that our departure from Fort Simpson would have been reported, therefore, as we were already overdue at Aklavik, it was important to get on before any search was started.

The last port of call before Aklavik was McPherson on the west side of the Mackenzie Delta. The snow looked perfect from the air but on landing we sank deeper and deeper until the aircraft was resting on its belly with the propeller cutting itself a groove. On climbing out of the cockpit I sank through the snow into water! I learned that this phenomenon was called 'overflow' and was caused by the lowering of the water level in the river during the winter causing the unsupported ice to crack in the middle: water flows up through the cracked ice and floats off the snow giving no indication of the danger.

Freeing the aircraft was hard work. The first step was to cut down some trees to provide a rough base for jacking. Having jacked up the skis high enough to clear the water the next step was to shovel the snow away to make a clear path exposing the water. This path had to lead to the bank of the river where the ice was not flooded. During this time we were inevitably floundering in and out of the water shovelling and jacking. We ought to have built a fire and removed our wet clothes to dry, while the water that had been cleared of snow froze over; but being inexperienced I failed to change my wet trousers and mukluks, only returning to the river water to prevent them freezing solid. However, in the end we managed to get the aircraft free and taxied close to the bank on solid ice. Knowing that it was only fifty miles to Aklavik, we decided to fly on immediately.

The decision almost proved fatal. Having climbed to 5,000 feet to get a good view of the delta, Wop put the aircraft into a shallow dive for Aklavik which was in sight ahead. Suddenly there was a thud and the nose went down into a gradually steepening dive. I looked out. The ski on my side had twisted round its axle and was lying with the tip down at about forty-five degrees to the airflow. Wop had the stick right back and was twisting on nose-up trim as hard as he could go to give the tailplane downward thrust. I scrambled out of my seat and over the top of the mail to join the two passengers on the back seat, trying to move the centre of gravity as far aft as possible. Slowly the nose came up. By the time Wop had reduced speed to 80 mph the ski had returned almost to the horizontal, normal in-flight, position. I could see clearly what had happened: the elastic shock-cord used for holding the ski in the correct position against the check-

cable had become frozen while under water in the overflow and had lost its resilience.

We landed safely at Aklavik. As soon as I got out I realised that my leggings were frozen rigid and the locals, seeing this, lifted me onto a dog sleigh and rushed me off to the nearest warm cabin. There my feet were placed into buckets of hot water and the ice thawed. My legs and toes were still all right but another twenty minutes and the story might have been different. Inexperience in the Arctic is dangerous and I was left in no doubt about this by my friends in Aklavik.

Aklavik was an important settlement with a Royal Canadian Mounted Police post, the Hudson's Bay store, Northern Traders and a Roman Catholic mission. The river had a deep channel to the Arctic Ocean a few miles away and Eskimos, who normally live on the coast, frequently visited it. After a bit of bargaining, I did a deal and obtained a good parka from one of them. They were a stocky, tough, independent people still living by hunting and constantly on the move. By contrast, the Indians, whose population had been decimated by a 'flu epidemic in the early 1920s, were very poor specimens. On coming in contact with the white man and abandoning the tribal life, they seemed to have lost their will to live; health habits which might have been acceptable in nomadic conditions led inevitably to disease when they took to living in shacks.

Even small communities such as the one at Aklavik have their social order and keep their distance, only meeting on special occasions. The local northern traders, with whom we dossed down for a couple of nights, were, however, very excited as they had recently rigged up an aerial which they shared with the RCMP and they found that for some reason they could listen in on all their private conversations! As they say, to be forewarned is to be forearmed. The two stations which provided the best reception on the 'wireless' were Schenectady and London 2LO. It was strange to hear Carroll Gibbons and his Savoy Orpheans. London seemed a very long way away but of course the distance over the Pole was much shorter than the way I had come.

I noticed small mounds of snow distributed around the settlement. These were huskies chained up and living permanently outside without shelter. During the night one dog would start a mournful howl sitting back on its haunches with its head thrown back. No sooner would one start than several others would join in, making sleep impossible. If someone gave a loud shout they would all stop howling and for a while a deathly silence would follow. Huskies are not domestic dogs but often a cross between a German police dog and a wolf, on no account to be patted. A lead dog in a team can find and will always use an old trail even though it is covered and hidden with fresh snow. It is able to feel the old path with its paws and in this way avoids some of the effort of breaking a fresh trail. It is interesting that within the first mile or two of starting a day's journey when a dog feels the call of nature somehow the lead dog gets the message and stops. The dog concerned will have its easement but instinctively draws off the trail to save fouling it for the future. If two teams travelling in opposite directions happen to meet on the same trail a fight to the death over right of way is likely to ensue, and in order to avoid this quite a large detour must be made. They also seem to have a great sense of pride in their strength as, however tired they may be on reaching a settlement at the end of a journey, their tails will go up, they will step out and enter all flags flying.

Aklavik had one very strange inhabitant. This was a horse which had been brought in by barge all the way down the 1,600-odd miles of the Athabasca and Mackenzie Rivers to this isolated trading post 300 miles north of the Arctic Circle. Its owner was a man called Peffer, who fed it on seal meat and fish, and hired it out for dragging timber and other heavy loads to the settlement. It seemed to thrive on this diet for a

number of years, and in Stan McMillan's words, 'It was well respected by both dogs and men.'

Our flight back to McMurray took two days with seven hours in the air on the last day. Altogether we made eighteen stops on the total sortie, covering 3,200 miles. Apart from the flying, we had to do all the parking, re-fuelling, morning warm-up and handle all the mail without any outside help. Our fuel caches had been put down on the river bank without much thought for convenience. Those who have ever tried to roll a 45-gallon drum of petrol through snow will appreciate the problem. We soon learned to park as near as possible to a cache and not to roll the drums but to tip them end over end. One also got very expert at opening the screw-on caps with an axe: a few well directed blows were more

The author on snowshoes in deep snow at Lower Post, Liard River, British Columbia on 30 January 1931.

Bellanca CH300 at the 27th baseline on the Athabasca River, Alberta on 8 January 1930. It was 50° below zero — note the frozen exhaust.

effective than any spanner. We carried our own wobble-pumps and hose and each aircraft had a very special elaborate filling funnel with a chamois-leather filter and water trap. Although in England the standard of maintenance insisted on by the Air Ministry was higher, the Canadians and Americans gave much higher priority to the fuel system. For instance, all the engine fuel filters could be flushed in flight in the event of an accumulation of water, whereas in England they were not only bolted but wired up and not part of the daily inspection routine. The one thing which will stop an engine dead is a fuel stoppage.

If an aircraft was brought to rest in deep snow it would often stick, and the only way to get moving again was to rock the wings by heaving up and down on the struts, or sometimes by pushing sideways on the tail. Similarly, if the aircraft was left overnight the skis would freeze on to the snow surface. A routine was evolved by which before stopping we would taxi in a figure of eight patting down the snow with our skis and then stop with the skis straddling two tree trunks with the underside of the skis clear of the snow. I was particularly keen on this technique after having once been left to walk a quarter of a mile through deep snow after unsticking: a more exhausting form of exercise it is difficult to imagine.

By the first week in April, the ice at McMurray was getting rotten and most of the snow had melted from the surface of the river ice. We removed the skis and replaced the wheels for the take-off for the flight to Edmonton Air Harbour, as it was called then. Arrival there was always quite an event. After a few months in the North our eyes had become so accustomed to whiteness everywhere that the first sign of colour or green fields was unbelievably brilliant and good. Having marched into the foyer of the Shasta Hotel clad in furs and looking like an Eskimo it was a joy to have a hot bath, clean clothes and a well-cooked meal. Our arrival in town was reported in the press and it was not long before a party developed; in fact, there were so many parties that in the end some of us were glad to get moving again and away from the artificial life and the bright lights of the city. This reaction may have been due to the sudden and complete contrast to the sort of life of austerity and adventure to which one became accustomed while flying in the North. Our city acquaintances were curious to hear about our experiences in the North but they had their own lives to lead with their own problems. It felt like being an utter stranger not really able to communicate.

6 Flying with Monkey

In preparation for the coming summer, the aircraft were overhauled and flown out to Cooking Lake about twenty miles east of Edmonton. Landing in a small field beside the lake we lifted the aircraft on a tripod and fitted the Edo floats. Our Managing Director, Cy Becker did the test flights and on 13 May we returned to McMurray. On a map Canada looks like a large land mass, but in fact about one third of the area is covered with lakes, while it is possible to fly, even in an aircraft with a short range, right across the Continent, hence the popularity of floatplanes there.

One of the engineers I got to know well was a Dutchman called Van der Linden. He had worked for KLM before going to the United States where he enlisted in the US Airship Service. He described life on board these big ships which would make flights lasting four or five days at a time. They cruised at quite low altitude, usually about 1,000 feet, the crew doing maintenance on the engines and constantly repairing leaks in the internal gas bags. These leaks were caused by the fabric chafing on the alloy rib structure, and I gathered that repairing them was quite a difficult job, rather like reefing sails on a square-rigger. Sleeping accommodation consisted of slinging a hammock between two girders, with nothing between you and Mother Earth except a piece of outer fabric covering. In any sort of bad weather the whole thing flexed like a jelly. In spite of his description, I have ever since longed to make a trip in an airship or a balloon but the opportunity has never come my way.

For most of the summer I flew with 'Monkey' Sherlock. He was a great character, very amusing and a brilliant pilot. He had originally been in the Royal Flying Corps and after the war had fought in the expeditionary force which Britain sent to help the White Russians fight the Bolsheviks. Retiring from the Royal Air Force in 1929, he had come to Canada to continue his easy going lifestyle as a bush pilot.

Like all fighter pilots, he was a press-on type always ready to have a go, but fighter aircraft up to that time had been very compact lively biplanes with thin wing sections which were liable to sudden vicious stalls, so understandably his flying technique was not ideal for commercial flying with nervous passengers. In the approach to land, he would 'stir the pudding', as he described it, moving the stick around feeling for the weight of the control and the aircraft's response to the movement, to assess how near a stall he was. On the other hand, in taking a heavy load off calm water, he had a delicate touch, just sensing when the lift was at a peak in relation to the combined drag of water and air. Similarly, in flight when turning back due to bad weather at very low altitude, he would use a lot of power and make a very gentle turn with a small angle of bank and allow the aircraft to turn gently without increasing the wing load due to G. One way and another he was a natural born pilot, and I am very grateful to have been fortunate enough to fly as his No. 2. He used to hand over to me to do all the routine flying when conditions were straightforward, and all the navigation whenever it was called for, as this was not his strong point. Our Bellanca, CF-AIA, became for all practical purposes our own personal transport, and for most of the time we were out of touch with the office and were our own masters.

Not much attention was paid to the all-up weight authorised in the Certificate of Safety of the aircraft. One simply took as much as one could lift off the water. There was an additional limitation for us, as the Bellanca cabin was designed as a six-seater and mail is very bulky in relation to its weight. The question of stowage required skill as every available square foot would be utilised, and it saved work if it was stowed in sequence for off-loading. A heavily loaded floatplane has to overcome a critical stage during take-off in getting 'over the hump' at about 15 to 20 mph. Resistance reaches a maximum as the floats try to start planing before the wings give the benefit of much lift. The engine of a floatplane inevitably receives a severe beating at full power with little air flow to cool the cylinders; on a hot summer's day the attempt to take off may have to be prolonged and even abandoned due to overheating. On 'AIA I reset the adjustable pitch propeller to give us more revolutions per minute, which enabled us to take off with more load, although once airborne our cruising speed was lower.

Whenever pilots met, there was often an argument about the best technique for getting a heavily loaded floatplane off smooth water. Some argued for 'rocking' the craft to get it onto the 'step', followed by the single leap method; others argued for the gentle touch. Similarly, there was argument as to whether to try taking-off down stream with the current, giving more airflow over the wings, or upstream against the current with more speed through the water and more dynamic lift on the floats. These questions were never completely solved as conditions were never identical but the handling of the controls at take-off required the greatest skill if a heavily loaded aircraft was to become airborne.

One danger was in landing on very calm glassy water, as the judgement of height is difficult under these conditions. On a river one landed close to the side using the bank as a reference line, but on a lake it was better to throw something overboard, such as a newspaper or cushion, and land on that

A heavy landing on the Great Slave Lake. The Royal Mail cypher on the Bellanca's fuselage is partly obscured by the strut.

as a reference. Another hazard for a floatplane is a floating log: in the spring the rivers rise and all the stranded logs float off; usually these float horizontally on the surface and can be seen, but if only one of the aircraft floats rides over a log it sometimes tips up and is struck by the revolving propeller. Later in the year, waterlogged tree trunks or dead-heads will float vertically with only the tip on the surface, and striking one of these will rip the bottom out of a float. Putting a patch on a partly submerged float is an unenviable job but it is surprising what one can do if there is no alternative transport and one is 1,000 miles from home.

Normally the weather in the North becomes very stable and settled for long periods, but from time to time patches of low cloud and rain persist for upwards of a week. We had one such spell in June 1930 on a flight to McMurray from Edmonton with three passengers and were forced to land on an unknown lake surrounded with reeds and marshes which made it impossible to get ashore. It rained all night and none of us got much sleep sitting in the cabin, cold, miserable and damp with the aircraft pitching just enough to add a slight feeling of sickness. By morning we were hungry but the emergency rations were stowed in a locker in the rear fuselage which I found very difficult to reach from a float. I had

not previously realised the difficulties of actually living on board a marooned floatplane: even the most elementary demands of nature called for an acrobatic balancing feat which our passengers did not appreciate. I did manage to make some flapjacks and tea for them, all done on our primus in the cabin. The Civil Aviation Authority would hardly have approved, especially with 100 gallons of petrol in the wing-tanks above us, but needs must when the devil drives.

As morning wore on there was a slight lift in the low cloud so we took-off. It was still hopeless, but while airborne we saw an isolated cabin on the edge of the lake and landed near it, making fast to a rickety wooden jetty. Several children ran down to see the aircraft, followed by their mother and father. He was the only one who could speak any English and looked either Scandinavian or Polish; as an immigrant, he had been given a piece of land and had literally carved a living for himself and his family from the virgin bush. I do not think the children had ever seen strangers before. They were very shy and would not come near us. Their mother made some hot soup as we were wet and cold, and in return a bottle of our rum was contributed to the party. She would not touch it, but the father took a liking to it and became very excited; by mid-afternoon he was singing and dancing, our own party fully entering into the spirit. It was a strange scene with six rather drunk men behaving like lunatics surrounded by half a dozen surprised and scared children and a resentful mother. Not an episode to be proud of.

By evening the clouds again showed signs of lifting, so being anxious to get away we took-off. Our navigation by dead reckoning was now adrift. In any case, the map only showed the Athabasca River but no other details so we took a northwesterly course hoping to hit it. The weather was still bad with a cloud base at about 200 feet and on seeing a stretch of water ahead, we landed. Unfortunately, the river, as such it turned out to be, was very fast flowing, almost a rapid with steep banks. A floatplane has a strong tendency to weather-cock into the wind, and turning downwind can present great difficulties as, by using a lot of power to give the necessary turning, effect, the craft itself gathers too much speed and this increases the turning circle. In the circumstances, we had no option but to get airborne again. We spotted a small lake and for 'want of a better hole' settled there. A second cold, wet night on board certainly had a sobering effect, especially as we were getting low in fuel. Every full-power take-off uses a lot more fuel and as we still did not know how far we had to fly before reaching McMurray the situation was getting critical. The Bellanca fuel gauges were glass tubes on the cabin end of the wing tanks, rather like a water gauge on a boiler, very accurate but we had been flying too low to drain either tank completely and as we had already flown nearly six hours since refuelling there was little showing on the gauges.

By leaning out the mixture and cruising at reduced speed I estimated that, at best, we had another hour's endurance. As luck would have it, next morning the weather improved and we were able to make it to McMurray in forty minutes flying time, a bit too close for comfort.

One evening we stayed the night at the Roman Catholic Mission at Fort Providence on the Mackenzie River and as the weather had deteriorated we eventually had to stay a second night. The nuns looked after us very well and for the first time in my life I ate bear steak and, later, wild goose. I was surprised to learn that wild animals at certain periods of the year are in such poor condition from lack of food that one can eat their flesh and yet starve to death. This is particularly the case with caribou. What we call lean beef from a domestic animal is really full of fat and weight for weight provides much more nourishment.

To spend the night in a bed was an unaccustomed luxury. Normal routine was to sleep on the floor in one's own sleeping bag using a sweater for a pillow. Washing facilities were non-existent except for a washing up basin and in winter water was a problem. The heat required to melt snow or ice came from burning wood which had to be cut down, chopped up and dragged to the cabin. If we ever had to make a forced landing we, for choice, would always pick an in-habited cabin, but failing that, it was an understood thing that one could go into any cabin and help oneself to shelter, warmth and food. However, before leaving, one wrote a message for the owner but, far more important, one left kindling ready to make an immediate fire; any food which was used had to be replaced at a later date and as soon as possible. Life in the far north has some elementary lessons for the so-called civilised man, as money ceases to have value in the fight for survival, and to leave money in payment for food used could well lead to death for the owner of the cabin.

Trappers were lonely men, always bachelors, although sometimes there was a squaw in the background. There were men from all walks of life and of different education who, for one reason or another (no questions asked), preferred a solitary life looking after their traps and selling some of the finest skins to be found anywhere in the world. There are people who criticise the killing of animals for furs but little do the rich wealthy city women realise the skill and hardship entailed in obtaining the skins. The real money is made by the middleman and furrier, not the trapper.

On 26 June 1930 Monkey Sherlock and I flew from McMurray to Aklavik, making ten stops en route to drop mail and refuel. We arrived at about two o'clock in the morning to find everyone up and about. I found the continuous sun at that time of year most disconcerting: there was no end to the day. It is interesting to note that Aklavik is nearly 70° north and as far west as halfway to Honolulu from San Francisco. One is moving up round the top of the world. It had taken us eleven and three-quarter hours flying time and was the first flight from the 'end of steel', the railway terminus at Waterways near McMurray, to the Arctic Ocean in a day. Those who fly seaplanes will know that one's anxieties are not over until the aircraft is safely secured on dry land. It was a very long day but we found the most restful part was while we were actually flying.

Our flight, although carrying only a few hundred pounds of useful load, was well covered by the Canadian press because it showed how effectively the aeroplane could in a few hours bring civilisation to the remotest parts. Today there are two flights a day to the Mackenzie Delta, only a short distance from Prudoe Bay, the largest source of oil on the North American continent, and on the Canadian side of the border a fully proved vast oil and gas field still waiting to be exploited. Little did Monkey and I know what lay below those barren wastes, because no one had even scratched the surface then.

The Canadian Government had bought a large herd of reindeer from the Russians with the intention of providing Eskimos with an alternative source of food and transport. The two Norwegian herdsmen who had flown with us to Aklavik in the previous winter were now ready to set up camp in anticipation of their arrival. The reindeer were being driven across the Beaufort Sea over the ice north of the Bering Strait from Siberia to the Arctic Coast east of the Mackenzie Delta.

35

We flew off with them along the coast in an easterly direction. It was a beautiful sunny day with unlimited visibility and the barrier ice could be clearly seen a few miles to the north. Our passengers picked a suitable looking place with a sandy beach with some low hills behind. After unloading their gear two of us decided to have a bathe. With a hot sun on the shallow water for twenty-four hours a day the water was reasonably warm!

The place chosen was completely barren but on a high bank well above sea level. At the time we named it Reindeer Point but later it was called Kittigasuit, an Eskimo name. We never heard the outcome of this experiment but both Monkey and I felt badly about leaving these men so sparsely equipped in such a desolate spot.

On the route south we were diverted to Fort Norman on a special charter flight for the Imperial Oil Company. In 1924 oil had been discovered on the east bank of the Mackenzie River, fifty miles down river from the settlement, but as there was no demand for oil in the North at that time, the well and other equipment had been abandoned. We were to visit the site and make a report.

We had a drinking party in the evening of arrival with the manager of the Hudson's Bay Company Store and two or three others. I was tired and although there was still daylight went off to sleep about midnight leaving the others to it. About five in the morning I was woken up with the news that we were just going off to the oil well. I did not immediately realise the state that Monkey Sherlock was in, not that I could have done much anyway, but we set off with two passengers in the back of the cabin. We found the site easily and went ashore to inspect. Everything movable had been taken as every boat going down river must have landed there to help themselves, but not knowing anything about the oil business I was surprised to find a pipe sticking out of the ground with a tap on it still intact. The stopcock was padlocked but with the judicious use of an axe I freed it and oil squirted out. We found an old empty food tin and filled it with the brown, dirty-looking liquid. To our surprise it proved possible to light it with a match without difficulty so presumably it was unusually volatile and I would guess that it could, after filtration, be used directly in a diesel engine. During World War II, a pipeline was constructed from this area, running for a few hundred miles over the Rocky Mountains to the new Alaskan Highway, that must have cost a lot of money and it would be interesting to know how successful this project proved to be.

Our flight back to Fort Norman from the oil well was very frightening. Monkey, still suffering from the night before, kept turning round to talk to his two passengers on the back seat, but in the middle of the conversation he gently pushed the stick forward until his passengers were suspended in mid air due to negative G! There were no such things as passenger seat belts in those days nor was there anything for them to hold on to, and their faces of surprise and alarm merely goaded Monkey on to do it again! He finished off by looping the loop which I knew was taking the wings and structure of the aircraft very near the limit of strength. Although we had the extra weight of the floats we fortunately had no load in the cabin and little fuel. Commercial aircraft are only designed for a wing strength of about four times that of a normal full load and this is easily reached in a pull out from a dive. The whole episode was a shattering experience. However, I thought I could stop him flying again while in that condition, and nothing like this ever happened again.

Monkey's usual drink was brandy, and it was not long before I too had taken a liking to it. It is a very different drink to whisky, which up to then had been my choice, but it does have a stimulating effect. It is known as 'eau de vie' and of course is used for medicinal purposes, but about this time I noticed my hands were getting shaky, so shaky in fact, that I had to use both hands to steady my glass to prevent it spilling. After this trip to Fort Norman, I swore never to drink brandy again, or anything at all before flying.

All our maintenance was carried out at McMurray, each engineer looking after his own aircraft. Wright Whirlwind engines were very reliable, the ignition being by dual Scintilla magnetos. These latter had rotating field magnets with fixed make-and-break, a great advance over any British magneto at that time. Engines were returned to the factory for major overhauls which became due at, I believe, 600 hours, but we did our own period checks and top overhauls.

One day I was greasing and adjusting the valve clearances when, on turning over the engine, I suddenly realised that it had started and was idling over slowly! At that time I was standing on a plank straddling the two floats with the propeller hub at about chin level. Not daring to move I shouted to someone to come and switch off, in the meantime holding myself clear of the hub with the blades whirling past my toes. It was a nasty moment and I can only assume that I must have knocked 'on' the American type of swinging arm contact switch with my knee while climbing out of the cockpit.

In the early summer, Lumsden heard he had been given the sack. He was too much of a man of leisure to stand the pace and was considering leaving anyway when the message arrived. It placed him in a dilemma as there was not much money in the kitty with which to buy his train ticket back east and the problem was whether he should travel the four day journey to Montreal first class or whether to go 'tourist' and take some bottles of whisky. Being a very human person who liked meeting people, you can guess which alternative he took.

The availability of our aircraft gave prospectors a wonderful opportunity of searching vast new areas for minerals. Their interest was primarily in gold and other rare metals

The author and a Norwegian herdsman at Reindeer Point (Kittigasuit) on 27 June 1930 after a bathe in the Arctic Ocean.

which could easily be transported as, although there is an abundance of other minerals such as zinc and copper in the North West Territories, these are more easily obtained elsewhere. We often flew these men and their supplies into some remote place in the early spring and arranged to collect them in the autumn before the freeze up. These camps were not identifiable on any map for the simple reason that no maps existed but they relied on our bump of locality and memory. It always worried me that should anything happen to us or our aircraft, they would be in trouble and would, at least,

have to wait until the freeze up before being able to travel to the nearest trading post.

On one such trip we were persuaded to carry a canoe to the site. It had been done before and using a lot of rope lashings we fastened it under the bottom of the fuselage which it fitted surprisingly well. However, in taking off, a lot of spray found its way inside the canoe which put the centre of gravity of the aircraft right outside the aft limit. In flight the water sloshed backwards and forwards making it impossible to hold a steady flight path. Fortunately, the distance was only 25 miles but we were glad to land safely and never took the risk again. In fact, it was our own fault because, although we knew canoes had been flown before, neither of us had actually seen it done. The proper method was to tip the canoe on its gunwale, and lash it upside down on to the outside of the struts of the floats so that water could not collect in it.

In mid July we were recalled to Edmonton to embark a party of politicians who wished to make an election tour of the Peace River District. The Peace River flows from the foothills of the Rockies in a northeasterly direction, feeds into the Slave River and ultimately flows north to the Arctic Ocean. This area must have been one of the last to be populated in North America as, although it was potentially good farming land, it was relatively inaccessible, being north of the main Trans-Canada railways.

After a flight of two and three-quarter hours we landed on the McLennan Lake. From there, the election tour really started with daily flights in different directions. It was all very sparsely inhabited, the meetings only attracting a few people. Although the charter was successful from our Company's point of view, I cannot believe the outcome of the subsequent election had any significant effect, except that it was the first electioneering tour by air of what is now a very wealthy oil province.

During the summer an old stern-wheeler called the *Northland Echo* made its yearly trip to Fitzgerald taking passengers and supplies. During summer 1929 our fuel dumps were established in time for the start of the service in the winter. In 1930, however, the steamer was unable or unwilling to do this and so the Company itself was forced to do it. A wooden barge and petrol-engined tug were built and the whole outfit set forth on its long journey. The Mackenzie flows very fast in places with sandbars and minor rapids, so that it was uneconomic to attempt to return against the current and everything that was used for the journey north had to be abandoned there. By the time the fuel was delivered to the most northern of the trading posts, it was very valuable and precious. From time to time one found a drum empty, lost either from evaporation or theft; for us this was almost as serious a matter as being short of food.

Most of the operational crews moved out of O'Coffee's hotel in the spring and joined together to rent a house. We took on a Chinese cook who more or less ran the place. As we were never there together it can be imagined what chaos this led to. I had never realised before how thin the veneer of civilisation really is; manners disappear, bad habits develop without check, and untidiness and dirt accumulate everywhere.

7 Yukon salvage

At the end of August 1930, 'AIA (which by now I regarded as my own aircraft) was allotted to Glyn Roberts, an ex-Royal Air Force Welshman. We were given a most interesting job, to fly a party of American big-game hunters into the Rocky Mountains to try to obtain specimens of the special mountain sheep which were known to live in these remote parts.

It had been decided to establish a camp at Dead Man's Creek on the Nahanni River, about 250 miles west of the Great Slave Lake. It was inaccessible both on foot or by canoe as the river flowed through a deep gorge which cut through a ridge of hills on its way to join the Liard River, a tributary of the Mackenzie. Everything had to be flown in, including three hefty men and all supplies for a month.

After waiting three days at Fort Simpson for good weather, we finally left on 10 September. From the air the whole area beyond the gorge looked formidable with high snow-covered peaks falling away to a heavily timbered valley. The river was fast flowing but it was straight for about a mile before the rapids leading through the gorge. On landing safely we taxied into the west bank and set about making a clearing and felling some timber for the camp. I joined one of the party fishing for the evening meal. It was unbelievable: every cast seemed to produce a beautiful large fish — it had evidently never been fished before. That night we had a further surprise as, while sitting round our camp fire, what I believe was a pack of wolves came to have a look. Their eyes reflected the light from the fire, but after taking a shot at one of them, they turned tail and slunk away. The valley was teeming with game of all sorts but it was not a place to go off casually shooting for the pot. Crossing one of the dried-out river beds we found the trail of a large grizzly bear. The prints were a good 12 inches long. After this we never left camp without rifles. A grizzly is one of the few animals which will stalk and attack a man without provocation.

While away collecting the next load of supplies, the hunters set off to climb the surrounding mountains in search of the sheep. The landing back at the camp three days later very nearly turned into a disaster. As previously mentioned, the river was flowing at about 6 knots. At the same time there was a wind upstream of 15 mph. Understandably, Glyn Roberts chose to land into wind but downstream. The width of the river was about 100 yards with banks lined with small boulders. Owing to the combination of wind and current making the aircraft weathercock, and not being equipped with water rudders, we found it difficult, in fact impossible to turn upstream. Every time we tried to turn we finished up heading straight for a bank. Finally, with the rapids looming up ahead, Glyn Roberts ran ashore into one bank at considerable speed with a great grinding and bumping of the floats over stony shallows as we were carried downstream. By climbing out and wading in the icy river I was able to swing the aircraft's nose up river and so to taxi back to safety. We had not improved the floats but they still seemed to be watertight. At least we would be able to fly out again successfully. I took the precaution of mooring the aircraft tail to the bank, as I knew that with leaking floats, or even a lowering of the river water level overnight, a floatplane parked nose towards the shore can finish up with the tailplane under the water.

The party were successful in their hunt and obtained some good 'heads' of the rare species for which they had been hunting. Their horns were rather similar to a bull's but were corrugated and curled round more at the tips. Mr Shultz, who was the leader of the party, was very pleased with their trophies. About a month after his return to civilisation a large packing case arrived at McMurray filled with an assortment of socks. It turned out that he was President of the largest sock manufacturer in the USA! My share lasted for years but Mr Shultz told me that the better the quality, especially of wool socks, the shorter the life, so there was little wool in them.

Returning to Fort Resolution on the Great Slave Lake, we received a message to go to Fort Rae on the north shore of the lake to take some mining engineers on a reconnaissance flight. Most of the places we used to land while on floats were well sheltered, but Resolution was fully exposed. On this particular day there were some big waves. The lake is like the open sea, being 250 miles long by 100 miles wide, and as we were carrying two 45-gallon drums of fuel in the cabin as well as two passengers we were on the upper limit of load. After a few violent bumps and premature leaps into the air Glyn Roberts managed to get the aircraft airborne without damage. Although the Bellanca never gave any structural problems there were a number of features which would never be accepted by civil aviation authorities today. The main throttle control was only a piano wire sliding through a tube; even the main elevator control cable ran over a sheave which relied on a weld to attach it to the middle of a cross tube of the fuselage.

Any aircraft which became damaged in the north was a write-off unless it could be patched up and flown out. There have been a number of amazing recoveries including one case where the crew made their own replacement wooden propeller, another when a badly twisted and broken rear fuselage was lashed up with wooden splints and galvanised fencing wire! The prospect of being marooned hundreds of miles from home without transport certainly proves the old saying 'necessity is the mother of invention'; improvisation is the order of the day, safety rules taking second place.

Before returning to the Nahanni River at the conclusion of the hunting trip, we were recalled to Edmonton. To my surprise, my brother David had turned up on his way back to England from Australia. He was a member of the London Stock Exchange and a keen sailor but, wanting a complete rest and change from City life, he had signed on as a member of the crew of the *Olivebank*, a 3,500-ton, four-masted square rigged ship. She took 168 days at sea to reach Sydney on the outward voyage from Finland.

We made the final mail delivery to Aklavik on 5 October 1930 before the winter freeze up. It was getting late and the weather was cold when trouble developed in the engine oil system. As we were still on floats, no winterisation of the engine had been thought necessary, but suddenly the oil temperature started to rise above the upper limit. Four times in one day we had to force land on the river to allow the oil to cool. The type of oil supplied incorporated the very latest advances in this field; in fact, we were being used as a kind of guinea pig. Unfortunately, it foamed badly and from the quantity of oil covering the exterior of the engine it was evident that a lot of pressure was building up in the crank-

case. Although we got home safely the trouble was almost certainly due to either the breather pipe becoming frozen or possibly coring in the oil scavenge line to the tank.

After a year of intensive flying I had acquired the airman's habit of thinking in terms of time and not distance and so, having saved some money, at the end of the season I returned to England for a holiday, four days by train to Montreal and then eight days in a ship. It was good to be home but England was a depressing place with upwards of three million unemployed. I suppose the life I had been living was unusual but one could not help contrasting the stodgy established order of things with the freedom of Canada. I could hardly wait to get back and the urge to fly was still very strong.

The return journey via New York and Chicago was interesting. The *Europa*, crack ship of the Hamburg America Line, broke down somewhere in mid-Atlantic. She was a new ship and the delay was only a few hours so it cannot have been very serious. From New York, I boarded the *Twentieth Century Limited*, a well known train, to Chicago; it made the trip overnight with a guaranteed arrival at 9.00 am. There was even a refund on the fare of a dollar a minute for delay!

I stayed with friends of my family in Chicago, but, not having room for me in their flat, I was made an honorary member of Mr James' club, a very sedate English type of establishment. The year 1930 was at the height of the gang warfare in the city and I was given strict instructions that if stopped on the street I was to hand over my wallet im-

The route flown to salvage the Junkers F.13 from Scurvy Creek.

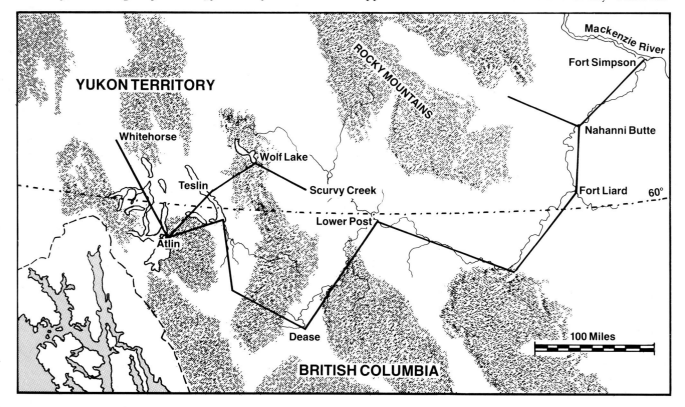

Salvage at Scurvy Creek, Upper Liard River, Yukon on 4 February 1931, with the Junkers on floats in the background. Emil Kading, a German engineer, is seen at our camp.

mediately without argument. Any foreigner was fair game. My clothes and hat were quite ordinary, but were probably different enough to look unusual in a mid-west city before universal television and rapid communications.

Mr James, an Englishman who ran a big power station, the State Line Generating Company, had a daughter, Margaret, a vivacious redhead with expensive tastes who was studying sculpture and, in the course of my artistic education, she took me to the opera. It was fun for a few days to enjoy a life of luxury. However, after another four days of second class rumbling over the bleak snowbound Prairies in a train, I came down to earth with a bump.

No aircraft was flying north to McMurray so there was no alternative to the weekly mail train. This was a new experience. The mixed freight cum passenger train consisted of four freight cars and one passenger coach and was due to take twenty-four hours for the 200-mile journey. The coach had a cooking stove at one end and a lavatory at the other. My fellow travellers consisted of about twenty rough and tough looking characters and we very soon got to know one another over crates of whisky and rum!

A game of poker started on leaving Edmonton and was continued all day as we crawled slowly north. We stopped at every wayside halt and even log cabins, where the engine driver and fireman would descend and have a chat with the locals. By evening the party was in full swing with singing and dancing (no girls!) until it gradually subsided into a drunken stupor. The next morning we crept into Waterways, the terminus near McMurray, very subdued.

For the winter I was to crew Stan McMillan, the celebrated Canadian bush pilot. In the previous year, 1929, Stan had been one of the pilots of the two seaplanes, one a Super

Fokker, the other a Fairchild FC2-W2, lost for fifty-four days in the Barren Lands in the Arctic. Colonel MacAlpine, President of Dominion Explorers, and his party had been visiting some of the company's prospecting parties in the area. It was the first serious organised search for minerals in the far North. They left Chesterfield Inlet on Hudson Bay in the late autumn intending to fly to Bathurst on the Arctic Ocean, but failed to arrive. No expense was spared in the search which was immediately organised as the freeze up was expected shortly, making floatplanes useless until equipped with skis. Most of the fuel caches were used up throughout the North before a wireless message came from Cambridge Bay of their safe arrival on foot, having waited for the sea ice to form and being guided there by Eskimos. They had force landed out of fuel at Dease Point.

The world press had been following the dramatic search in the Arctic Barren Lands and their subsequent rescue. The experience gained of operating aircraft under such adverse conditions owed a great deal to the fortitude of the pilots concerned. In all, five aircraft were lost through failures or accidents, but no lives; sadly, several of the pioneering bush pilots who took part were killed in the following years.

Many bush pilots have disappeared without trace in the North. An aircraft is difficult to spot, especially in winter when the top surfaces would probably be covered in snow. Our Bellancas were painted post office red, which stood out well, but nowadays fluorescent orange is used, as the colour is easier to see. It is a strange fact that when a pilot is lost, it has been found that he tends to turn in a westerly direction, so when first searching for him, the search is always made to start with on that side of his planned route.

Stan was a very different character to Monkey Sherlock, being quieter and far more painstaking in planning a flight; furthermore we never carried any alcohol! His experience the previous year when the MacAlpine party came so near to starvation, may have made him more cautious, but he was a good steady pilot, never taking any unnecessary chances. He realised, as I began to realise, that the hazards of bush flying are as great on the ground as they are in the air. The North is such a vast almost totally uninhabited and inhospitable area, that any unexpected minor mishap can easily lead to disaster. Stan knew how to survive and I could hardly have had a more experienced true bush pilot to teach me.

After a few northern flights with mail we were sent on an entirely different and unusual charter trip. A Junkers F.13 flown by Paddy Burke and carrying a prospector and an engineer had been forced to land on a river in bad weather during a flight in Northern British Columbia. The river was shallow, a rock had punctured the floats and the aircraft, although otherwise undamaged, had had to be abandoned. The insurance company thought it might be possible to salvage it and commissioned us to do the job.

It was a sad story. Paddy Burke, an ex-RAF pilot, had been persuaded to make the prospecting flight late in the summer. Following a river through the Rockies he had been forced by bad weather to fly lower and lower until he had no alternative but to land. The floats, being damaged, filled with water and the aircraft was left with the floats submerged but the fuselage and wings high and dry. The three men on board waded to the bank and set up camp. With the oncoming winter no rescue was possible until the freeze up. After a few days they decided to try to walk to Wolf Lake which they knew was at the head of the valley about 75 miles away.

None of them had any real experience of living rough and off the country. Burke, the Irishman, a German engineer called Emil Kading, and a city-type mining engineer made all the mistakes one might expect. Seventy-five miles may not sound too far but there was a lot of undergrowth along the banks of the river, all the icy tributary streams had to be crossed and they had to carry all the camping gear. On top of this they had little food. After a week on the trail they had covered 20 miles, then had the luck to see and shoot a deer. None of them had even gutted an animal before and in their efforts with a knife wasted a lot of meat. After feeding themselves up they set forth again but three days later they were so hungry that they went back for the head and other bits. Burke was getting very weak. A few days later he died. The others managed to reach a trapper's cabin on Wolf Lake.

We left McMurray on 27 January, following the scheduled route as far as Fort Simpson. There we loaded all the fuel we could carry into drums and branched off to the west, landing at Fort Liard on the Liard River. After staying the night we set off next morning to fly over the Rockies for Atlin, British Columbia, where the land undercarriage for the skis and other spares were awaiting collection. The only map we had was one of Western Canada torn out of an atlas with a scale of about 80 miles to an inch, which showed the distance as the crow flies as being about 340 miles. It appeared as if the best route would be to fly up the valley of the Dease River, over the height of land and by steering west we should then hit a river which flowed north westerly, taking us in the direction of Lake Teslin and so to Atlin.

We followed up the Liard River with the mountains rising steadily on either side. Carrying about 80 gallons of extra fuel in the cabin we had hopefully expected to pump this into the main wing tanks during flight. I could not make the lash up system work; in any case, it was bumpy and some of the precious fuel was spilling. I had had no experience of mountain flying, nor I think had Stan. It became evident that with an adverse wind and the heavy load trouble lay ahead.

Although the Whirlwind engine was mildly supercharged, the impeller was more to improve the distribution of the mixture than to provide power at altitude. The height of land we had to cross was about 10,000 feet but the westerly wind was pouring over the top like a waterfall and as we approached our rate of climb turned into a rate of descent. After three hours in the air, Lower Post, where the Dease River joins the Liard River, came into sight only 160 miles from our point of departure. Here was the first sign of human habitation, a log cabin with smoke and trails leading to it. We landed in very deep snow to be greeted by a very surprised Scotsman. I do not think he had seen another human being for a year or two, certainly not an aeroplane. For us it was a relief to have landed safely and found shelter, and to receive a warm welcome in such inhospitable country was a real pleasure. We stayed there overnight.

The snow was so deep it was like a feather bed and Stan and I were forced to use snowshoes but all was well and taking off next morning we reached McDame, a small trading post, an hour later. Here I pumped the remainder of the fuel into the tanks and was glad to get it out of the cabin. We stayed the night before setting out on the final leg.

The height of land was a flat featureless, snow covered plateau 50 miles across but there was no sign of any river or valley to guide us to Lake Teslin. I was beginning to think that the position of the river had been inserted on hearsay! The lie of the land and mountains was in a north westerly direction so after turning that way a long narrow lake eventually appeared. This proved to be Teslin. The route onwards to Atlin was through a narrow gap in the mountains, which acted like a funnel for the strong westerly wind, bumping us violently all over the sky, I was glad that most of our fuel had been used as I looked anxiously at the flexing of the wings.

Atlin, a gold mining town on Lake Atlin, duly turned up but to our embarrassment we saw that the lake was open water and we, of course, were on skis! Not much hope of landing there. Luckily we had spotted a small lake about five miles away which was frozen. Hardly had we landed than a Snowmobile or tracked Model T Ford appeared with many helpful people. I think we must have been the first to fly over

The salvaged Junkers at Atlin, on 11 February 1931. From left: the author, Stan McMillan, Van der Byl and Joress. The paddles proved useless.

the Rockies in such northerly latitudes. It was strange to find relatively mild weather with over 20 feet of snow. We were definitely wrongly dressed for the occasion without parkas, mukluks and Arctic gear. However, I was glad to get there as a large boil had developed on one of my fingers and it was beginning to affect my left arm. All was well after it had been lanced, but it took quite a long time to heal up in the cold weather.

Gold was still being mined near Atlin. Somewhat to my surprise the manager offered me a job at twice my salary to look after the mining machinery. A nice, cushy job with no risks but I was not in the mood to be tempted. We immediately started making plans to fly the skis and other equipment to the wrecked aircraft but before doing so we had to report to the Provincial Authorities at Whitehorse across the border of British Columbia in the Yukon. It seemed that the wreck was in their territory. The flight there was via the White Pass on the old Klondike route from Skagway. It looked very desolate, as no doubt it did to those who took part in the gold rush of '98. The landing strip was a clearing in the forest a couple of miles from what remained of the ghost town of Whitehorse, which at one time had had a population of some 30,000. The reception party took us straight to the Police Station before joining us for a meal. It was the only occasion in my life when I was asked to produce my licences both as pilot and engineer. I felt we had come a long way into the wilds to be so insulted!

Back at Atlin, Emil Kading and a freelance pilot called Van

der Byl were waiting. It was then that we heard details of the difficult journey to Wolf Lake and, understandably, the engineer was not too keen about going back. Nevertheless, next morning one ski for the Junkers was lashed under our fuselage and we all left for Wolf Lake en route to the accident.

The trapper at Wolf Lake had more or less nursed Kading and his companion back to life using up many of his precious provisions on the starving men. So he was very glad to see us and the food. He made his living by shooting wolves and claiming from the Government the bounty of eight dollars per tail. It takes all types to make a world, but this must surely have been one of the loneliest of men, completely cut off from civilisation, content to live a life of isolation.

We found the Junkers somewhere on the Upper Liard River and gave the place the name Scurvy Creek. The aircraft looked like a sort of white scarecrow, all the upper surfaces were covered with the full winter's snow, about three feet on the wings, yet the struts of the floats held the aircraft well above the surrounding snow bound river. On examination, I was doubtful whether it could be salvaged as the wing tips were sagging downwards at least a couple of feet under the snow's weight. The first job was to establish camp.

There was a very small clearing near the aircraft which had been used by Paddy Burke and his crew. One of the trees had a flat surface hacked out with an axe. On it was carved an arrow and a message: 'Leaving for Wolf Lake, October 1930, Burke'. We cut the tree down and took back the part with the message for his widow, a somewhat macabre present. We felt she might like it. I never heard she received it.

We built a comfortable camp on the bank near the aircraft and we had no intention of going short of either food or drink. First, fresh spruce boughs were laid on the snow followed by a ground sheet, tent, collapsible cooking stove and even a stove pipe. The first night we were all in a fairly relaxed mood having celebrated well and truly before crawling into sleeping bags. During the night I crept out quietly in order to relieve the call of nature and, looking round, saw a rifle pointing at me through the flap of the tent. One of the party had woken up, seen a shadow outside, and assuming it was a bear scavenging around was just about to take a shot when he heard my shout! We had, as usual, left a loaded gun handy just in case of intruders, but for me it was a lucky escape. After that we took more water with the rum!

The usual method of clearing snow or frost off the wings was to throw a rope over the wing and for two people, one either side, to 'saw' the rope backwards and forwards, gradually moving inwards from the wing tip. It was most successful on the Junkers until suddenly there was a 'thump' and the aileron flipped up as it was relieved of the weight of snow. The other aileron went down hard to its maximum travel, so hard, in fact, that it bent the lever arm slightly. The control circuit was not designed for that particular load, but we were pleased to see the wings spring back without any apparent set or damage from the weight of snow. We were not accustomed to this heavy damp snow but to a powdery dry snow known as sugar snow which does not pack.

Stan and I made three more flights to Atlin to pick up the second ski and various parts of the undercarriage, while the engineer got busy checking everything. The Junkers was an all-metal low wing monoplane, a very advanced design at the time. The aluminium sheet covering both wings and fuselage was corrugated to provide stiffness and this type of construction was still in use by the German manufacturer during World War II when a three-engined design, the Ju 52/3m was used as a troop transport. Another unusual feature of the F.13 was that the aircraft had an open cockpit for the pilot and an enclosed passenger cabin. My first flying instructor, Colonel Henderson, was killed flying a similar aircraft while returning to Croydon from Le Touquet with a party of well-known celebrities. The aircraft was seen to dive into the ground at Meopham and it was later reported that the cause of the disaster had been due to the top engine cover becoming loose, swinging back and covering the cockpit.

Fitting the undercarriage was not easy but with the use of jacks and several tree trunks it was finally accomplished. Then the even bigger problem arose of removing the float struts. There were a very large number and anyone who has tried cutting through steel tube with a hacksaw will appreciate how easy it is to snap the blade. It was a question of whether the supply of blades gave out before the F.13 was free. In emergency it is amazing what can be done with an axe!

The big moment arrived with the starting up of the engine, a six-cylinder Junkers L5. Water-cooled engines are not the preferred type for use in the north, but all was well, it fired up immediately and ran smoothly. Both aircraft took off and flew in company, the F.13 flown by Van der Byl, landing safely at Atlin after brief stops at Wolf Lake and Teslin.

Stan McMillan and I took a good view of Atlin and northern British Columbia. Although only 100 miles from the Pacific Ocean, it is separated from the sea by the long narrow strip of Alaska which runs 350 miles to the south nearly as far as Prince Rupert. Whoever drew the boundary between Canada and the USA seems to have made a mistake here. Perhaps the separation and consequent isolation was the key to the independent, free life they seemed to live. After two days of celebration on finishing the job we set off home.

En route for the Mackenzie we landed at Lower Post with a present of liquid refreshment for our trapper friend who had been so kind on the way out. He was very pleased to see us but unfortunately for him, the weather closed in and during the ensuing two days the supply dwindled a bit. The flight time to Fort Simpson was six hours including stops at Nelson Forks and Liard to top up with fuel from the drums which we carried in the cabin. One more day picking up mail at the usual trading posts found us back at McMurray.

As the engine of the Bellanca had by now reached its normal time for an overhaul it was decided to remove it and return it to the manufacturer. It did not go according to plan. The replacement engine was in the manufacturer's standard large packing case; as this had two convenient wooden beams underneath we used these as skids and got Paddy, the local jack of all trades, to drag it down to the river with his horse. In the meantime I had disconnected the various pipes and controls from the old engine in preparation for pushing the aircraft out of the nose hangar to lift the engine out. It was a cold, crystal clear night with a bright moon and we had a good fire going in the stove so as to be able to work in comfort. When the time came to slide the aircraft backwards I found the skis had frozen to the snow and, using the usual method of rocking the wings by pushing up and down on the main struts, proceeded to heave away. What I had completely forgotten about was Paddy's horse which had been waiting patiently under the other side of the wing. He evidently was also taken by surprise by the sudden battering on top of his head. The horse bolted and our precious engine disappeared at speed round the bend and out of sight up the Clearwater. A search party was quickly organised, but it was three hours before the whole outfit was retrieved.

Glyn Roberts also excelled himself about the same time. The weather was clear but exceptionally cold, around 50 degrees below zero. As was his usual morning custom, he used to take a blow lamp with him to the privy to warm up the place and with an extra touch of delicacy would complete the job by running the flame round the seat. On this particular morning the inevitable happened and he set the place on fire. The badly singed seat was never the same again.

8 Farewell to the Barrens

Following the opening up of a new prospecting area at the eastern end of Lake Athabasca, there was a great stirring of activity in the mining world towards the end of February. Stan and I made a number of flights from McMurray carrying personnel and their gear, landing them at Crackingstone Point, Foud du Lac and Stoney Rapids. Sometimes one was at a loss for a name to enter into our log books, and the map was of little help. Early explorers put their own name to places and rivers or picked up local names from Indians or Eskimos. These names live on, but visits by aviators were often too transient to leave any record of their ever having been there.

One day one of our aircraft had a tragic accident at Chipewyan on Lake Athabasca. The day was overcast and conditions made the finding of the direction and strength of the wind very difficult. Smoke from a chimney merges into the snow background and any movement of trees or cloud shadow was, of course, not visible. To make matters worse a recent early spring thaw had been followed by frost leaving an icy surface on top of the snow. After flying round, the pilot decided to land along the row of spruce boughs which had been laid out to indicate the best landing strip. Unfortunately, he landed with a 5 mph tail wind and on touch down the aircraft just skidded along the ice with no resistance, running helplessly a considerable distance gradually losing directional control. At the same time the local children had come out to greet the arrival of the mail, the big event of the week. They did not realise that the aircraft was out of control and one was hit and later died.

The normal magnetic compass becomes very unreliable and finally useless in the area of the magnetic north pole. This is not located at the true North pole but 500 or 600 miles to the east of Aklavik. The magnetic compass in an aircraft is always a bit misleading when flying on a north-south course, as on banking into a turn the needle gives momentarily the wrong direction. This is because the lines of force are not horizontal to the earth's surface near the poles, but dip downwards towards the earth. At the magnetic north pole itself the lines of force are vertical and, therefore, the north seeking end of the compass needle, which is mounted horizontally, cannot respond. Many aircraft have been lost in the far North for this reason. For any long journey over the Barren Lands towards Hudson Bay, the only alternative at that time was a sun compass. This was simply a sundial, the base of which was revolved by clockwork at the speed of the rotation of the earth. To hold a course, the shadow was kept lying along the central line, but it had its limitations!

To fly in the Barren Lands of the far North is a lonely and yet a very satisfying experience. In winter the landscape as seen from 2,000 or 3,000 feet is featureless as far as the eye can see in all directions, and everything is still. There are no trees to move, no water to ripple, no smoke to be seen, often there are no clouds or wind to blow the surface snow, no sign of man, in fact utter peace.

Our mail route did not cross the Barren Lands but followed the course of the mighty Mackenzie River making its way to the Arctic Ocean. The banks had a fringe of trees and scrub but in flat areas what would normally be marshes was muskeg. Here, even in summer the ground was frozen two or three feet below the surface so that no crops or food could be grown and even the burial of the dead presented a problem!

The Mackenzie River drains an enormous area of Canada but it is unusual in that the flow is northwards into a frozen sea. For all practical purposes the Beaufort Sea near the delta is not navigable by ships and this is the reason why the area with all its minerals and possible oil fields has not been opened up. It was the arrival of aircraft which changed the picture.

From the air the trading posts looked tiny, consisting of a warehouse and only three or four cabins, with a population of white and native of perhaps a dozen souls. Quite insignificant in comparison to 'God's own country', as it has been called. Some of the men living in these outposts had no wish to return to civilisation or the outside world, and were unkindly described as being 'bushed'.

During a late trip to Aklavik, the last of the 1931 scheduled winter services, the Royal Canadian Mounted Police asked us to fly two of them to Blake's Cabin on the Porcupine River about 50 miles away. They had found a man there dead for no apparent reason but suspected murder by poisoning. We waited while the grisly job of removing the intestines was performed by two totally unskilled surgeons and departed with a strange looking object in a jam jar pickled nicely in alcohol. It seemed a waste of good alcohol but we could think of no alternative. However, in due course it was delivered safely to the hospital in Edmonton for analysis. They say the Mounties always 'get their man' but, as so often happened, we never heard the end of this story.

During the flight south, we picked up a trapper who was taking with him his entire catch of white fox and a pair of live wild mink in a box. He was hoping to catch the market early in the season and so obtain a better price for his fur whereas the live mink were fetching a very high price for breeding purposes. Mink farming was a development which came later and, of course, led to an enormous expansion in the market for expensive coats.

The settlement of Good Hope was one of the scheduled stopping places on the route. It happens to be almost exactly on the Arctic Circle. Its only claim to fame concerned the manager of the Hudson's Bay Post there. The story goes that year after year in his returns of stocks and request for stores he would put in a demand for two gallons of red ink. After this had finally been noticed by head office in Winnipeg, they had written to ask why he was using such an exceptionally large amount for the limited office work involved. With a mail delivery only once a year this entailed a further delay and the correspondence dragged on for some years. What they apparently did not realise at head office was that red ink is almost pure alcohol.

In Canada the buffalo was almost extinct. As the tide of immigrants flowed westwards with the coming of the railways so the buffalo herds were slaughtered for food and driven out. However, some of the early conservationists in Ottawa had designated an area to the north west of Lake Athabasca as a reserve and our company had received a small contract to make a survey and report.

The Government was particularly interested in a census of the animals which had been preserved. The reserve was not clearly shown on our map but covered an area to the west of the Slave River and north of the Peace River where the land was relatively flat and partially wooded. Stan and I flew to the Government Hay Camp, a log cabin where the warden lived. We all flew round looking hopefully for buffalo. I had expected to find a few silhouetted against the snow but, in fact, there were two big herds with animals packed together. As soon as we flew low to make a count they stampeded, hurling themselves through the deep snow in panic. It was impossible to make any sort of count but only a rough estimate, but at least they seemed to be thriving.

About 25 miles north of McMurray the Athabasca River showed signs of a black tar like substance oozing through the sandy banks. It seemed a curiosity but as we quite often landed at a prospector's cabin there with mail we had all noticed it. It seems that the area is now considered to be the world's largest area of oil-bearing sand and of immense value. Until recent times it was not known how to separate the oil from the sand, especially as the ground is permanently frozen a few feet below the surface. However, with the current price of oil and with the expenditure of very large capital sums on extraction plant, the Alberta tar sands are now producing oil.

We made our last flight north as far as Resolution on 10 April 1931 before the break-up. By then the sun was getting high and the ice at McMurray began to look rotten with pools of water lying on top of it. When it breaks, the river carries it away very suddenly but large chunks of ice jam together or get stranded in shallow water. Where this occurs a barrier can form and within minutes the river will rise twenty or thirty feet and overflow its banks. After twenty four hours it will flow clear of ice. A week later the snow will have disappeared and the mosquitoes will be out in force.

Another sign of the arrival of spring was the return of the snow geese. One day we were following the course of the river flying just below the low cloud at about 200 feet. The tops of the trees on either bank were hidden in the cloud but visibility beneath was about a mile. Suddenly about 200 yards ahead at exactly our height we saw a skein of geese. They were in Vee formation flying in the same direction and there really was not much room. We were cruising at about 90 miles an hour and our closing speed seemed quite slow and prolonged. Finally, when we had almost joined their formation, the leader must have spotted us and they scattered, missing us by inches. One had somehow expected the wing birds to break first but they neither saw nor heard us, or at least took no action until the leader gave the signal. I suppose they had as much right to the route as we did but it was surprising to get a traffic jam in flight.

During our flights together I got to know Stan well. Sharing the hardships, the frustrations, indifferent food and all the hazards of the unknown, cements a friendship, and it was a strange experience to return recently to Edmonton with my wife, after forty-eight years, to see him and his wife Dot. They were just the same welcoming friends, and Stan and I, in spite of the lapse of time, picked up exactly where we left off, the real test of friendship. He still has a flying licence after 22,000 hours, and has retired, but he takes an active interest in Canada's Aviation Hall of Fame, a Museum dedicated to bush pilots and other famous Canadian pioneers. He showed us some cine camera films, which really brought back memories. One particular sequence was of our trip through the Rockies to Atlin, another was of McMurray, which looked exactly like a typical Western town film set, a single dirt road with a raised wooden sidewalk, flat fronted clapboard houses with ridged roofs. It now has high rise office blocks and a population of 50,000. The prosperity, as a result of the extraction of oil near there now extends to the whole of Alberta which, from being the poorest Province in Canada, is now the richest. With the rising price of oil, even the tar sands, 20 miles away, are beginning to yield their frozen wealth.

Communications between our operating base at Fort McMurray and the Edmonton head office were few and far between and the brief announcement in April 1931 of the company's take over by Western Canada Airways was a shock. Up to that time the life in the far North had been isolated from the depression which followed the collapse of the Stock Markets. Commercial Airways had been financed during the public euphoria for aviation generated by Lindbergh's flight across the Atlantic and the easy money of the Wall Street boom. The whole staff were given the sack but some were offered jobs with Western Canada at greatly reduced salaries. Most of us spurned the offer and thought we could get better jobs elsewhere. Unfortunately, there were no such jobs and aviation, being largely dependent on Government support, entered the very depths of hard times.

My salary had been $100 a month and 2 cents a mile. Out of this I had saved some money and on reaching Edmonton I went to the Canadian Pacific office and booked a passage home to England going westwards across the Pacific and picking up a P & O liner at Hong Kong. To me it was just another way back to England and I knew nothing of our ports of call. Boarding the *Empress of Japan*, a new ship, at Vancouver, it was with astonishment that five days later we sailed into Pearl Harbor at Honolulu. The contrast of the warmth and colour of the tropics after so long in the frozen north was to my eyes almost unbelievable. To be greeted by an Hawaiian band, and as one stepped ashore, to have a lei of flowers thrown over one's head added to the impression of entering another world. By the time my journey finished at

A DH Moth (Cirrus) of the London Aeroplane Club, of which the author was a member, at Stag Lane, 23 April 1933. (Richard Riding)

Plymouth, however, my savings had dwindled to practically nothing and obtaining a new job was a very urgent matter.

As aviation was still so dependent on Government finance, it was hardly surprising that it was one of the first industries to feel the squeeze. Technically, we were very much in the vanguard of progress and had won the Schneider Trophy twice running, but when it became our turn to stage this international seaplane race, the Government flatly refused to pay for the building of an aircraft to defend the title. It was only through the generosity of a private individual, Lady Houston, that the £100,000 required was found. The Supermarine S6B not only won the race outright at an average speed round the course of 340 miles an hour piloted by Flight Lieutenant J. N. Boothman, but soon gained the world speed record of 407 mph. The design team headed by Mr R. J. Mitchell, CBE went on to design the Spitfire based largely on experience learnt from the S6B.

It was difficult to find a job in aviation in 1931 as the country was in the throes of widespread unemployment and a business slump. There were still a number of aircraft manufacturing companies building aircraft, but they only survived on small Government orders of military aircraft, the main object being to keep the design teams together. On the civil side, where we lagged sadly behind the Americans, the only serious operator was Imperial Airways, which was responsible for carrying airmail to the Commonwealth

The author's Klemm (Salmson) seen postwar. (Richard Riding)

countries. I applied to them for a post and was offered a job as second pilot, but I found on presenting my Canadian licences to the Air Ministry that they would not accept them. After passing the required medical examination for a 'B' licence, I borrowed £150, joined the London Aeroplane Club at Stag Lane and hired a Moth. The necessary hundred hours solo flying took only two months, but on returning to the authorities for the licence, I was told that I was no longer fit and had tachycardia. In spite of all my efforts and pulling every string, they were adamant. It was a bitter experience as I lost the offer of a job, was left in debt and could see no way of carrying on with my career.

Twelve months later, by which time my self confidence was at a low ebb, I was glad to be taken on as a clerk in the City at £5 a week. My original private 'A' licence was still current and somehow I scraped enough money together to

do the necessary three hours a year for its annual renewal. In 1935, however, an uncle died and with a legacy of £1,000 I bought a Klemm which was kept and looked after by my old training school friends at Brooklands.

The Klemm was unusual as it had been built in Germany and was fitted with a French engine, not at that time a very likely combination. The Salmson was a 7-cylinder air-cooled radial of about 45 hp. It had single ignition and had a bad habit of oiling up the lower plugs so that after taxiing out to take-off it would often only be firing on about five cylinders. Although I flew only a few hours before selling it I did have one memorable flight. This was after a weekend sailing at Itchenor when a friend, Pat Wigan, joined me for the return flight to Brooklands. We had intended to leave immediately after dinner on Sunday evening but, having wined and dined exceptionally well, we were late taking off, leaving only just time to get there before dark.

As luck would have it, there was a thunderstorm inland and it got darker and darker until we were flying in pouring rain and visibility of about a mile. Neon lights and streams of car headlights appeared but with no cockpit lights to help I continued hopefully on course thinking that I was bound to hit the main Southampton to Waterloo railway. Finally the four-track railway appeared but no aerodrome, which was hardly surprising as it had no lighting. Turning west I saw a large field and decided to land.

The Klemm fortunately had a low landing speed and we settled gently into a crop of fully grown barley. Rather shaken, we picked up our weekend kit, which included a half bottle of brandy, and made our way to the railway. By now we were soaked to the skin and glad of a nip. After trudging along the edge of the tracks for two or three miles, we came to a station where the ticket clerk was somewhat startled to see on a Sunday night two City gents complete with bowler hats, soaking wet, and rather the worse for wear, asking for tickets to London, and when we said we had just landed from an aeroplane, he obviously thought we were quite mad. The only damage in the whole adventure was to the farmer's crop for which he charged me £5.

Having sold the Klemm and determined to keep my flying licence in being, I took to hiring aircraft. The Cierva Autogiro Company at Hanworth was at the time trying to popularise their new C.30 and was offering an hour's flying to any 'A' licence holder for £5. This was to the best of my knowledge the first rotating wing aircraft to obtain a certificate of airworthiness. The rotor was spun up on the ground to about 180 rpm by the main engine through a hand clutch and lightweight transmission. The pilot then disconnected the drive by declutching, released the wheel brakes and, with full power, took off in about 20 yards. All the flying controls were similar to a fixed wing aircraft with rudder, elevator and ailerons mounted on stubby wings. It flew extraordinarily well and could be landed in its own length, but one had to be careful not to raise the nose on the approach as an autogyro will fly backwards as well as forwards, and this can be embarrassing. In spite of all the early development of rotating wing aircraft which took place in Britain, this was abandoned on the outbreak of war, leaving the whole field open to the Americans, another of our lost opportunities.

In 1938 when the second war seemed inevitable, the Government came forward with support for the flying clubs in a scheme called the Civil Air Guard. One of the conditions of obtaining cheap flying time was an undertaking to assist in some way in the event of an emergency and so I applied to join the RAF Volunteer Reserve, but I was again rejected as a pilot for a new reason, this time for not having the required standard of eyesight.

Everlasting arguments between the Royal Air Force and the Navy over control of air defence at sea had only finally been settled in May 1938, when it was decided that in future all shipborne aircraft were to revert to the Navy. This was fortunate for me as it left the Navy, on the outbreak of war and the withdrawal of RAF personnel, extremely short of experienced pilots and engineers, with the result that medical standards and other requirements such as age were relaxed and a considerable number of civil pilots were engaged purely for second line or training purposes.

First solo: Avro 548, Brooklands,
August 1928

Sports flying:
D.R.R., Tipsy and Richard Muspratt,
Lympne, 1946

Supermarine test pilot: Sea Otter, 1942

"TiPsY"

G-EBVE

PART II

NAVAL WINGS

Supermarine test pilot:
Spitfire Mk XXI and XII prototypes, 1942

Naval fighter pilot: Fulmar, 1940–42

Naval pilot:
D.R.R. and Sea Gladiator, 1941

9 Fleet Air Arm

War was declared on Sunday, 3 September 1939. On the Monday morning, armed with my log-books and Canadian licences, I went to the Admiralty. Goodyear, the chief instructor of the London Aeroplane Club of which I had been a member for years, had given me the name of the recruitment officer. Entering by the side door near Admiralty Arch in the Mall, I asked to see the officer. To my surprise I was immediately ushered into his office and within a quarter of an hour emerged with the promise of a flying commission if I was passed by the medical examiner. There were a number of recruits milling round the converted offices in Lower Regent Street where medical officers were doing the tests and I passed without any trouble. In the rush and confusion it did not take much sleight of hand for one recruit, who thought he had diabetes, to find an obliging

friend to give the necessary sample! On 15 September, an impressive document arrived signed by Admiral Little on behalf of Their Lordships appointing me Temporary Acting Sub-Lieutenant (A) RNVR.

Some months after war had broken out I was called up by the RAF to join the Balloon Corps. It was with some satisfaction that I was able to report I had a flying commission in the Royal Navy.

The assessment of the new officers' flying ability was carried out at Eastleigh, then a Naval aerodrome, but shared with Vickers Supermarine who were building Spitfires in the old hangars on the west side. By a stroke of luck the chief instructor was Lieutenant Commander John Wintour, whom I knew well. He had been axed from the Navy in 1931 under the ten per cent economy cuts, and like me became a clerk in the Stock Exchange. We often had lunch together at Lyons Long Room in Throgmorton Street and reminisced about aeroplanes. Even more fortunate was that he and his wife Daphne had taken a house in Southampton, and they

The Hawker Nimrod, the Naval version of the Fury, was the final refinement of the biplane fighter. (Richard Riding)

invited my wife and me to share it with them.

Tests of flying ability were carried out in a Miles Magister, and on passing these, we were initiated into flying a variety of service types. We all had had considerable civil flying experience so after being shown the taps, off we went. After a short period we were selected and sent to report to the various observer, air gunner and wireless operators' training squadrons. The object was to release the fully-trained regular Naval pilots for the first-line duties in operational squadrons.

All the aircraft were deck-landing types, mostly made by Faireys although there was a sprinkling of more modern biplanes made by Hawkers, including the Osprey and Nimrod. These two aircraft were naval versions of the RAF Hart and Fury, the last of the biplanes, beautiful aircraft in their day, very eager and responsive to fly having been developed to the *n*th degree. The new monoplanes just coming into service, namely the Hurricane and Spitfire, with their much higher performance, made the biplanes obsolete almost overnight, but I am glad I had the opportunity to fly them, and to handle a Rolls-Royce water-cooled engine for the first time. A rare antique collector's piece, was a Fairey Seal in good condition and complete with wire and interplane struts in two bays all arranged to fold back along the fuselage. The air-cooled engine, a 600 hp Panther, was

mounted al fresco, in a prominent position on the nose—this was kept very busy in flight.

The headquarters of the Fleet Air Arm were at Lee-on-Solent, an ex-RAF station renamed HMS *Daedalus*.

There my wife and I rented a small house on the seafront and I settled down to flying air gunners and radio operators on their various exercises. The Blackburn Shark was a strut-braced biplane with folding wings and an Armstrong Siddeley Tiger engine of 760 hp. It was a well-engineered aircraft and rugged, but heavy. Standard practice in all military biplanes was to arrange for the pilot to be positioned with his eyes in line with the upper wing in order to give the least obstruction to his view both upwards and downwards. In the case of the Shark this drew attention to two unusual features. One was the very steep angle of glide and secondly, the fact that in heavy rain rivulets which formed on the upper surface of the centre section ran uphill and forward, indicating a less than perfect airflow.

At Lee-on-Solent, the injection of a relatively large

The Blackburn Shark (760 hp Armstrong Siddeley Tiger engine) was relegated to training wireless operators and air gunners. This Shark is at Lee-on-Solent in October 1939.

The Fairey Seal (500 hp Armstrong Siddeley Panther engine) was a relic of the early 1930s. (Flight)

number of wartime RNVR personnel, many of whom had run their own businesses, inevitably altered the well-established routine of service life there. The Navy makes a point of trying to fit square pegs into square holes and gradually people found their feet. In my own case this was a transfer from an observer training squadron into the Service Trials Unit commanded by Lieutenant Commander Kilroy, a tough regular naval officer and an exceptional leader. The unit had been formed as the Navy had had no facilities for undertaking any special trials the Admiralty required.

In the spring of 1940, we were joined by Lieutenant Lewin DSC, just back from the *Graf Spee* battle in the River Plate, where he spotted for the guns of HMS *Exeter*. Lieutenant Commander Grenfell, a retired naval officer who had been axed in 1931, was our Senior Observer and expert on communications. To be appointed to the STU was indeed lucky for me.

One of our two Fairey Swordfish had an extra petrol tank

taking up a large part of the observer's rear cockpit. I was sent off to do some trials to make sure it functioned properly and that it drained completely as well as to do a check on the engine fuel consumption. Robin Kilroy went away for the weekend with it, but it was only weeks later that I heard that he had in fact flown from an RAF station in Norfolk to somewhere in Norway, then occupied by the Germans, presumably to pick up a passenger. He never gave the slightest indication that he had been on a secret mission, and he had even made the flight in his everyday working uniform without any extra warm clothing, not much fun in an open cockpit. But Kilroy was like that, complete control of mind over matter, and incidentally he was a gifted painter.

As a number of reports of anti-submarine bombs failing to explode had been received, we were instructed to carry out some trials. These consisted of loading a stick of six AS bombs onto a Swordfish, flying round the east end of the Isle of Wight (a prohibited area) to St Catherine's Point and having made sure that no shipping was about, dropping them and counting the duds. There were plenty.

The Blackburn Skua was the most modern aircraft in use by the Fleet Air Arm, a two-seater monoplane fighter with

The author first flew a Fairey Sea Fox (Napier Dagger I) in January 1940. Lt Lewin flew one to spot for Exeter *against* Graf Spee. *(Flight)*

the 820 hp sleeve valve Bristol Perseus, a two-position fine and coarse pitch propeller and a retractable undercarriage. Unfortunately, the centre of gravity of the prototype was found to be too far aft, and about 18 inches had to be added to the engine mounting to make the aircraft stable aerodynamically. However, the undercarriage was still in the same position, with the result that a touch on the brakes or a soft bit of ground led to a tip up on the nose. On my second flight in one I was sent to Farnborough to pick up Ralph Richardson, the actor, who had just delivered a Proctor there. With the wind in the north-west the grass field was very short, especially coming in over the hill and trees from the south-east; good training for deck landing, but 75 knots with the nose well up and lots of power does not come naturally to a land-based pilot.

Two of our aircraft, a Swordfish and a Walrus, were fitted with highly secret equipment. I was not allowed to see it or even go aft of the cockpit. However, we used to fly south into mid-Channel and from the directions which I received from the observer, usually Harold Grenfell, it became obvious that it was a method of intercepting ships when they were out of sight. Air Ship Visual (ASV) as it came to be called, was a very early version of radar. The range was 10 to 15 miles, but this depended on the size and silhouette of the ship. After an interception we flew down to bridge height to read the name and obtain her tonnage from Lloyds register. Most ships' names had been painted out but often a name board would be held up for us to read. Sometimes I would be directed off on a wild goose chase and find nothing, due to reflections picked up by the antenna giving a false reading.

A key man in these trials was Able Seaman Banner who had also been axed from the Navy in 1931. In the meantime he had become Managing Director of one of our largest radio manufacturing companies and had made the ASV sets which were fitted to our aircraft. After each sortie Banner, Harold Grenfell and a captain from the Admiralty would sit down together to discuss and decide on the next step, an unprecedented break with Naval discipline.

As part of the trials, we were sent to Tenby in South Wales. There are a number of small islands off the coast and

The Vickers Supermarine Walrus, an amphibious workhorse which was descended from 1920s designs but survived into the 1940s, saved many aviators' lives during the war. (Flight)

we used these to calibrate the radar tube. On crossing the coast I would shout 'Now', at which Banner would pencil a mark on the tube. Repeating this at various heights, and crossing the coast at different angles, a fair polar diagram was established. Being posted to Tenby made a welcome change as my wife was able to join me, and we still talk about the super Dover sole we had at one meal at the Imperial Hotel.

One day when we were grounded by bad weather, Grenfell and I went for a walk and he started talking about ASV. Apparently, their Lordships were not convinced of the use of ASV for the Navy. Decisions to proceed were painfully slow and money was sluggish in forthcoming. Grenfell was impatient, to put it mildly, and he told me that he had given Mr Banner an order for twenty sets which he himself promised to pay for if the Navy would not. I never heard the final outcome as our paths went different ways, but after the war I read that he became chairman of one of the biggest mining companies in Africa. It now seems incredible that the usefulness of airborne radar could have been questioned.

At Lee-on-Solent there were still a few floatplanes which had been pensioned off as the catapults were removed from the larger warships. They were like magnets to me after my years in Canada where half my flying time had been on floats. Lieutenant Commander Esmond, an ex-Imperial Airways flying boat pilot and later to win the VC for leading the torpedo attack on the *Scharnhorst* and *Gneisenau* in the Channel, cleared me for flying the Walrus and I went off by myself on the floatplanes. The Blackburn Aircraft Company had modified a Roc, a gun-turreted fighter, to a floatplane using floats designed for the Shark biplane. There was, at the time, a very urgent demand for a fighter in Norway and someone must have thought that this aircraft could be used from the fjords. It had a two-pitch position propeller and after a tremendously long run from Lee Tower to Calshot Spit, I left the water; in another five minutes 1,000 feet was achieved but on going into coarse pitch, height could barely be maintained! It was not a great aircraft and the final straw occurred when on reaching the slipway a pebble went through the bottom of a float on beaching. The floats had been designed for some reason, probably inexperience, without on external keel but with a beautiful smooth bottom. It was an interesting experience for me but not much help to the war effort, and, of course, the project was dropped.

Lieutenant Commander 'Butch' Judd was in command of the Walrus training flight. He was a fierce-looking character to any young pilot coming for a conversion course on boats with his red beard and abrupt manner. The Walrus was not fitted with dual control and it had a strong tendency to swing on take off. Judd's method of training was to grip the trainee pilot's right ear and twist it until the message got through to check the swing to the right. In his midshipman days he had been a shipmate of my friend, John Wintour. Having a party in his cabin one evening and being short of a glass he went to John's cabin to borrow the tooth mug. Finding some water in it he threw it out of the scuttle. Next morning John could not find his false tooth, the one replacing that knocked out by Judd in a fight they had had years before.

The Fairey Albacore, a larger version of the Swordfish, was the first aircraft to do its acceptance trials at the Service Trials Unit. The Navy was less interested in its speed or rate of climb than in its range and weight carrying capacity. Its Bristol Taurus sleeve valve engine was also, I believe, an unknown quantity as it had not previously been used in any production aircraft. I was detailed to carry out some of these trials and it gave me the opportunity of putting in many

flying hours. Most sorties were away from the heavily defended south coast area and I got to know the geography of the west of England and the Cornish coast well, while doing long flights measuring consumption.

Being a Naval aircraft, the radio and other electronic equipment represented a heavy electrical load. In fact, the generator could not cope and even the windscreen wiper had to be discarded. I invented a small vane device to move the wiper aerodynamically and to my surprise it was not only put into production but years after the war I received a cheque for £50 and Their Lordships' grateful thanks.

The Admiralty was for some unknown reason interested in the installation of automatic pilots. An early design called the PB was fitted to one of our Swordfish. It was obviously a hand-made prototype and occupied most of the rear cockpit. One day, flying along peacefully on the automatic pilot at

Blackburn Roc seaplane, L3143. Intended as a stop gap for the Norwegian campaign, it was a dead failure both in performance and as a rear gun-turret fighter. The ingenious wing folding hinge, also used on the Skua, and the plated over undercarriage wells can be seen clearly.

The Fairey Albacore (Bristol Taurus sleeve valve engine) was uninspiring and no big advance over the old Swordfish, possibly due to overlap of control by the RAF and the Navy. (Charles E Brown)

2,000 feet somewhere between Winchester and Salisbury the rudder bar suddenly whipped over to full lock. I could not get at the override release quickly enough as the aircraft did the first half of a flick roll before I was able to regain control. The gyro must have toppled when the power supply failed and there was no automatic disconnection as is the case in the very sophisticated systems fitted to airliners.

In the spring of 1940 the new Naval aerodrome was being built at Yeovilton. I was sent down at regular intervals to take aerial photographs to record its progress. A big debate took place in the ward room at Lee as to whether the ammunition dump should be placed next to the officers' quarters, and the WRNS quarters on the opposite side of the main road, or vice versa. In the end it was decided that it would be safer to put the dump next to the officers' quarters.

When some urgent ferrying was required three of us were ordered to fly the Skuas up to Evanton in Scotland. The supply depot was at a secret underground hangar at an aerodrome in the Midlands where the aircraft were stored tipped up on their noses and nestled like chairs in a public hall to save space; it was a surprise to find such quantities. We heard that these aircraft were destined to go to our gallant allies in Finland, who at the time were fighting the Russians single-handed. This bitter Winter War must have been one of the biggest bluffs in history as it made the Russians appear incompetent with their obsolete equipment and untrained soldiers. At least it persuaded the Germans that they would be a push-over. Fortunately, at the last moment, someone in Whitehall must have persuaded Churchill not to send the Skuas.

Delivery of aircraft was, in the early days of the war, a very haphazard business. There was no preflight planning, no weather report, no radio, just a signal from the watch officer to the intended destination to notify the departure time. The number of accidents was staggering until the Air Transport Auxiliary pilots took over. I had great admiration for these men and women who, for one reason or another, were unable to pass the stringent tests for active service, but who came forward to help their country.

In June 1940 during a search operation in the Channel by one of our aircraft carriers, an Albacore had been forced to land at Jersey with high oil temperature. I was sent there in a Walrus to accompany the aircraft on her flight back to the UK. The weather was poor with low cloud and rain but after passing Cap de la Hague, Jersey appeared right on the nose. A Wellington landed just behind me and the pilot was very annoyed. He had been fired at by French guns at Cap de la Hague. I think they must have been alerted by my noisy Walrus, but they were obviously very nervous with the German panzers sweeping down the French coast roads behind them. During lunch at St Helier the radio broadcast the surrender of the French. It came as a bombshell to those at tables around me as they realised the possible implication for themselves.

Before departure an official from the Governor's office gave me a letter to be delivered to the C-in-C Portsmouth and I also bought some wine and brandy thinking it would be a pity to leave it for the Germans. What I did not know was that the British Government had already decided that it would not be in the country's best interests to evacuate the civilian population who were to be abandoned to their fate. The letter was, I believe, a request for ships to be sent immediately: perhaps the Governor had not been told of the original policy decision?

10 Fighter course

The Fleet Air Arm was very heavily engaged in the Norwegian campaign of 1940 when the Germans invaded from the south. The distance from the United Kingdom was too far for the RAF to give fighter cover to our troops and an endeavour was made to provide this from aircraft carriers. During the three months before our final evacuation, losses in pilots had amounted to thirty per cent of the first line strength. These men were part of the peacetime regular Navy, the natural leaders for the growing number of RNVR pilots who were being trained to fly in Canada and elsewhere, but not yet ready as replacements. These losses were serious and left the Service desperately short of pilots.

The fall of France and the call for the 'little ships' to help take off our troops from Dunkirk, suddenly brought the war closer, and was followed immediately by an Admiralty request for volunteers for first line pilots. So far most of the RNVR pilots, like myself, had been confined to training air gunners, wireless operators, positioning aircraft and such activities; this was our opportunity to see active service. On 20 June I was sent to Eastleigh again on an air fighting course.

An odd collection of fighter aircraft had been assembled; some Blackburn Rocs, Gladiators, Skuas and to everyone's surprise a Spitfire. Spitfires were, of course, built at Woolston and some were assembled at Eastleigh. Our particular aircraft was a very early version with a manually operated retractable undercarriage and a two position propeller.

After half an hour in a Gladiator to familiarise myself with its handling I was surprised to find myself flying in vee formation with my CO, Lieutenant Commander Brian Kendall, leading. He took us up through broken cloud, insisting that we get closer and closer. Finally, we broke into clear, brilliant sunshine. The other aircraft stood out sharply silhouetted against the white clouds or hanging stationary in the blue sky with highlights from the wings and fuselage reflecting the brilliant sunlight; I had never been so close to other aircraft in a flight before. To fly in tight formation is in many ways easier than in a loose formation when any loss of position takes longer to recognise. But close formation requires very heavy concentration and a determination to keep one's wingtip in the right position and the wings parallel. On entering a turn a lot more power is required by the outside wing aircraft both in order to climb a little and to increase the speed for the greater distance due to the bigger radius of the turn; conversely, the inner wing man has to cut back the power sharply.

One loses sense of direction, height and even horizon in concentrating on maintaining one's position in relation to the leader and I was surprised, therefore, when ordered to lower the flaps for landing. Flaps on the Gladiator had to be pumped down with a lever on the starboard side of the cockpit. This was awkward in formation as it meant releasing the throttle and changing hands on the stick. The sight of grass a foot or two under the leader's wheels then appeared and soon we rumbled to a stop.

For me the Skua was the first aircraft I had flown which incorporated all the latest devices to improve performance, such as a retractable undercarriage, flaps and a variable-pitch propeller. In order to ensure that these were correctly set for take-off, we were taught to run through the word REPUF, i.e. Rudder, Elevator, Pitch, Undercarriage, Flaps. In my early flying days one had just made sure that the petrol was turned on; in a modern airliner the second pilot has to read out and check off a somewhat longer list of at least 30 items.

Apart from the training in how to make an attack, how to make use of the sun, how to break away, the Naval side also had to be covered: simulated deck landing on the aerodrome, dive bombing, open sea navigation, night flying. During the two and a half months of my training there were seventeen serious accidents in our squadron, but the worst one of all occurred one evening to a visiting aircraft. A Lockheed Hudson belonging to the Air Transport Auxiliary landed to pick up a few pilots who had just delivered some Spitfires to the Supermarine assembly hangar. The whole Southampton area was surrounded with balloons which, of course, were down at the time. Unfortunately, an enemy air raid was reported as being imminent and the balloons went up. As the Hudson taxied out evidently intending to take-off, Johnnie Wakefield, of Castrol Oil fame, who happened to be Officer of the Watch in the Duty Pilots Office at the time, ran out on to the aerodrome and fired a red Verey light. By this time most of the balloons were at about 500 feet but one right in the take-off path was already at about 2,000 feet. The pilot must have thought there was a gap, as with the low, shallow windscreen of the Hudson, he could not see upwards, and proceeded to take-off. Again Johnnie fired another red Verey light low across his bow, to no avail. On reaching about 500 feet the aircraft struck the cable, slowed up, stalled and spun in right in the middle of the town of Eastleigh. All eighteen people on board and two on the ground were killed. I felt sickened, as all who saw it did, at such a tragic accident.

Deck landing training was usually carried out on Skuas. A special area would be marked out on the aerodrome and an experienced deck-landing officer or 'batsman' would be in charge. By holding his bats in an upward V, horizontally or

The Gloster Sea Gladiator (Bristol Mercury engine) was a very manoeuvrable fighter but was outdated in 1939. It was a pilot's aeroplane, but not much of a weapon. (Flight)

in a downward position he indicated that the approaching aircraft had to go higher, was correct for landing, or had to come lower, respectively. In a ship these signals are direct orders from the batsman, and so long as the instruction is followed, no blame for any subsequent crash is attached to the pilot. The landing technique is quite different from a conventional landing on an aerodrome as the aircraft is placed and held in the landing attitude, i.e., nose up, at about 200 feet and the final approach made with a lot of power. The rate of descent can be controlled by delicate use of the throttle, but, being near the stall, it is against one's natural instinct to throttle back in order to lose height. If out of line, the aircraft must be eased into a gentle side slip, but no attempt should ever be made to turn.

We were sent over to Gosport for catapult training. There are various types of catapult, this one (removed from HMS *Hood*) used cordite as a propellant. Cordite is good as it

pushes harder and harder as it nears the end of its throw, whereas compressed air does the opposite. The acceleration is just enough to make one black out temporarily and providing no mechanical failure occurs the sensation is not unpleasant. While I was sitting in the aircraft waiting to be shot off an RAF corporal came round to the side of the cockpit and showed me a couple of white sacks on a tray, rather like a waiter bringing a specially cooked chicken for one's approval in a good restaurant. Never having seen cordite before I did not know what was going on until afterwards when I enquired. It seemed that there had been an unpopular Commanding Officer at Gosport at some time in the past who, having decided to give a demonstration of catapulting to a course under instruction, mounted his aircraft. But someone had decided to get his own back and increase the cordite charge so that the aircraft went off with a tremendous kick. After that station orders were amended: all pilots were to be shown the charge before being catapulted off!

The author after his first flight in a Gladiator, N5546, on 24 June 1940, during an air fighting course at Eastleigh.

The Blackburn Skua (820 hp Bristol Perseus sleeve valve engine), designed to Naval requirements, was a good dive bomber but was too slow as a fighter. Note the extended engine mounting.
(Charles E. Brown)

The Skua had been designed as a dive bomber to give it the capability of attacking a ship or any other small target. The technique, which the Navy adopted, was to fly past the target at about 8,000 feet and when it became visible under the trailing edge of the wing, the aircraft was pulled up into a stalled turn at the same time partially closing the throttle and applying the dive-brake flap. In this way all the forward speed was lost and the aircraft could be pointed vertically at the ground. It was then possible to do an aileron turn to bring the target into line over the nose before gaining too much speed. The more vertical the dive, the more accurate the attack, but what feels nearly vertical to the pilot merely appears steep to the onlooker. Part of the aerodrome at Worthy Down was used for target practice, with smoke bombs, and one was encouraged to dive really steeply because any bombs overshooting the target tended to land in the Captain's garden and incur his displeasure!

The balloons round our home base at Eastleigh were a menace. Often while training as fighter pilots, we would return home to find the balloons up and had to land and wait

The Blackburn Roc (Bristol Perseus) Naval fighter, introduced in 1940, had a power-operated turret. (Charles E. Brown)

at Worthy Down. The aerodrome had a ridge along the centre with relatively steep slopes on either side. It may have been suitable for World War I aircraft, but for Skuas and Spitfires one had to touch down short and to stop by the crest of the hill. It caught out many an innocent stranger and must have cost the country millions of pounds in damaged aircraft. I even saw one aircraft virtually written off while parked. The pilot had parked facing up the hill with the tail to the south. In the south westerly wind which was blowing, the rudder was swinging from side to side thus releasing the air pressure for the differential brake/rudder control. On finally losing all the pressure, the aircraft started to roll backwards until it reached a shallow ditch alongside the approach road.

The tail wheel fell into this and the whole fuselage buckled just in front of the tailplane.

On receiving news of the balloons being pulled down there was always an ugly rush to get home first. One evening we heard that one balloon had broken its cable after a hang-up on the winch, but it was only after the daily inspection of our aircraft next day that two deep, ugly cuts were noticed on one of the engine cowlings. The strange thing was that the cuts were horizontal and the culprit had, therefore, been in a vertical turn. We never heard any more of the incident but it did discourage the evening race to the bar.

In the early years of flying the accident rate was appallingly high. My own parents, with their memories of the losses in the Royal Flying Corps in World War I, were very much against my learning to fly, but I had the urge and, like all youth, would not listen. Even in 1928, the general attitude to civil flying was still slapdash. Perhaps training in the armed services was better organized, but even here the ratio of accidents to the number of flying hours was fairly constant. By noting every mention of an accident in the press it was possible to make a reasonable estimate of the number of hours that that particular service had flown. Every now and then there would be an outcry in the press about excessive losses in the Royal Air Force and a call for an inquiry.

I saw many crashes and had many good friends killed. Somehow one hoped one's luck would hold, but it would be untrue not to admit that one was constantly aware of the danger, just one small mistake due to thoughtlessness, misjudgement, or any other of the many human failings is enough to cause disaster. An aircraft is very unforgiving of any error: no excuse, no second try, it must be right the first time. The discipline of thought and action does not come naturally, but only as a result of training and experience. The lesson must be well and truly understood — No mistakes.

Once airborne and flying there is little danger, for as Monkey Sherlock used to say, 'It's the last half inch which helps the undertaker'! I remember Duncan Davis, my early instructor, telling me never to make a climbing turn, but to fly straight on until reaching 1,000 feet, then put the nose down to gain speed before making a turn. Taking off is the most critical period of any flight and by far the most dangerous, but to visit the Farnborough Air Show nowadays it appears as though the new generation of pilots can disregard the old training; my heart is in my mouth for them when I see those frightening climbing turns.

The one thing which I believe all pilots dread more than anything is fire, the most usual outcome of any aircraft accident. The best action to take in a crash landing is always to get out as quickly as possible, even with the mildest bump. Once as a passenger in the old Canadian days, I learned a trick from Lumsden, which as a passenger was to sit as near the tail as possible and to open the rear door a crack, by putting your foot in it! Doors almost always jam in a crash due to the fuselage distorting.

By August 1940 the Germans were only 80 miles away across the Channel and the air war was in full swing. Some pilots from my course were seconded to the RAF who were very short of fighter pilots, but I was told to go on a week's leave. On ringing Ella to tell her to pack the bags I was surprised to hear that Lee had been bombed. Ninety Stukas had attacked Gosport and the aerodrome at Lee. Forty-five out of the forty-seven aircraft dispersed on the aerodrome were either burnt out or riddled with bullets, the two main hangars had been burnt down and everything was in a shambles.

The attack had been made in broad daylight and was intended for Gosport which is only two or three miles away from Lee. However, Gosport was not in use as an aerodrome by the RAF. The orders at Lee were, however, for the Duty Pilot to fire off coloured Verey lights in the event of an enemy attack or the sighting of parachutists and this he did. The Germans must have thought that they were attacking the wrong target and switched their efforts to Lee where all the activity was. In fact, Gosport and the Dockyards were heavily defended with anti-aircraft guns while Lee was fully exposed and virtually without defence. For fifteen minutes the Stukas, after dropping their bombs, flew round the perimeter having a good squirt with their machine guns at anything worthwhile.

The Navy had only recently taken over control of ship-borne aircraft and the naval air stations had only just been handed over from the RAF. The question of the defence of aerodromes was a point of contention between the RAF and the Army until the Aerodrome Defence Regiment was formed from RAF personnel. In the meantime the Navy decided it knew how to defend itself and at Lee, the head-quarters of the Fleet Air Arm, the defence plan consisted of a large number of officers and men who were posted all round the perimeter of the aerodrome every night. We adopted a shift system of Naval watchkeeping hours, marching up and down between all the tents. If we only had had enough men we could all have held hands and our defence arrangements would then have been perfect. We all carried revolvers and there was even a Maxim machine-gun (a relic of the Boer War) on the watch hut overlooking the slipway.

eturning from leave, I was sent to No. 807 Squadron, a new squadron being formed with Lieutenant Commander Sholto Douglas in command, and equipped with the first Fairey Fulmars to come off the production line. These were in many respects similar to the RAF's Fairey Battle day bomber, but were built to Naval Specification 08/38 with folding wings, four Browning machine guns firing forward and, of course, a hook for deck landing. It was a good reliable flying machine, but hardly a fighter. It was conceived before the days of radar and an observer was considered essential for communication and navigation at sea, hence the second enclosed cockpit.

We started working up the squadron at Worthy Down, and were sent to St Merryn in North Cornwall for air firing practice. I knew this remote aerodrome well, as my parents had lived at Constantine Bay for many years. Before the war, my wife and I had lived in a flat in London but, when I joined the Navy, we gave it up and put all our possessions in store. While we were in Cornwall, I received a letter from the Army and Navy Stores to tell us that as a result of an 'incident' on 11 October, their depository had been burnt

by an incendiary bomb, and was a total loss. They went on to say that any claims were to be made to the War Damage Commission, and not to them. To add insult to injury, they enclosed a bill for storage due from 1 October to the night of the fire, for the sum of twelve shillings and sixpence. Considering we had lost everything we owned, it seemed a bit callous, especially as their letter was a printed form with a rubber stamped signature.

On returning to Worthy Down I was sent to Lee in charge of a flight of three Fulmars. We were briefed to make an attack on an unmanned radio controlled, high speed power boat undergoing special trials operating in the West Solent. It was fun to fire one's guns at a live target but due to the lack of good radio communications, the whole episode was a mess. Our aim and/or gun alignment was also wide of the mark as we scored the minimum of hits on the craft during several attacks. After this I always insisted on setting up my own

The author flew the Fairey Fulmar (Rolls-Royce Merlin) two-seat Naval fighter on active service in 1941–42. (The Aeroplane)

Personnel and a Fulmar of No. 807 Naval Air Squadron at the unit's commissioning at Worthy Down in July 1940.

guns and sight, taking the greatest care to see that the aircraft's attitude was correct for the expected attack speed and that the gun pattern was focused on a point at the correct distance. Considering the cost of the weapon as a whole, the aircraft, the guns, the crew, the training, the best natural shot in the world is no good unless he knows his weapon and how it fires, yet it was surprising to find that many fighter pilots accepted a new aircraft from a supply depot without making their own check of the gun alignment.

Our Commanding Officer, Lieutenant Commander Sholto Douglas RN, had an extraordinary experience and an unpleasant shock one evening when we were working up No. 807 Squadron at Worthy Down. He was returning to his home near Winchester, and was just about to drive under a railway bridge, when he saw a man fall or jump from the parapet on to the road in front of his car. He was killed instantly, so Sholto Douglas drove to the nearest house and telephoned the police. He went back and waited for them, when they arrived, after they had searched the body for identity, one of them asked Sholto Douglas for his name and address, and when he told them, the policeman said, 'No, we want *your* name'. It turned out that the man lying dead on the road was also a Sholto Douglas.

While waiting to embark in HMS *Ark Royal* a signal arrived from Admiralty detaching a flight of three aircraft which were to fly forthwith to Sydenham, the aerodrome by the Belfast Docks. I believe the inspiration for this move

came from Mr Churchill himself. We had been losing ships at the rate of one a day while they were approaching the Northern Irish coast in convoy. A four-engined German aircraft, the Focke Wulf Fw 200 Condor, operating from Stavanger would appear off the west coast of Ireland at dawn every morning, give a weather report, the position, course and speed of any convoy, pick off any stragglers with a bomb and fly on to land at Bordeaux. These convoys had no anti-aircraft defence except their escorts and these were seeking out submarines. The object of our operation was to provide fighter defence by loading Fulmars onto a catapult ship called HMS *Pegasus*.

We towed our three Fulmars through the dockyard area early one morning and loaded them aboard. One in a hold, one on the hatch cover and one on the catapult. *Pegasus* had started life as a tanker in World War I, but was converted for aircraft training purposes in catapulting and recovery at sea and used in the Solent for perhaps one afternoon a week in the summer. Hardly suitable for the North Atlantic in mid winter! However, her crew was increased to over 200 and some extra life rafts were added. We set sail in February 1941 under the command of Captain Wodehouse (who I believe was the brother of P.G.) and joined an outward bound convoy from Liverpool. The aircraft on the catapult was at immediate readiness. This meant that the pilot and observer were in the cockpit fully kitted up, the engine was kept warm, all ready to be fired off at a moment's notice. From dawn to dusk a fresh crew relieved those on duty every four hours. After a sortie our orders were to dump the aircraft in the sea near a destroyer or to fly back to Belfast if it were feasible. By using a secret code, the ship kept in constant radio touch with a land-based direction finding station, and as soon as the Condor broke radio silence we were informed. After reaching a position of 25° west without incident we broke away from the convoy and wandered aimlessly about the middle of the Atlantic hoping to intercept the next incoming convoy.

We were kept informed of the position of the eastbound convoy which, due to enemy action, was running behind schedule. I was shown how to decode these signals, and then plotted them with the navigating officer.

Our Chief Engineer, who was nearly 70 and brought back for war service in *Pegasus*, was very nervous, as were we all. The area was stiff with submarines and with our maximum speed of 8 knots and no watertight compartments we did not reckon our chances high in the event of a torpedo attack. The wardroom, however, was amidships just under the main deck and it had an old fashioned double brass rail and glass covered hatch above the dining room table; by removing the screws from the latches we eased the Chief's worries a bit as this allowed one to step straight out off the top of the table on to the upper deck.

The incoming convoy was delayed first by one day and then another. Meanwhile, our navigator, ex-Merchant Navy, had not been able to get a good sight to fix our position since leaving Ireland and was getting worried but a great cheer went up when at last smoke appeared on the horizon. We tucked ourselves into the middle of the back row, the safest position in a convoy.

That night the convoy was attacked. I was asleep, but a tremendous crash woke me up and I thought that the main engine connecting rod had gone through the side but all was dark on deck so I went back to my bunk. Then there was another even bigger crash just as if the ship had been hit with an enormous hammer. An oil tanker was on fire and another ship was burning. At dawn the tanker was still afloat and after much deliberation and signalling, one of the escort ships was sent off into the blue for 50 miles before breaking radio silence and asking for a tug to be sent. The main convoy plodded on at a steady 6 to 8 knots with no sign of a Condor.

I noticed some drops of oil on the deck below our aircraft; sure enough, on close examination, there was a very small leak in the corner of the oil cooler. It was impossible to switch aircraft — even in harbour it was difficult let alone in the prevailing sea — and so we kept the oil tank well topped up hoping for the best. A day later the Irish Coast came into sight. When about an hour's flying time from Sydenham I was catapulted off as it seemed the simplest way of changing round the aircraft. Hardly was I airborne before oil started coming up into the cockpit through the slot of the radiator flap lever. It covered everything including all the inside of the windscreen and my eyes and goggles. Opening the hood increased the flow and made it worse. However, I got down

all right, but soaked to the skin in hot dirty oil. On landing I was immediately called to the telephone to speak to the NOIC (Naval Officer in Charge). Thinking I had broken some local flying regulation I was surprised to be told that my wife was waiting for me in the Grand Hotel! How she pulled strings to get there I shall never know, but she had a room with a bath, clean underclothes, shirt, socks, shoes and my No. 1 uniform. I have never been so pleased to see her in my life.

Belfast was relatively free from rationing and with the bars open from morning to midnight we all had quite a time. We even had a dinner party on board HMS *Pegasus* one night, Consommé Mussolini, Halibut au Fulmar and Widgeon Roti Catapultie. An unusual event in wartime.

Leaving Belfast to join our next convoy we made the routine run over the degaussing range as a precaution against magnetic mines. We promptly turned back as the ship's signature was too pronounced. After a loving farewell in the early morning, Ella was surprised and delighted to see me back at midday. The same thing happened at least twice again as the electricians could not get the ship 'clean' to clear the range. Finally, my relief pilot arrived, Bob Everett, the 1939 Grand National winner, and I was ordered to return to

Invitation to the author and his wife to dine aboard Pegasus.

H.M.S. PEGASUS

The *fours* widowers + bachelor(s) would be very pleased if you and Mrs Robertson would dine with them, onboard, on Friday Evening February 7th at 1930.

February 5th 1941.

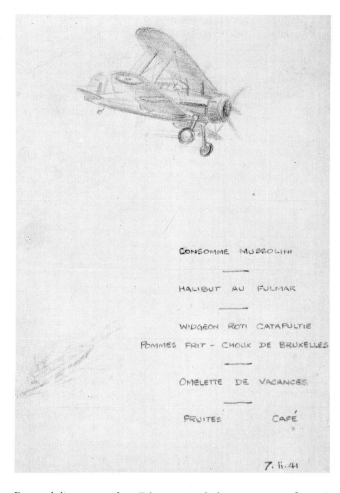

CONSOMME MUSSOLINI

HALIBUT AU FULMAR

WIDGEON ROTI CATAPULTIE
POMMES FRIT - CHOUX DE BRUXELLES

OMELETTE DE VACANCES

FRUITES   CAFÉ

7. ii. 41

Pegasus' *dinner menu for 7 February 1941 had a contemporary flavour!*

the formation of the first Fulmar squadron, No. 807. Buster was a lieutenant RN and had had a somewhat unusual career since joining the Navy as a cadet at Dartmouth. After qualifying for his sea watchkeeper's certificate, he volunteered for flying in the FAA. At the time the FAA was partly under RAF control, and naval pilots had to take a temporary RAF commission, so that although wearing naval uniform, they came under Air Force discipline when not embarked in ships. The whole business of dual control of this vital arm of the Royal Navy between the wars, was a most unsatisfactory arrangement.

In 1937, when he was flying as a young lieutenant with the Torpedo Development Unit at Gosport, Buster was court-martialled by the RAF for low flying over the nearby coast en route to the torpedo range only half a mile away, the number of his aircraft having been reported to the AOC by a local poultry farmer. At this time, the Minister for Air was being criticised by the press, and questions were raised in Parliament about low flying nuisances by the RAF. Buster and another naval officer had their flying careers terminated and the Minister concerned was able to announce that 'action had been taken against two flying officers in order to put a stop to unauthorised low flying', though he failed to mention the true facts.

Buster immediately resigned his commission, but this was not accepted by the Admiralty, and he was sent to sea. He left the Navy shortly afterwards and was put on the Emergency Reserve List, being reinstated in 1939, when the Admiralty was at last granted autonomy over the FAA. After an outstanding war record during which he was awarded the DSC, commanded two fighter wings and a Carrier Air Group, he ended his naval career as Captain of Greenwich.

This whole episode was an example of the controversy and bitterness which existed between the heads of the two services over control of Naval Aviation, and from which the Fleet Air Arm had suffered for years.

Buster and I both enjoyed flying Gladiators, of which we had two in NAFDU (Naval Air Fighting Development Unit) in April 1941. I had not been trained to fly by the Service and, therefore, had little experience of aerobatics. However, the 'Glad' was very manoeuvrable with precise controls, and between us we worked out a little routine act. Starting in line abreast, about 100 yards apart, we would do a dive followed by a loop, another dive with a pull up and a roll off the top, then a stall turn and a dive followed by an upward roll.

my squadron, now at Yeovilton. On the following trip of the *Pegasus* Bob was catapulted off and had a chase and a shot at a Condor. I never heard whether its loss was confirmed but Bob himself was lost shortly afterwards. The message that some of these convoys had a fighter escort soon got back to Germany as the Condor, being basically a converted civil airliner, had no rear defensive armament and was very vulnerable to attack by fighters. This particular menace diminished from March 1941 onwards.

Back at Yeovilton I was disappointed to find my squadron had already left and was in the Mediterranean in HMS *Ark Royal*, but glad to meet up again with a good friend, Nigel 'Buster' Hallett. We first met at Worthy Down in 1940, on

12 Gun trials at Duxford

From Yeovilton I was posted to the RAF station at Duxford near Cambridge, which was the headquarters of the RAF's Air Fighter Development Unit. I joined the Naval Air Fighter Development Unit under Lieutenant Commander Brian Kendall. I had no fighter experience but we were concerned with making our guns work and developing predictor sights and new sighting patterns. The Fleet Air Arm was already becoming dependent on American aircraft and equipment, but these sadly lacked any background of operational experience. For example, the Grumman Martlet, just entering service, had two .5 inch machine guns. They would fire a few shots and then break their forward attachment mounting on the front wing spars. This did not stop the gun, which would continue to fire through the top skin of the wing. The guns would jam if fired while making a turn at 2 or 3G and they lacked any heating or cooling system.

I personally liked the big American air-cooled engines with which all their aircraft were fitted, having learnt respect for their reliability in commercial flying in Canada, but we soon found one could expect trouble if one used full power in a very steep climb or by using high rpm and full boost for any length of time.

While at Duxford our nearest air firing range was on the north Norfolk coast. We had the RAF's permission to use Matlask near Sheringham, a satellite aerodrome of Horsham St Faith. It was a grass field convenient for dropping our target flags and the officers' mess was nearby in a delightful old mill house straddling a stream.

The Admiralty had no reliable information on the speed, rate of climb, or range of the American aircraft, including the Martlet. This we did our best to supply, although we were not properly equipped or qualified to measure aircraft performance. Lieutenant-Commander Kendall was particularly interested in fighter tactics and thought there was a big future for predictor sights in fighters. One version had been in-

The Grumman Martlet was the FAA version of the F4F Wildcat, an American naval aircraft with a good range, and good handling characteristics, particularly off a deck, but lacking in armament. Nevertheless, it was a very welcome addition to the Royal Navy when it was desperately short of aircraft. (Charles E. Brown)

The Fiat CR.42 was the Italian equivalent of the Gladiator, but was not in the same class. This one, given the RAF serial BT474, was part of Mussolini's Balbo against England, but force-landed in England with high oil temperature (The Aeroplane)

vented by a Professor of mathematics, and he had been given a laboratory at Exeter airport to develop a practical instrument. This was ultimately installed in a Hurricane which we had, and I became involved in the trials. The sighting point was a cross of light which moved ahead of the target on a reflector sight. It gave the right deflection to allow, provided the range was correct. The range was fed in from a twist grip control on the top of the throttle, which lengthened or shortened the cross of light. It was never adopted, the old-fashioned method of getting in really close being more effective.

Our Naval party all fell in with the routine of life on an RAF station and shared in their duties and entertainments. Shortly after our arrival there was a big army defence exercise and we were detailed to defend the aerodrome. There happened to be a main road passing through the station and so it seemed sensible to block this partially with short lengths of railway line lowered into previously prepared holes in the

road. A couple of tanks appeared from an easterly direction and tried to squeeze through the gap, but it was just too narrow and after grinding away, showering sparks from their tracks, they reversed clear only to make a rather bad tempered charge. This time they got stuck on top of a spike, their tracks unable to get a grip, so we threw some whizz-bang fireworks under them and waited. The bang was almost swamped by the verbal onslaught; it appeared that we had obstructed the friendly force, not the invaders.

Two captured enemy aircraft, a Fiat CR.42 and a Messerschmitt Bf 109, were being assessed as combat aircraft in comparison with our own equivalents. The CR.42 had landed somewhere in Essex when Mussolini had sent his big Balbo to help his friend Adolf win the Battle of Britain. It had force-landed with high oil temperature, but as no trace of this recurred it seemed rather a poor excuse. It was a biplane with a big air-cooled radial engine, rather like a Gladiator but not in the same class to fly, although the Italian pilots were reputed to indulge in all sorts of aerobatics during combat. To start the engine, there was a small motor-mower type engine driving a compressor to pump up the compressed-air bottle first, all very complicated and heavy for a fighter.

The Bf 109 had a Daimler-Benz engine with fuel injection and an electrically operated variable-pitch propeller, the con-

A captured Messerschmitt Bf 109E (1,150 hp Daimler Benz DB 601Aa) at Duxford in 1941, which was used for comparison and assessment against British aircraft by the Royal Air Force Air Fighter Development Unit at Duxford. (The Aeroplane)

trol switch of which was mounted at the end of the throttle lever. I liked the positive response from the throttle and the negative G capability, but the manually operated propeller pitch change required constant attention, especially in any sort of a simulated dogfight. The aircraft's handling characteristics, except for very heavy ailerons, were good, particularly in a dive, but not outstanding in other respects. The Spitfire could always outclimb it and turn inside it but, of course, not all engagements developed that way.

The Admiralty was determined to try the effectiveness of various gun alignment patterns — first, focused on a point; secondly, as an ellipse; and thirdly, as a rectangle. We used a flag target about 30 feet long and 5 feet deep towed behind a Roc or a Skua. The Martlet or Fulmar were loaded with 400 rounds each and a series of beam attacks was made until the ammunition was exhausted. The flag was then dropped back on the aerodrome and the holes counted. It was a wonderful opportunity to get some real firing practice in and we made the most of it. Previously, I had only used 100 rounds in one gun and then on a circular drogue fired at from astern.

The Martlet's guns were now working well and the average number of strikes varied from 11.5 to 22% but, as with any shooting, one had one's off days. On one occasion, having fired a long burst and finished my ammunition, I was returning to Matlask when suddenly one gun fired a single round. The trigger was on safety but the gun must have jammed and the heat of the breach set off the charge. This was my one and only experience of a 'cook-off' as it is known among the experts.

Towing a target is a thankless task usually reserved for anyone who has put up a black of sorts: it can be dangerous, and is very hard work and deadly boring. One day when I was in charge of the firing party the winch operator was either very stupid or very frightened. He failed to tell his pilot that he had not winched in the target flag in preparation for dropping, nor had he actually dropped it, so that they came in and landed towing a quarter of a mile of wire cable with the target flag on the end. Apart from nearly stalling the aircraft on approach he had shorted the power line, knocked down telephone wires, frightened the local cows and infuriated the farmer. It was especially embarrassing as we were the guests of the RAF who also took their share of the blast.

The author with a Hurricane from the Naval Air Fighter Development Unit of Yeovilton, in 1941.

The Naval airman culprit told me that he had forgotten to take his wire cutter (standard equipment) and when the winch jammed had not liked to tell the pilot. After I had had a go, Petty Officer Martin gave him the benefit of his advice in no uncertain terms. It seemed hardly believable, but three weeks later the same man was operating the winch in a Skua. This time he did not reeve the cable correctly and failed to notice that the cable was not passing over the sheave where it went through the bottom hatch but was resting on the edge of the hatch itself. He just winched it in regardless, watching the wire cut through the hatch, the fuselage skin and the ribs nearly back to the tail wheel. To saw the aircraft in half must be the nearest thing to cutting off a branch on which one is sitting. I thought Martin was going to have kittens; what made it worse was that he had just completed a major overhaul of the aircraft.

An RAF officer at Duxford had been given the job of installing a big gun in a Blenheim. It was about 40 to 50 mm bore and because of the size had to be mounted externally underneath the fuselage. The aircraft had to be kept serviceable while the bits were made up and a fair exchange was arranged, he to fly the Martlet, and I the Blenheim. There was no official permission ever given but these exchanges were often made and I never heard of any accident. I was glad to have a twin-engined aircraft in my log book, as up till then I had only flown singles.

In July, I received a signal ordering me to report to HMS *Argus* for a deck landing course. She was an old ship reported to have started life as an Italian liner. She had four screws directly driven by turbines, which gave her the necessary speed as an aircraft carrier but were probably grossly inefficient in fuel consumption. All the upperworks had been removed and replaced by a flat deck without any obstruction. There was, however, a slight step up in the deck towards the bow, which was quite helpful in getting airborne in the short deck. Strangely enough this idea has now been revived to assist the latest jump-jet Sea Harrier to shorten its take-off run and save fuel or to carry a heavier load.

HMS *Argus* was based on the Clyde and for convenience used to lie in Lamlash Bay, Isle of Arran. After completing the required six deck landings in a Fulmar, I returned to Duxford and continued the firing trials. In action, an attacking aircraft's wings and wing mounted guns are usually parallel with those of the enemy, that is in a stern attack. Our target was a flag with the leading edge vertical which meant that all our firing trials were from the beam. To make an attack on the beam meant a deflection shot from a turn with the wings banked at about 80°. In doing this, the convergence of the guns to the aiming pattern would only be correct at a fixed range and, in any case, put a tremendous premium on the pilot's skill in aiming. However, inexplicably, I found that whereas with the two .5 inch guns of the Martlet I averaged 18% strikes, with the eight .303 inch Browning guns of the Hurricane I could not do better than 12%. The American .5 inch gun was very high velocity with a streamlined bullet, but it had a lower rate of fire and wore out the rifling in the barrel very quickly. After 200 or 300 rounds some of the bullets would become 'tippers', that is instead of revolving and flying straight they would go arse over tip! They also lacked enough punch to be able to pierce an aircraft's skin and then go on to knock away any armour plate.

Two twin-engined captured enemy aircraft at Duxford were a Messerchmitt Bf 110 and a Heinkel He 111 bomber. Endless simulated attacks were made on these to try to find their weak points and vulnerable angles of approach. In the Heinkel the pilot sat far back in a kind of streamlined greenhouse, and as a result visibility was bad; it seemed a poor exchange to give away pilot's vision for a small increase in speed due to the streamlining. Fortunately for us the *Luftwaffe* were largely equipped with 1935 designs, already getting out of date by 1942, whereas, though we were very late in re-equipping our Air Force with fighters, at least they were up-to-date.

13 Russian Approaches

On 7 December 1941, the day of Pearl Harbor, I was ordered to report to Lieutenant Savage RN, Commanding Officer of No. 809 Squadron at Hatston in the Orkneys. This was the second Fulmar squadron to be formed and was earmarked for HMS *Victorious* in the Home Fleet. Savage was keen on flying discipline and we were kept very busy with formation flying and squad drill. It was the equivalent of square bashing in the Army: the four flights of three aircraft had to perfect their own precise formations and, when flying as a squadron, to change position quickly and neatly.

On joining the ship we developed and perfected a technique of taking off from the deck in quick succession. By jinking to port, to clear our slipstream for the next aircraft taking off, proceeding straight ahead for a given number of seconds, depending on the order of take-off, and then turning to port each aircraft was able, by taking a short cut, to join the formation in a very tight sequence. Meantime, the leader,

who took off first, had made a rate one turn after going straight ahead for the longest period (one minute 30 seconds), so that on passing the ship on a reciprocal course the whole squadron was already in Vee formation. It was quite impressive when well done.

While at Hatston, the American aircraft carrier USS *Wasp* in company with the battleship USS *Washington* arrived at Scapa Flow and flew off her aircraft, mostly fighters but also a few torpedo bombers. The US Navy is dry but this was certainly an occasion for a celebration and we made our visitors welcome. The following day we were invited to their return party, the slight difficulty over the shortage of alcohol being solved by their forethought in milking their torpedoes.

HMS *Victorious* was in Scapa Flow and we landed on during the afternoon of 24 December. Although, as pilots in the Fleet Air Arm, we had no nautical duties in the ship, it was a stirring experience finding oneself in a new world steeped in tradition and prestige. The ship's routine, the pipes, the discipline and the whole naval atmosphere, par-

HMS Victorious, *with the Albacore squadron ranged on deck.*

No. 809 Sqn Fulmars ranged for take-off from HMS Victorious.

ticularly while at war was, I found, intensely interesting and exciting. My first day happened to be Christmas Day and to hear 1,500 men, assembled in the steel hangar, singing 'For those in peril on the sea' was very moving, as was the old tradition of the youngest boy in the ship donning the Captain's gold braided cap and solemnly doing the ship's daily round of inspection with his attendant staff.

Victorious was a new ship, although she had already been involved in the chase and sinking of the *Bismarck*. Like all British Fleet carriers, she had an armoured flight deck. This was 3½-inch thick armour steel reputed to have been made in Czechoslovakia by Skoda and shipped out after the war had started. It is interesting to note that although the Americans lost many of their aircraft carriers, which had wooden decks, the Royal Navy never lost one from aerial attack. Even when, later in the war in the Pacific, a *Kamikaze* pilot made a suicide attack on *Victorious*, he only dented her deck.

While at sea, those with the responsibility for war damage control were distributed throughout the ship, slinging their hammocks in gangways and other odd spaces. The object was to avoid the possibility of losing all the experts in any particular trade. In contrast, the majority of the flying officers had their own cabins close to their aircraft.

Control of fighters from an operations room on board was in its earliest stage of development at that time. As fighters, our prime job was to protect the Home Fleet from aerial attack while at sea and never to go far afield. It was, I believe, an RNVR officer, Lieutenant Commander Borthwick, who realised the importance of controlling the fighters, and he was given full authority to organise an operations room. His nickname was 'Meatball' but it was years after the war before I realised why; his family firm was the largest in the London meat market! Most of our early exercises while flying from *Victorious* were devoted to the technique of interception of incoming target aircraft while under the control of the Fighter Direction Officer.

In order to give all the Home Fleet's guns an exercise — as up to then there had only been a visit by one rather half-hearted German reconnaissance aircraft — we were ordered to simulate an attack with our Fulmars. Savage decided to split the squadron into four flights and attack at low level from four directions simultaneously. We worked out a route to all our respective targets as we knew where the big ships

A Fulmar of No. 809 Sqn on patrol north of the Arctic Circle, with part of the destroyer screen visible.

were lying in the harbour. Mine was the battleship *King George V*, the flagship, and our approach was to be over the hill from the south east and into Scapa Flow. We took off from *Victorious* in the Pentland Firth and each flight made a big sweep round into position well out of sight behind the low hills. At the appropriate moment we all converged and made our attacks, flying very low. The observers fired a red Verey light to indicate that a dummy bomb had been dropped. I do not think there was much aiming done that day as they had not expected that type of approach. In fact, in spite of the expectation of an attack they were caught with all their big guns pointing at the sky and the short range weapons unmanned. Our own run in to the target went very well but I was shaken when my observer, Sub Lieutenant Rogers,

fired his Verey pistol. The flare bounced across the ship's deck and fell on the edge of a barge moored alongside. It had been hidden during the approach and we had not thought of the possibility of the ship loading food or ammunition. We heard no more of it, but nor were we ever asked to make a raid again.

A few days later we were again exercising in the Pentland Firth. There was little wind but a biggish swell and such wind as there was, was along the swell, just about the worst conditions for operating aircraft off a deck. The ship had to do 25 knots along the swell to get the necessary wind speed and this made her roll. A squadron of Albacore was also exercising and the Commander Flying decided to land them on first. About the fifth aircraft made a very heavy landing and had to be craned up and dangled overboard. The next aircraft went into the barrier but after delay it was dragged forward out of the way. The remainder landed on successfully.

Meanwhile, our flight of three aircraft had been airborne over three hours and were short of fuel, and when the last Albacore landed I had expected to be given the signal to land straight away. Instead the ship turned round with her destroyer escort onto a reciprocal course. My petrol gauge was bumping on the empty stop and we had been forbidden to break wireless silence. It was too far from land to reach an aerodrome so we flew round the ship in loose open formation at minimum speed to save fuel. I remembered an old trick of Monkey Sherlock's aimed at attracting attention which was to switch off one magneto and go into weak mixture so that the engine pops back and misses badly. They very soon got the message on the bridge. It was a difficult decision for the Captain to take to turn his ship again, as he told me later he had been on one course far too long already and was afraid of a lurking submarine. However, although shaken, we did save the aircraft from being ditched. It is impossible to land on a deck without power and we were on the point of having to land in the sea.

When HMS *Ark Royal* was torpedoed and sunk in the Mediterranean about this time, we were at Scapa Flow. The Germans had claimed to have sunk *Ark Royal* many times before, so in an effort to confuse them, we in No. 809 Squadron immediately took over her old fighter squadron call sign CAYMAN, which we used in all our exercises in the Orkney area, hoping that our calls were being monitored.

Shortly after the sinking of the *Ark*, *Victorious* was used for stability trials. The *Ark* had been hit in the area of her starboard boiler room, the side of a carrier on which the 'island' is sited. This extra weight is not balanced by any equivalent structure on the port side but merely with water in the port ballast tanks. It had been reported that on being struck she heeled to an acute angle and water flooded not only the starboard boiler room, but flowed through the air intake ducts over the top of the fore and aft compartments flooding other boilers leading ultimately to the loss of all auxiliary power and consequently the bilge pumps.

While at our moorings and after lashing down all our aircraft very thoroughly, *Victorious* was heeled step by step, while measuring the required shift in the water ballast. After reaching an angle of about 30°, she was righted again. Like all warships, she was subdivided into quite small watertight compartments, except for the single large hangar deck, with watertight doors and hatches between each. At sea all the doors were kept permanently closed except for a small hatch through which a man could pass, and even these were closed in action. When down below, one might just as well have been in a submarine. There was something to be said for being a pilot.

One soon got to recognize the signs of an impending operation. Black puffs of smoke indicated extra boilers being fired up, the early recall of liberty boats, aircraft to have their

daily inspection completed, followed by the series of pipes mustering the sea duty men in preparation for casting off the mooring or raising the anchor. Once the ship was at sea the Captain would speak on the public address system and tell us what the operation was and where we were going. Particularly in wartime a ship's company becomes very much of a team, each man is dependent on others and all have respect for the other man's abilities. Beyond that is the knowledge that the ship itself is one's home and its defence is vital in order to survive. This spirit extended to the flying personnel, too; we became part of the ship and however far one was from the ship one knew that if you went down in the sea they would come looking for you, no matter what the cost. This feeling of belonging was a great morale booster.

Although Scapa Flow was the normal base for the Home Fleet we spent more time at Hval Fjord on the west coast of Iceland. On going ashore in Iceland we all wore civilian clothes as it was a neutral country, but it had a very left-wing Government with leanings towards our new ally Russia. For political reasons, the United States was sending vast supplies of weapons to Russia and these convoys converged on Hval Fjord before being escorted to Murmansk, their destination. As the Germans were occupying the whole of Norway, this involved passing close to their fighter and bomber equipped

Max Newman (left) and the author going on church parade at Hval Fjord, Iceland.

The Home Fleet in line astern, covering a convoy to Russia, March 1942.

aerodromes in the far north, and also within easy striking distance of the *Tirpitz*, a very powerful ship based at Trondheim. The job of the Home Fleet was to prevent the interception of these convoys by surface ships, but not to venture into the area where the Germans had air superiority. Winter provided the cover of darkness, but in summer losses in merchant ships were appalling. While waiting, morale among the merchant seamen was very low and we used to invite parties of them over to *Victorious* for hot baths, hot meals, drinks and a cinema show, but little did we know that many of these brave men would shortly be the victims of the ill-fated convoy PQ 17.

While covering the Russian convoys against interception by German warships, our Albacores flew anti-submarine patrols during the daylight hours while the fighters stood by at readiness. Although we knew that enemy aircraft were shadowing the fleet we were not allowed to leave the deck. All movements of our aircraft had to be authorized by the Admiral whose flagship was *King George V*. Normally, all

HMS Victorious *takes a green one, damaging her flared bow.*

HMS Victorious *near Spitzbergen.*

signals were made by lamp or by flag. Why the Admiral chose a battleship for his flagship instead of *Victorious*, which had the necessary accommodation for his staff, was difficult to understand. It was all part of the pre-war thinking of big guns and armour versus the newfangled aeroplane, a kind of status symbol!

While covering one convoy, news came through of the passage up the Channel was a slap in the face both for the *Gneisenau* through the English Channel. Two friends, Mike North and Esmond, were both killed making an attack with torpedoes; in fact, the whole flight of six Swordfish and crews were shot down. The whole episode of the ships' passage up the Channel was a slap in the face both for the Admiralty and the RAF. A day or two later reconnaissance aircraft reported that two warships were proceeding up the fjords of Norway, apparently intending to join the *Tirpitz* near Trondheim. At the time our position was about midway between Iceland and the northern tip of Norway. *Victorious* was detached from the Home Fleet and proceeded south at 28 knots escorted by three destroyers. Meanwhile, twelve Albacores were ranged on the flight deck and loaded with torpedoes and the crews briefed on the operation. They were to take-off at 1 am, fly in 50 miles to the Norwegian coast, and make a southerly sweep through the fjords with ASV. If the enemy ships were located they were to make a

night attack and then fly on to land at Sumburgh in the Shetlands. A hazardous operation and a lot to ask of crews who had never made a night torpedo attack, barely had the fuel for the distance, and did not have the radio frequency of Sumburgh to get direction finding assistance. *Victorious* could not hang about but after flying them off would be 150 miles away to the north by dawn.

However, the RAF, in the prevailing bad weather, had been unable to confirm the position of the enemy ships and shortly after dark the ship turned round and the whole operation was called off much to the relief of the Albacore crews. The next day at noon the show was on again. Again we went south and at 1 am the Albacores took off under the command of Lieutenant Commander Plugge RN. It was snowing but patches of moonlight were visible on a heaving dark sea giving some horizon to fly by. The heavily loaded aircraft went off, slowly gathering speed along the deck and dipping over the bow to gain more speed before disappearing into the night, flames streaming from their exhausts.

The next day we listened anxiously for any news of our aircraft, but it was not until the following morning that we changed course for Scapa Flow. It was a lovely day of high

All hands on deck to clear snow during a Russian convoy in March 1942. Note the raised barrier.

wind and bright skies with patches of clear-cut clouds as we slid quietly through the following seas on our way south. A call to action stations on the reported sighting of a torpedo bomber was called off as by this time we were near the Shetlands and a number of RAF Beauforts had appeared and were circling the fleet.

Before refuelling *Victorious* at Scapa Flow, we were told that the Albacores were going to land on. Three were missing. They saw nothing of the *Scharnhorst* and *Gneisenau*, two had collided in the darkness, the Commanding Officer, Plugge, was lost, and the remainder of the squadron had had to jettison their torpedoes when desperately short of fuel before reaching Sumburgh and landing in darkness. A very expensive, fruitless operation but it was bad luck, as they had, in fact, just missed the German ships by about an hour.

While escorting the next convoy, the fleet ran into a severe storm. The wind was in the region of 60 knots with mountainous seas and speed had to be reduced to 6 knots, the minimum to retain steerage way. In spite of this we were pitching so badly that every now and then we took a green sea over the bow setting a cascade of water sweeping down the flight deck. Eventually, the overhanging flare of the bow, which was 70 feet above the normal waterline, took an awkward wave and was bent upwards. Down in the hangar we had the aircraft well lashed down, but water poured through the catapult rail slot into a trough beneath where it slopped salt water over our aircraft, engines, instruments, guns and ammunition, all of which were fully exposed as the wings were folded. Looking out astern from the well protected quarter deck, even the battleship *King George V* was making heavy weather of it, sometimes 50 feet of daylight could be seen back under her bow. The damage to our bow was not exactly a cause of sorrow as it meant a week's leave for most of the ship's company while it was being repaired at Rosyth.

The flying training programme continued whenever the ship was able to proceed to sea. Two or three times we were catapulted off in the fjord, flew to Reykjavik and rejoined the ship at sea. Reykjavik was a staging post for the delivery of American aircraft and had a good runway. I once landed my flight of three aircraft in formation, which did not please the Air Traffic Controller.

By an extraordinary coincidence I was in the canteen one day when in walked Lew Parmenter, a Canadian I had not seen for ten years. He had been air engineer to Punch Dickins, the famous pilot with Western Canada Airways in the pioneering days of 1929. Now he was chief engineer, and was delivering a Boeing B-17 for the US Army Air Forces. He told me that Punch was in overall charge of the whole ferry operation.

Back to sea again with the convoys, one soon got back into the routine. I enjoyed flying over the sea — there were no mountains to hit or power lines: one could fly low, very low.

HMS Victorious *with an icy deck north of the Arctic Circle.*

A kind of voice pipe. A Petty Officer tells a gun crew 'all clear to rotate the turret', on HMS Victorious *in March 1942, with HMS* King George V *in the background.*

A kind of sixth sense developed giving a hunch for direction and position. An aircraft pointed in one direction travels fast in a moving element, the air, and one's point of reference was, of course, a ship which was itself moving along a mean line of advance (a zigzag course) on another moving element, the sea. The sun, the direction of the waves, the tops of distinctive clouds or holes in the clouds, all give significant information to be stored in one's memory, but in some ways the best guide of all is the ship's wake which may leave a visible trail for a mile or so, and can be seen more easily than the ship itself.

Landing on a deck requires precise flying. After two or three hours in flight one becomes mesmerised by the noise

and speed. Before landing on it is important to shake off this feeling of lethargy and stiffness and concentrate on being alert. I used to open the hood to let in cold air, and bring the aircraft's speed right down to near the stall, in order to get the sloppier feel of the response to the controls. The batsman or deck landing control officer is a great help as he can tell from the relative steadiness of the ship whether the approach is likely to lead to a successful landing. From the deck it is easy to see a crash coming seconds before it occurs. Even at the last moment it is possible for a pilot to avoid the worst, either with a burst of throttle or a twitch of the rudder. I believe the same theory applies to an accident on the road; never give up till the very moment of collision. The smallest gap is softer than the middle of a telegraph pole.

The battleship HMS King George V *in a rough sea.*

A Fulmar gets a wave off: go round again.

One of our duties was to censor the outgoing mail, and return it to the sender if there were any references to the location of the ship, or in fact anything that might remotely help the enemy. One letter which has always stuck in my mind was one from a sailor to his mother, thanking her for his birthday cake, and asking her, in future to send him quantity instead of quality. Rather to my surprise, we were allowed cameras, and to take any photograph of life on board, the only restriction being that all films and prints had to be processed by the ship's professional photographer when, of course, the same restrictions regarding censorship applied. Pictures of deep snow on the flight deck with the ship's company clearing it away overboard were unusual, so to me was the order to 'clear the lower deck'. This meant all hands on deck, with only those who had duties exempted. Pale-faced stokers, tired looking engineers, electricians, armourers, storekeepers, the lot all appeared from the depths of the ship to shovel snow.

In the days of sail, whenever a man was lost or died at sea, his effects were sold or auctioned off 'before the mast' and the money raised sent to his next of kin. This tradition still survives, and often when we returned to harbour the appropriate pipe would be made and a man's kit sold. I bought a collection of Jean Sablon's records, which I had heard being played by a brother officer in the cabin next to mine. These frequent pipes were a constant reminder to young flying

HMS Victorious *rolling in swell with low wind speed over the deck, the most difficult condition for landing on: Fulmar catching a wire.*

One of No. 809 Sqn's Fulmars nearly goes over the side.

types of the risks they were running, although not all fatalities were to airmen.

To live cooped up in a steel box in artificial light, and with forced air ventilation, sometimes for months on end, was not the most healthy atmosphere. Young pilots joining the ship and with only an occasional opportunity to fly, did not find the waiting easy on the nerves.

Most accidents to aircraft were of course due to errors in landing on a deck, but the whole operation of handling aircraft in a ship involved hazards to both aircraft and men. On one particular day when the fleet was in usual line astern formation, one of the destroyers sweeping the waters ahead picked up by asdic a signal indicating an enemy submarine. Instantly the fleet was ordered to make an emergency turn to port, which meant the immediate application of full rudder without warning. Cruising at the usual 22 knots, the ship took a 15° list to starboard, causing the chocks of one of our Fulmars to slip and the parked aircraft to run wildly across the deck. The tail wheel was knocked off by the raised edge of the deck, and the Fulmar finished up half overboard. One more aircraft unserviceable until we reached harbour.

On another occasion, when a flight of three aircraft were ranged for take-off, an enemy aircraft was spotted. They could not take-off as the fleet was steaming down wind, but the 4.5 inch guns were brought to bear. The crew of one

Fulmar, whose engine was running, watched helplessly while the twin guns in 'Y' turret, swung round, checked just above their heads, and loosed off. The gun crew were following the various dials below deck, with no view of the aircraft. The pilot and observer were badly injured by the blast, and the Fulmar was more or less written off.

I had a lucky escape when being catapulted off one day. The catapult was a type which had a piston with compressed air on one side and water on the other. Unfortunately, at the moment of release of the catch holding back the cradle which propels the aircraft, there was a bit of slack in the cable, and one of the two legs fell away on the deck, and I was pushed off with a very big jerk with only one strut. The violent jerk made me black out momentarily, and I came to flying over the sea knowing nothing about the mishap until told later. If the catapult fails to push at the critical moment of releasing the catch, the aircraft merely trickles forward under its own power, and falls off the bow into the sea, more or less perfectly aligned to be chopped up by the ship's propellers.

When flying operationally, it was not always possible to park the aircraft below in such a way that the serviceable ones were conveniently placed. Sometimes several unserviceable aircraft would have to be ranged on deck in order to get at those required. This caused great annoyance and frustration to those waiting on the flight deck, and we used to say 'Uncle Fred has been at it again.' This referred to a prewar music-hall comedian Fred Carno whose slapstick act consisted of house decorators carrying ladders, planks and paint, in which

HMS Victorious' *flight deck showing the forward lift down and the deck marks to give wind direction in conjunction with the steam jet.*

everything went wrong, but somehow the chaotic situation was always saved at the very last moment.

The forward and aft heavy armoured lifts formed part of the flight deck, and could be operated at either high or low speed. The higher speed required enormous electrical power and was extremely unpopular with the engineers and so was rarely used, but to save time in No. 809 Squadron we made a practice of starting up our engines while the lift was rising, so as to be able to taxi forward the moment we reached deck level, leaving the spreading of the wing until we were parked. Naval aircraft used Coffman cartridge type starters which were not too reliable, and not infrequently twenty men had to be called upon to push the aircraft clear.

The flight deck and other aircraft handlers faced continual dangers from revolving propellers, being squashed by folding wings, hit by arrestor wires, falling down lift shafts with everything being done at the double under conditions of noise, sometimes a howling gale, and darkness. They had my admiration but it was no wonder that sometimes accidents occurred.

14 Frustrating Tirpitz

While the bow damage was being repaired at Rosyth, I was given a week's leave. Both the Savoy and Berkeley Hotels very generously gave special concessionary rates to officers on leave and at thirty shillings a night, including dinner, bed and breakfast, Ella and I made the most of it. The return journey north, however, was also to be remembered. Three of us from No. 809 Squadron left Euston at 10.30 one morning to rejoin our ship at Scapa. The train had no heat and no restaurant car, not even drinking water. Next morning when we pulled into Aberdeen we made a rush for the station restaurant. Halfway through bacon and eggs, the train started to move, two of us just made it but one man was left behind. By next morning we had reached Thurso there to embark in a trawler going to the Orkneys. Crossing the Pentland Firth was miserable, as there was no cabin and the only shelter was to stand on deck in the lee of the wheel-house, every now and then being covered with a shower of cold salt spray. We were dropped off at a depot ship only to hear that *Victorious* was in Iceland. An hour or so

later we were transferred to a destroyer, HMS *Icarus*, which was taking the mail to the Home Fleet in Hval Fjord. I was as sick as a dog and had to make constant sorties to the deck which was cold, windy and half awash in the rough sea. The crew were dead tired and yet I could not help noticing that in spite of complete informality in personal relationships they worked in the strictest discipline as a team. On reaching Hval Fjord our first stop was to an oiler to top up tanks and then on to distribute the mail. The Navy attach great importance to news from home even, as we saw, by sending a destroyer to Scapa to collect it. Never was I more glad to see *Victorious*. It was almost like getting home.

While at sea and during daylight hours, an Albacore loaded with two depth charges would supplement the destroyer screen searching for submarines. I was having a cup of early morning tea one day when there was a tremendous bang and I thought we had been struck by a torpedo. In fact, what had happened was that an Albacore taking off for a patrol had swung off line and struck the island with the starboard wing. The impact had swung the aircraft over the side and on hitting the water the two depth charges were ripped off and the safety pins pulled out. On reaching the set

HMS Victorious *at Hval Fjord, Iceland in 1942.*

A Naval pilot lends a hand to HMS Victorious' *anti-aircraft defences with a Thompson machine-gun from the flight deck.*

depth they exploded, fortunately just as the stern cleared the position. The crew of three were killed. Later, from the vibration, it became clear that one of the ship's propellers had been damaged.

On the same operation when we were returning to Iceland I realised for the first time why we had not been allowed to fly off and attack the German aircraft which had been shadowing us from ten miles astern. It had been on our radar all afternoon and by evening our position was about due north of Iceland. The pilot's report, intercepted by our radio, to his base gave our position and added that we were obviously returning to Hval Fjord and that he was returning home. What he did not know was that he was being watched and that this course was a deliberate attempt on our part to mislead. We had had an Admiralty signal reporting that the *Tirpitz*, with one escorting destroyer, would be at a certain position 50 miles off the Norwegian coast next morning at 8 am on a certain course and speed.

On the departure of the shadowing aircraft we turned round and went east at full speed to be in position to make an attack next morning. It was during this high speed dash that

the damage to the propeller became obvious. The vibration in the stern was very bad and it forced a reduction of speed to 28 knots. On visiting the heads (in the stern) I noticed that the lead pipes from the overhead cisterns were chaffing on their clips and that there were pools of lead powder on the deck. Hardly a reason to slow up but the vibration was so bad that if no action had been taken it would certainly have led to major mechanical trouble.

Our Captain was sceptical of the Admiralty report and decided to fly off four Albacores with ASV to make a search at dawn. Sure enough, a few minutes after getting airborne they got a radar contact and returned to the ship. There was a delay while the torpedoes were loaded but an hour later twelve aircraft took off under the command of Lieutenant Commander Lucas, the new CO who had replaced Plugge. The two other replacement crews had not yet had an opportunity to fly with their squadron. The wind was from the east and to get into position to make an attack the squadron was in full view of the *Tirpitz* for a good half hour. Finally, having reached 10,000 feet, they dived. Unfortunately, not having flown together before, and being led into a different method of attack from previous training there was a misunderstanding and a very ragged attack was made. Not one torpedo got a hit and one Albacore was shot down. It was a poor show, and a great opportunity was missed but the blame for the failure lay at least partly in a combination of unlucky circumstances.

Back at Scapa No. 809 Squadron returned to training and air-firing practice. All our new pilots had to do six deck-landings before being accepted for operational flying. One of them went over the side. He had caught a wire successfully

One of HMS Victorious' *2-pdr multi-barrelled anti-aircraft gun positions — the 'multiple pom-pom' or 'Chicago piano'.*

Ice in the Arctic covering one of HMS Victorious' *starboard for'ard twin 4.5-in gun turrets.*

but was drifting sideways across the deck and, after resting on the edge for a few seconds, went on over. I saw him climb out and swim away a few strokes but by the time the destroyer, stationed just astern of us, had swung round and picked him up, probably under five minutes, he was dead, presumably from the shock of plunging into icy cold water from a warm cockpit. In harbour that night it had been decided to bury him at sea but the next day the Fleet was ordered to sea, being at four hours notice, and I was detailed off to take the body ashore. I had no idea of the routine but a bearer-party of four was organised and a trawler came alongside. The coffin was being lowered by the ship's crane when suddenly the Captain appeared and a bugler played the last post while our party all stood to attention on the trawler's deck. A signal to the hospital at Hoy had requested an ambulance to meet us, but on reaching the jetty no ambulance had arrived. Eventually, we had to go as the ship was about to sail, so we staggered up the slippery seaweed covered steps carrying the coffin to be confronted at the top by a mob of sailors recalled to their ships from an evening ashore in the canteen. The sight of our little party sobered them up but the sentry on duty was most reluctant to accept responsibility for the body. The whole

episode was painful to all of us in No. 809 Squadron as we should have liked him to have had a dignified burial at sea.

We always flew in our ordinary day-to-day naval uniform although there was an issue of a flying suit to those flying open cockpit aircraft such as the Swordfish. The Fulmar had a warm front cockpit as there was a gap in the floor leading to the radiator. However, naval officers' uniform calls for a white shirt and stiff white collar and a black tie (in memory of Nelson). This was the worst possible rig for swimming so we made it a rule to slacken off the tie and loosen the collar. In addition, for landing on the deck, the hood would be opened and the Sutton harness locked back to prevent one's face hitting the dashboard in the event of going into the barrier. As a further precaution and to permit a quick exit I used to undo the chin strap of my helmet, release the bayonet fastening of the oxygen pipe and pull out the RT plug lead. This still left the parachute and dinghy attached to one's body and some pilots released these too, before landing on.

The best place to watch aircraft operating off the deck is from the protection of the upper deck of the island just abaft the funnel. From this position one can see the approach and is close enough to the point of contact to be able to study the movements of the controls and even the pilot's face. Unless the hook, attached to the bottom of the fuselage, catches one of the eight arrester wires there is no hope of stopping before hitting the barrier. The pilot's objective, therefore, is to catch a wire and not just to make a pretty landing. When this happens and the aircraft is snatched out of the air, the tremendous relief is apparent on his face. On being arrested, the aircraft is allowed to run backwards a few yards to release the wire from the hook, while in the meantime the barrier has been lowered and immediately the aircraft is taxied forward, using a lot of power, to the forward half of the deck where the wings are folded. It is not possible to 'strike down' the aircraft on the forward lift as fast as they land on and a traffic jam occurs, hence the barrier to prevent damage to aircraft and accidents to the flight deck crew from over shooting aircraft. A well trained squadron and flight deck crew can under ideal conditions land aircraft at twenty second intervals but so many parts of the operation can go wrong that this rarely happens. Nevertheless, to an observer the whole operation is an astonishing scene particularly when the faster and more heavily loaded aircraft land, for it hardly seems possible that they can be stopped in time.

When at sea the Fleet would steam in line astern with an outlying screen of destroyers searching for submarines. To lessen the danger from submarines a zigzag course was often adopted, all the ships turning to a new course simultaneously at a predetermined time, usually every twenty minutes. As well as a steering wheel on the bridge, a second control

position was located several decks below, well protected from damage by enemy fire. One day the Captain happened to be on the bridge when the ship failed to make her regular turn at the appointed moment. The Coxswain was on the lower steering deck at the time, and on being asked what was going on replied in an anxious voice: 'The wheel's come loose in me 'and, Sir.' The rudder had failed to respond to the wheel due to a failure of the operating mechanism. Control was immediately taken over on the compass platform, where some of us thought it funny, but the Captain was not amused.

An Albacore makes a heavy landing. Note how the propeller blades are bent forward.

Urgent. Clear the decks, others short of fuel. Note the Albacore flying by the port beam.

HMS Victorious *in May 1942. A bent but salvageable Albacore is dangled over the side, leaving the flight deck clear for the rest of the squadron, short of fuel, to land.*

Arctic convoy warship escort in line ahead (above) *and on the opposite
tack* (right) *in echelon after the defensive zig-zag.*

Jason Borthwick, our Fighter Direction Officer, was a
keen dinghy sailor and before the war I used to crew for
Gavin Anderson at Itchenor where we raced Sharpies. One
day at Scapa a sailing race was organised for the whole Fleet.
We had noticed the hull of a dinghy hauled up underneath
the flight deck out of the way and the Commander gave us
permission to get it out. It was about 16 feet long, clinker
built but beautifully fitted out and brand new. Launching it
from the quarter deck was not easy but with many willing
hands helping we lowered it into the water. There was a fair
breeze for the race and about a dozen starters. Competition
was not too hot, but we led the race all the way to within a
quarter of a mile of the finish when we were beaten to the
post. We both felt it had been a great honour to represent
Victorious among such an august gathering but everyone was
pleased, at least we had not disgraced our ship.

In the late spring I received a letter from the appointments
Board at the Admiralty. It advised me that with the coming
into production of the naval version of the Spitfire, the
Seafire, there was an opening for a civilian test pilot with
Vickers Armstrong at Eastleigh and that as I had recent deck
landing experience and also of Naval operating conditions
they felt I might fill the position. It was for me a very difficult
decision; the war at sea was at its height and to take a civilian
job looked like opting out. I wanted advice and fortunately
decided to request an interview with my Captain, Caspar

John. He pointed out that I was thirty-four and that a steady
stream of young fighter pilots were by then completing their
training and that Appointments Board were asking me to
take the job.

Although Spitfires were designed and built by Supermarine at Southampton, this was a subsidiary company
of Vickers Aviation Limited whose headquarters were at
Weybridge. I was interviewed there by the chief test pilot
Mutt Summers and he drove me down to meet Jeffrey Quill
at Eastleigh; Jeffrey had the final say and was to be my
immediate boss and I was delighted when he accepted me for
the post.

15 Supermarine test pilot

Spitfire production at the beginning of the war all was based at Supermarine's Woolston factory on the river Itchen. The very first enemy night raid in the spring of 1940 by a single aircraft was aimed at this target, probably to test the strength of the defences, but no damage was done. The Southampton area was heavily defended with anti-aircraft guns and a balloon barrage, but this did not discourage a second really determined attack by a squadron of bombers in daylight. This also was a failure as they missed the main factory, their bombs falling near the chain ferry, but by then the message had got across to the Ministry that the south coast of England was not a healthy place for the production of our premier fighter with the *Luftwaffe* only 70 miles away.

Jeffrey Quill demonstrating the Spitfire Mk I to French Army Reserve officers at Eastleigh, 12 May 1939.

Feverish activity on the part of the works engineer, Len Gooch, led to the commandeering of all the large bus depots in the triangle formed by Reading, Salisbury and Southampton, and stuffing them with all the production jigs and tools. These were dispersed so that if any one depot were bombed it would not mean the loss of all production of any vital part, such as a wing, tail plane or aileron. Within one week of the departure of the last jig, the Germans attacked again and flattened the place completely. This fortunate dispersal operation was a key factor in our ultimate dominance in the air, and those concerned never received the public recognition to which they were entitled as, of course, the whole move was a well-kept secret.

After Mutt Summers had made the first flight in the prototype Spitfire in 1936, he handed over the whole development to Jeffrey Quill. Jeffrey was not only a great test

Spitfire 'basic six', 33,000 feet. One altimeter pointer is obscured.

pilot, he also had the ability to explain clearly and in great detail the interaction and subtle effects on an aircraft of every kind and movement of the controls and its response. The third dimension is a new factor in man's experience and, as few can analyse their thoughts and put them into words, the technical team at Supermarines were undoubtedly greatly helped by his reports.

He later became one of the very few test pilots to reach a boardroom. In my opinion, he should have been promoted to a senior position in Vickers Armstrong years before, but the loss was theirs, as on becoming Director of SEPECAT, the Jaguar consortium, in 1965, and later of Panavia based in Munich, his abilities were quickly appreciated. He really knew aeroplanes and their weapons, and was very well briefed in the tactical and strategic situation in Europe. He could and did lecture to NATO chiefs and has more than done his share in launching the Tornado as the fighting weapon of the future.

I got to know Jeffery well. We both lived at Bursledon, and we usually shared a car to the aerodrome to save petrol. Over the years, he has become a great family friend, the sort of friend one can pick up with again, even if months have gone by since our last meeting.

The Spitfire was the only first line fully operational fighter aircraft in use by the Allies from the beginning to the end of the war. The general public had no idea of the technical battle to keep ahead. The aircraft retained the same smooth lines with beautiful elliptical wings and slim body as originally

designed by R. J. Mitchell, but its continuing success was largely due to the very close links between Supermarine and Rolls-Royce who worked together hand in hand. The technical story has been told elsewhere, but the continuous improvement in performance, in particular its ability to outclimb other aircraft, always gave the pilot the advantage of being top dog, able to pounce, hence its popularity.

By July 1942, when I joined the Company, the principal production of the standard aircraft was at Castle Bromwich near Birmingham, where ultimately a peak of 320 aircraft per week was reached, together with another 100 per week from the Southern Regions. All the experimental and development work and some production was controlled from Hursley Park, a large country house near Winchester. The special limited production types were assembled and flight tested at five small grass aerodromes in the southern area, whereas all the experimental aircraft under development were located at the Royal Naval Air Station Worthy Down. This involved a lot of travelling for the pilots and there was a collection of small, civil aircraft at Eastleigh which we all used. It seemed strange to commute by air but I enjoyed the almost daily flight to Worthy Down, passing over Winchester jail where the unfortunate inmates were often exercising in the yard.

Every Monday there was a weekly meeting at 9 o'clock at

*Seafire Mk III folding wing actuation and locking mechanism; note the
split duct (centre) for hot air for gun heating (Vickers-Armstrong)*

Folding wing Seafire Mk III at Worthy Down, 1942.

Hursley where Joe Smith, the chief designer, presided; Alan Clifton, aerodynamicist, and Mansbridge, the technical officer, were also always present. Progress on each of the experimental aircraft was discussed and priorities decided. Joe Smith had direct access to Whitehall and the various ministries involved in aircraft production and he would frequently ring up during a meeting and get an immediate reply to some vital change in the development programme.

George Pickering, who had been a Supermarine flying-boat test pilot before the war, was just recovering from an accident when I arrived. He was an amusing character and his description of the occasion when the wings came off his Spitfire and he found himself flying through the air strapped to his seat, but without any aeroplane round him, was very funny. He landed by parachute safely after ridding himself of the armoured seat, but lost a finger in the process. A few months later he was killed when he went for a ride in a Bren gun carrier which overturned while crossing a bank.

Seafires were just beginning to come off the production line at Chattis Hill, previously a celebrated racing stable near Stockbridge. The early ones were not fitted with folding wings and, therefore, had limited Naval use, but by November 1942 the first folding-wing prototype was completed. In the meantime I had been flying other development aircraft at Worthy Down. In the quest for speed, the designer was often looking for quite small increases such as from the effect of different air intake scoops, blanking off air leaks and retractable tail wheels, all details from which a few miles an hour could be squeezed. At other times the whole spectrum of performance from ground level to the ceiling would be covered but in every case accuracy of flying and consistency were important and sometimes this involved half a dozen sorties in a day. The early Spitfire only carried 85 gallons of fuel and this would give time for five or six full throttle level speeds to be measured in a flight of about fifty minutes. Worthy Down was a Naval Aerodrome and was used primarily for training radio operators flying in Proctors. Coming in to land in a Spitfire, short of fuel, with twenty or more Proctors in the circuit was to be avoided. I soon learned that the time to be avoided was just before the bar opened at 12.30.

The Photographic Reconnaissance Unit (PRU) at the RAF Station Benson had a special version of the Spitfire which was equipped with cameras and long-range tanks in the wings, but no guns. It depended for its survival on speed at height. The pilots were engaged in photographing the results of the bombing of the previous night, a hazardous task as the enemy fighters were expecting and waiting for them. The usual technique was to climb until a trail formed behind the aircraft around 30,000 feet and then descend a couple of hundred feet. The Spitfires were flying too fast to be intercepted from below and an enemy attacking from above could be seen by its trail. In early 1942 losses started to mount

alarmingly for no apparent reason but it was known that those lost had dived to lower heights.

We had one of their PRU aircraft to investigate. It was suspected that the trouble was due to the cold air at 30,000 feet affecting the oil circulation. Heated vents were fitted to the oil tank breathers but the difficulty was to reproduce any failure. I made many long flights at 30,000 feet to simulate the conditions, followed by a dive to sea level at maximum diving speed. It was surprising what a relatively long time it took to lose height, and how rapidly the density of the air increased below 10,000 feet so that it felt thick and soupy near the ground. At 400 mph on the ASI, one could feel the air resistance build up. The atmosphere around us is, in fact, a relatively thin skin only about 1/80th of the earth's diameter.

After several flights without result, we noticed while re-fuelling one evening that the petrol was blowing back through the filler cap. On closer investigation it was found that the flexible fuel tank had collapsed inwards and had kinked the vent pipe which would have eventually stopped the engine through fuel starvation. The end of the vent pipe itself was in the radiator duct and cut off at an angle of 45°. Unfortunately, the 45° cut off faced aft and not forward as intended, so that at very high speed it was sucking on the tank instead of pressurising it. From such small mistakes in assembly are aircraft accidents caused.

Talking one evening to one of the labourers who was responsible for pushing the aircraft into the hangar at Worthy Down he told me how much he was looking forward to the end of the war. I asked him what his job was, and he said that he worked at Porton Down, the chemical warfare establishment near Salisbury and told me quite seriously that he was a guinea-pig for the mustard gas section. Every time he got a blister from a drop of mustard gas he got £5 bonus and a week off work.

As was to be expected, Naval aircraft only represented a very small proportion of the testing done at Supermarines. Apart from the fitting of a hook, the biggest development was in redesigning the wings for folding. The aircraft behaved in exactly the same way as a fixed wing Spitfire although under heavy G loads there was more wing deflection. By pushing and pulling on the control column during a high speed dive the tips of the wings moved about seven inches, an amount quite visible to the eye and about double that of a standard Spitfire. One naturally did these G and diving tests at a reasonable height and approached the maximum figures step by step making a careful inspection between flights.

Carrier operation of the Spitfire had never been even remotely considered in the original design and understandably the Seafire was not an ideal deck-landing aircraft: the forward view was badly obstructed by the engine and most pilots developed a technique of making their final approach

The prototype Spitfire Mk XII (Rolls-Royce Griffon), DP845.

in a gentle turn. Secondly, the flaps were on the small side permitting only a touch of power during the approach to the deck; on other aircraft with large flaps the extra slipstream from the propeller flowing over the wing root gave considerable lift, so that on cutting the power the aircraft drops immediately onto the deck. Finally, the undercarriage had a very limited travel and consequently the springing was stiff and would cause a bounce if the main wheels touched first. A bounce on a grass aerodrome does not matter but on the deck it means that the hook misses the arrester wires and the aircraft floats into the barrier. To overcome this, special hydraulically damped legs were installed, but the leg travel was still inadequate, owing to the restriction of the existing wheel housings in the wings and propeller tip clearance.

Naval aircraft designed for the US Navy all had soft, long-travel undercarriage legs, large flaps, and were more robustly built; they also had much longer endurance, as it was a requirement in their area of operations. However, what they gained in the practical aspects of operational reliability they partially lost in fighting performance. Their aircraft carriers had two hangar decks and carried at least twice the number of aircraft that Royal Navy ships could, but the Admiralty regarded the ship itself as the vital weapon with the aircraft as rather expensive ammunition. Their argument was that it took six years to build an aircraft carrier but only three months to build an aircraft. In these respects the requirements of the naval staff of the two countries were quite different.

The greatly increased power from later versions of the Merlin and the Griffon led to some handling problems from torque at take-off from a deck. I was sent to the Hawker factory at Langley to fly the Tornado which had a complex 24-cylinder Rolls-Royce Vulture engine with contra-rotating propellers. It certainly overcame any take-off difficulties but one wondered what would happen in the event of a heavy landing and the blades getting mixed up. When an aircraft landed heavily on deck the revolving blades usually bent forward, not backwards as happens on an aerodrome. Sometimes it proved possible to fit another propeller without changing the engine; the engineers just put a dial gauge on the propeller shaft and if it was not bent too badly it was accepted as being serviceable.

An interesting experimental aircraft was the first Spitfire to be fitted with the new Rolls-Royce Griffon engine, which Jeffrey Quill first flew in November 1941. This engine was similar in layout to the Merlin but, with an increased capacity of 37 litres, delivered more power at lower rpm. With a two-speed single-stage blower, it delivered 1,735 hp and had been installed in a suitably modified Mark III airframe, DP845. It was a thrill to fly, rather like driving a 3-litre Bentley instead of a buzz box like an MG, and had a phenomenal performance at low altitudes. Now a legendary aircraft, DP845 was the prototype of the RAF's Spitfire Mk XII, which was used for low level sweeps over the north French coast, pinpointing and photographing the V-1 flying bomb launching sites. The Naval version was the Seafire Mk XV where this engine's performance matched the Navy's operational needs for a high performance fighter.

16 Stretching the Spitfire

bsorbing more and more power became an increasing problem on the Spitfire. It started life with a wooden two-blade propeller and went progressively to three-blade variable pitch, four-blade, five-blade and, on the later version of Seafire, the Mark 47, to six-bladed contra-rotating propellers. As the propeller disc area became more dense with blades, so the directional and longitudinal stability decreased. The revolving weight also led to undesirable handling characteristics due to gyroscopic effects; for instance, if at high rpm in a dive the aircraft was yawed from side to side it would pitch quite violently up and down

requiring a considerable stick force to correct. The rotation of the slipstream also affected control. If the aircraft was trimmed for level flight and pulled into a steep climb the change of airflow over the rudder led to a yaw. Any fighter pilot will tell you that it is no good shooting with any yaw showing on the top needle of the turn and bank indicator. The revolving bullet leaving the gun will curve away from the target rather in the way that a spin bowler introduces a curve into a ball's flight, so altering its normal trajectory.

The original design of the Spitfire was, as in all aircraft, a compromise. Mitchell biased all the options towards performance but he certainly struck a happy balance. Perhaps his finest achievement was the elliptical wing with its curved leading edge and thin wing section. Typically, he insisted on extreme accuracy and would not even tolerate any rivet

The Spitfire Mk XIV, with two-stage two-speed intercooled Rolls-Royce Griffon engine, was the best of the bunch. Note the anti-spin parachute guard on the fin.

heads forward of the spar. This accuracy was achieved by stretching a single sheet of aluminium over a mould. As a result, a specially prepared aircraft was able to reach, in a dive, a Mach number of .9, far ahead of any other aircraft of its time.

Most people can appreciate that the Spitfire's wing is easy on the eye, almost the work of an artist, but the truth is that the wing *is* the aeroplane, as Mitchell proved so successfully. What the powers that be had also missed was that he boldly designed the whole aircraft using the skin as the load-bearing structure; this meant that the potential for development was vastly increased. As an example, one day after a series of high speed dives, some wrinkles appeared in the rear fuselage just in front of the tailplane. The technical staff were delighted as it showed that their stress calculations were about right, and that there was no built-in excess weight. By increasing the skin thickness by one gauge there would be ample strength.

A chief designer's eye for line and the overall concept in

The prototype Spitfire Mk XXI, DP851, at an interim stage with curved windscreen, extended wingtips, and a bigger, broad chord rudder. In 1942, it was the fastest and highest flying Spitfire, the work of Joe Smith (see signature), R. J. Mitchell's successor. In the background is the prototype Mark XII, DP845, with a single-stage Griffon, developed for speed at low level to counter the Luftwaffe's fast, low, fighter bomber incursions, and later used to photograph the flying bomb launch sites.

effect stamps his signature on the aircraft. Mitchell's design of the elliptical tailplane and the curvature of the fin and rudder of the Spitfire followed naturally from the wing and gave it symmetry. Joe Smith, who took over on Mitchell's death, never altered these particular features except to enlarge their area. The Air Ministry specification for a fighter called for an angle of, I believe, 10° over the nose to permit the pilot to see his target in a turn and allow the correct deflection, but Mitchell would have none of this and went for the minimum frontal area. He even persuaded Rolls-Royce to alter the position of the constant speed unit on the Merlin to eliminate the hump it made between the cylinder blocks. Not so the Hurricane, which met the Ministry specification and perhaps in consequence received the first large orders.

Although from the ground the Spitfire's silhouette did not change throughout the war there were at least five new wings. This was due to changes of armament and to the additional strength required to carry the more powerful engines with their greater weight. The all-up weight increased from 5,400 lbs to 12,000 lbs or, as Jeffrey Quill used to put it, from a single-seater to a thirty-two seater. There was a very close link between the Supermarine design team and Rolls-Royce; they worked hand in hand to such an extent that whenever Rolls-Royce had a new engine, Supermarine had an aircraft in production able to take it. This was achieved by incorporating in any new wing enough extra strength to take more weight than the specification called for. The sequence of new wings was that the Mark V (eight machine-guns) became the VB (four machine-guns and two Hispano 20 mm drum-fed cannons), and the VC (four machine-guns and two Hispano 20 mm with ammunition tanks and belt feed) became the Mark IX (two-stage, two-speed intercooled Merlin 60 Series). The Mark VIII wing, designed to an RAF requirement to take the advanced but heavier Merlin 60 Series, became the Mark XIV with a two-stage, two-speed intercooled Griffon, the final version being the Mark XXI with a completely new, stiffer wing and four cannons. By this process of leap-frogging the Spitfire kept its lead in the battle for performance and this was one of the major factors in the Allies' command of the air. From the technical aspect, it was the supreme example of a good original design being developed to the nth degree.

Apart from the handling problems introduced by the large propellers, probably the weakest point was the relatively poor rate of roll. The ailerons had a nose balance but became very heavy at high speed when they also tended to 'float up' or distort upwards. There was no lateral trim control so any tendency to fly one wing low had to be corrected on the ground by reflexing the metal trailing edge of the aileron upwards. Slight variations in manufacture made big differences and a bad aileron would cause so much 'wing low' at take-off that it was wise to land immediately.

Great efforts were made to improve the rate of roll by fitting geared tabs and other methods but at the request of Fighter Command, towards the end of the war, the wingtips were removed. This certainly increased the response but at a small cost in loss of rate of climb and ceiling. Another variation was an aileron with a bulged upper surface, which had been thought of by the design staff at Westlands, who were also building Spitfires. It certainly improved the lateral control but as Joe Smith did not approve it, it was never fitted

to production aircraft. He was probably worried about the wing strength in torque. If an aileron is very powerful it can twist the wing in the reverse sense of the direction to that in which the aileron is working. Up to that time the value of a very rapid rate of roll had not been fully appreciated, but when flying at a very high speed, it is not possible to make any quick change of direction in the pitching plane due to the build up of G and consequent black-out of the pilot. A quick roll or an aileron turn in a vertical dive is a much more effective manoeuvre to throw off an enemy fighter in pursuit.

A great deal of work was done in an attempt to improve the fore and aft stability. Because the aircraft was in mass production, no major alteration such as a larger area tailplane could be readily contemplated. A great scare arose when, for unexplained reasons, a number of aircraft lost their wings. These aircraft had all been built at the main production factory at Castle Bromwich. Jeffrey flew off to various Spitfire squadrons and immediately hurried back to report that every aircraft being delivered to them was unstable. He found that the centre of gravity had been allowed to move aft by the unauthorised addition of extra equipment, the effect of which was to make the aircraft tighten into a turn and thus increasing the G force, a handling characteristic which is quite unacceptable. There were a lot of these aircraft already in service and an immediate solution was called for. Within a week 'bob weights' were being made and issued to attach to the front of the control column and thus apply a forward force on the elevator control during a turn. Not an ideal solution and unpopular with certain pilots, but it worked.

At Worthy Down we had experimental aircraft fitted with special long chord elevators, different tailplane incidence and alternative areas of elevator horn balance. Of these, the most effective improvement in stability was obtained with a larger horn balance. This surprised me as increasing the area forward of the hinge line might be expected to do the opposite. The only disadvantage was that on take-off, particularly on rough ground, there was a certain amount of twitching of the elevator control.

In a fighter, one of the most important characteristics is the stick force required per G force in turns. A difficulty arises in a high-altitude fighter, such as a Spitfire, because the longitudinal stability decreases at height due to the air being less dense. If the stick forces are reasonable at high altitude they become too heavy low down. Modern aircraft overcome this problem by having powered controls, but in the days of reliance on inherent aerodynamic stability this was not possible.

The flow of completed aircraft from the dispersed southern production units was not a steady stream as at the main factory at Castle Bromwich, but the pressure from the Ministry of Production for numbers was nevertheless intense. The weekly figures were telephoned to the Ministry every Friday evening at 5 pm Jeffrey and I would often help out the local test pilots on Friday afternoons, as there was always a build-up of completed but untested aircraft towards the end of the week, and bonuses to the men in the factory were geared to results. A production test flight would commence with a quick circuit and if necessary a landing to correct aileron trim. For this a man would be waiting at the downwind end of the aerodrome, ready to do the reflexing. From experience, one could usually estimate the amount required in one flight. Having made this adjustment, a climb to 20,000 feet followed to check that the supercharger automatically changed into high gear at the appropriate height, plus checks of all operational equipment and systems, followed by a level speed and boost check, then a dive to maximum permitted speed, watching for upfloat or poor aileron trim, and a landing. As zero hour approached I have seen the shop foreman waiting on the tarmac for the thumbs-up signal, indicating acceptance by the pilot, before running to the telephone to claim another aircraft completed. In order to meet zero hour, I have even seen a propeller changed in twenty minutes, which is double quick time for a complicated fitting operation.

The prototype Spitfire Mk V seaplane, W3760, launched at Follands' slipway on Southampton Water, September 1942. Note the increased rudder area and the keel for directional stability.

The Dowty propellers which were fitted to most Spitfires had blades made of compressed wood and resin. From time to time a bad batch would cause production delays. The Spitfire was very sensitive to small variations in manufacture and, although all the propellers were correctly balanced, sometimes it would vibrate badly on take-off. The motion was relatively slow and caused the nose of the aircraft to move in a circle with a whirling movement. The only cure was to try another propeller, sometimes several, before the aircraft could be accepted. It was thought that the trouble was due to the propeller being out of aerodynamic balance by one blade producing more thrust than another.

With the developing war in the Far East the Chiefs of Staff foresaw a necessity for a high performance fighter capable of operating not from an airfield but from lagoons or inside coral reefs. This led to the conversion of a Spitfire to operate on floats. The Supermarine design team had won the Schneider Trophy in 1931 with their S6B seaplane and in many respects the Spitfire itself was a direct development or at least was strongly influenced by their previous experience, so that the design and fitting of the floats was no problem to them.

Folland aircraft at Hamble fitted the floats and, being located on Southampton Water, they also had a convenient slipway. Jeffrey made the first flights and reported that it lacked directional stability but was quite safe to fly. Although highly secret, one could hardly fail to hear it flying round the Hamble area as it made a strange sound like an organ, due to

Jeffrey Quill makes the first flight of the Spitfire Mk V seaplane.

the open end of a cross-tube used to locate the axle of a pair of launching wheels.

Under political pressure from the highest level, the urgency of measuring its performance was very great so it was decided to defer the curing of the directional stability until later. We decided to do the performance testing between Southampton and Poole. As this was only about 80 miles from the German fighter aerodromes and the area was heavily defended, special arrangements had to be made before every flight. This included a two-hour warning and a broadcast to every gun-site.

During a preliminary handling flight around Hamble, I made several take-offs and landings. It had so much thrust at take-off that the normal seaplane technique was not necessary: it was over the hump before the throttle was fully open. In flight the increased side area of the floats caused a permanent yaw with the rudder trailing slightly out of line, although the aircraft could be held straight by continuous corrections with the rudder.

I set off at the appointed time for Poole flying over Christchurch en route. As the object was to show the aircraft to the gun crews, a height of 1,500 feet seemed appropriate. At Poole another Spitfire flew up alongside and after circling around the harbour the pilot waved to me and sheered off. When over the Royal Poole Motor Yacht Club I suddenly noticed some red tracer shells coming from a Bofors gun emplacement just ahead of me. Having no radio and thinking that perhaps an enemy aircraft was about, I hastened to get out of the way. To my surprise, other guns opened up, obviously aimed at me! The red tracers seemed to come quite slowly towards me rather like a catch in the deep field at cricket, but were travelling fast as they came close. I knew that the aircraft when pointing in one direction was moving in another (due to the yaw) and made full use of this. Whenever the shells missed me to port I changed to the other yaw angle, and sure enough, they missed to starboard. I was also making violent changes of height and speed but there seemed to be a lot of guns firing and so at about 100 feet I tore out of the harbour entrance over the chain ferry and on out to sea.

Leaving the harbour I noticed some black puffs in the distance in the direction of the Needles but it hardly seemed possible that they were aimed at me as they were at least two or three miles away. Climbing up to 1,500 feet and getting my breath back I thought that the best place to cross the coast was Christchurch where the gun crews could hardly have failed to see the aircraft on the outward flight, so I flew towards the town and to make doubly sure of being recognised I flew up and down the shore about a mile out and then flew quietly straight over the town. All the local Bofors

The Spitfire seaplane made a noise like a church organ.

opened up with a grand firework display of which I took a very poor view. Diving down at full power to tree-top level I then flew inland over the New Forest where I knew I should be too low for them to be able to take aim. It was still a few miles to Southampton Water, where I just hoped that the locals would recognise the familiar aircraft and let me land.

Climbing up to 1,000 feet I headed east for Hamble. Keeping a good look out astern, I saw to my horror a squadron of Spitfires coming my way. Pretending not to have seen them I continued flying steadily east at cruising speed, meanwhile keeping a very careful watch in my rear view mirror. They were in a loose formation but too close to each other to be able to manoeuvre freely. When the leader was about a quarter of a mile astern I suddenly banked 90°, put on full power and pulled about 5G. They immediately sheered off, obviously having seen the distinctive wing shape, of a Spitfire, not to mention the RAF roundels.

I reached Southampton Water safely and, not knowing whether the floats had been hit, landed, keeping well above the hump speed till I approached the slipway. I got out, and could see no obvious damage, so I made my way to the nearest telephone to ring the controller to report what had happened. A very high pitched excited voice told me: 'Get off the line at once, there's an enemy raid on!' As I was presumably the 'enemy raid', I returned to the aircraft absolutely furious, and when a few moments later, I had an urgent message to call the controller, I refused to speak to

him, and sent him a message telling him what he could do with his 'enemy raids'.

That evening, Ella and I had been invited to a drinks party at the headquarters of the local anti-aircraft regiment in Hamble. We were greeted by the Commanding Officer, who said to Ella: 'I bet your husband was scared stiff this afternoon by his unfortunate experience.' Ella replied without out a moment's hesitation: 'Not at all, he realised that if your men couldn't recognise a Spitfire after three years of war, there was little chance of them being very good shots.' That was the end of the conversation, but not of the whole incident, which was taken to the highest level. I must say it was no joke being fired on by our own people. They had fired eight 4.5 inch shells, ninety Bofors, and 400 .303 inch bullets. To add insult to injury, most of the Bofor guns were manned by women.

After some delay, tests were resumed, but this time with an RAF escort of two Spitfires from Tangmere. We had no radio communication but arranged the whole sorties by telephone. While doing the level speeds between 15,000 and 20,000 feet I drew ahead, and only saw them on turning round for the next run. Understandably, they were reluctant to use full throttle at maximum revs. In fact, their aircraft were theoretically 30 mph faster than the seaplane version. However, in the limited amount of testing we were able to do we got a good indication of the maximum speed and rate of climb to 20,000 feet. In view of all the local difficulties, it was then decided to move the whole programme up to Beaumaris in Anglesea, where in all some twelve aircraft were due for conversion.

17 The quest for performance

In the spring of 1942 the latest version of the Spitfire, the Mark IX, was wheeled out. It was an outstanding aircraft, having a much higher power to weight ratio, and a very lively performance indeed. The latest version of the Merlin engine had a two-stage compressor, intercooled and with two speeds, which really gave it the kick of a mule, and when it began to lose boost at around 18,000 feet the second gear clutch engaged and with a shudder the engine came to life again taking the aircraft up to over 40,000 feet. Within Rolls-Royce there was a friendly battle between the Merlin protégés and the Griffon ones as to which could be made to produce the most power, and this undoubtedly spurred on the development of the Merlin in spite of its smaller capacity. All the development was concentrated on higher supercharger pressure and not on increasing the rpm.

The higher altitudes achievable with these aircraft led to a requirement for pressurising the cabin. An aircraft, a Mark V, was suitably modified in order to gain experience of the problems likely to be encountered. For military purposes, it was considered that a maximum of two pounds per square inch pressure was enough. On my first flight I heard a loud bang, and noticed the sensitive altimeter needle making about one revolution per second, quite a rate of climb! A quick access panel had blown out of the side of the windscreen, but even that sudden pressure drop was quite disconcerting.

The hood was held in place with four cam type levers, the handles of which were pushed home with the pilot's elbows. It was rather like sealing oneself in one's own coffin and, although I do not suffer from claustrophobia, I did not like it. There was also the danger of suffocation in the event of the failure of the mechanical pump. On coming down from altitude the interior of the windscreen would mist up and the cockpit became unbearably hot. Most of the development was directed towards trying to improve the ventilation with different air scoops and spill valves. Fortunately, after limited production, the Mark VI project was soon dropped.

The Mark XXI had a two-stage, two-speed, intercooled Griffon which made it the fastest and highest flying aircraft under development among all the Allied Air Forces. One day we had a surprise visit from two civilians, who turned out to be from MI5. Apparently the *Luftwaffe* monthly news magazine had not only mentioned the Spitfire Mk XXI, but

Jeffrey Quill flying a Spitfire making a trail at about 32,000 feet.

The view through a Spitfire's armoured windscreen of Jeffrey Quill's Spitfire.

also its performance. The most recent issue had given its top speed as being 431 mph, which was in fact the very speed which had been calculated by the technical office from figures which I had obtained three weeks before. Obviously, there was a serious leak of information and we were questioned in detail on all our methods of operation. In flight, test figures were jotted down on a pad strapped to one's right thigh. The paper or card was held in position with rubber bands and I usually wrote down the headings for the columns of figures required before taking off. For a level speed these would be height, outside air temperature, engine rpm boost pressure, charge temperature and indicated air speed. On landing, the figures were copied out on a form and sent to the technical office at Hursley Park. With special experimental engines, such as the Griffon in which Rolls-Royce were particularly interested at this time, their representative at Worthy Down would telephone the vital figures straight off our pads to his office at Derby.

After the MI5 visit the whole system was changed. At the end of a landing run and before taxiing in the test pad record was removed and put into one's breast pocket. A motor-cyclist with a padlocked box then took this card direct to the technical office. The whole episode made everyone very security conscious; clearly the enemy were very interested in what we were doing at Worthy Down, and it came as a shock to hear that we had an informer around.

A lot of Spitfire flying involved going above 30,000 feet, sometimes several times a day. We had no radio or navigation aids and the filing of a flight plan was unheard of, but most flights were short in duration through lack of fuel tank capacity. One developed a kind of homing instinct. The sky at height can sometimes be lonely and beautiful, especially in

This illustrates the obstruction caused by the engine cowling to the forward view from the Spitfire.

The Supermarine Sea Otter was intended to be a replacement for the Walrus. (Charles E. Brown)

the early morning and evening. One particular evening when the sun had set on the ground and I was flying in bright sunshine at 40,000 feet I noticed that a sheet of cloud had formed below me at about 30,000 feet. The sun was setting in a red glow on the bottom of this cloud which gave the appearance of a huge red carpet with the murky darkness of the earth out of sight. Fleetingly, I was in another world and revelling in the beauty of the sky.

Occasionally, Jeffrey and I would have a simulated dog-fight at about 35,000 feet in order to assess the handling characteristics of new or different aircraft. In a dogfight one loses one's sense of direction and speed in one's determi-

nation to get onto the tail of the other aircraft or to shake it off. One day when Jeffrey got onto my tail and we had been tearing round the sky for a few minutes, I suddenly glanced at my airspeed indicator while pulling up in a zoom. It showed only 70, and thinking the aircraft was about to stall, I pushed the stick forward. To my surprise, the response was a lot of negative G; a slight misjudgment of my speed as the needle of the airspeed indicator had already gone round once and my actual speed was really about 500 miles an hour!

Shortly afterwards the engine stopped and it sounded like lack of petrol, although we had only been airborne for 35 minutes. After a long glide I finished up at Blackbushe. Although it had a long runway from east to west, there was a strong southerly cross wind and I chose the north-south short runway. This runway crossed the old main London to Southampton road but, coming in off the glide rather fast, I was still doing 30 miles an hour or so as I rolled over it. Fortunately, there was no traffic crossing at the time, although normally this road carried a lot. It was a dry tank! The petrol gauge was not standard but a new type being tried out. It did not get a good report from me.

As a complete contrast to the Spitfire, Supermarine had also designed a replacement for the old Walrus amphibious flying boat. This was the Sea Otter which, although also a biplane, was more sophisticated with a single engine driving a variable pitch propeller mounted in front of the wings. The Walrus had been demoted from operational use as a ship-borne spotter aircraft and was being used, largely by the RAF, for Air-Sea Rescue. Although probably designed in the late 1920s, it was very tough and could be landed in fairly rough seas, whereas the Sea Otter was more a fair-weather boat. With an engine and whirling propeller just above one's head it seemed in many ways a retrograde step; those who have any experience of landing in rough sea will appreciate the tremendous pounding that ensues — the engine and propeller could easily land on one's lap!

The retractable wheels and landing gear of an amphibious boat add another hazard to flying. I myself had three incidents. The first was entirely my own fault when I landed on the grass at Lee-on-Solent with my wheels up. There had been a lot of aircraft in the circuit, and one in particular came much too close. It turned out later that he was trying to warn me not to land. On another occasion a photographer I had picked up at Weymouth harbour could not see how to free one undercarriage leg which had got stuck in the up position when I attempted to lower the wheels for landing at Lee aerodrome. It was frustrating, as the spring-loaded plunger of the catch was easily accessible inside the cabin, but I was unable to leave the controls and had to land on the sea. The old-fashioned method of a well directed kick immediately freed the offending catch! Shortly afterwards, when I was a

passenger, the pilot asked me to check that the gear on my side was locked up before landing on the sea, but he proceeded to land with the wheel on his own side trailing. The aircraft slewed round to about 45° throwing up a cloud of spray. We were lucky as with the gear locked fully down a Walrus would flip upside down on the water. This was a not infrequent event with pilots in training.

The first batch of Spitfires made use of the retractable gear similar to that used on the Walrus, but later on an engine-driven hydraulic pump replaced the hand-operated one. Although relatively crude by modern standards, the system was simple and light and the somewhat spidery undercarriage proved very reliable in service.

Another unusual aircraft which made its first flight at Worthy Down was the S24/37, or Mayfly as it was known locally, not I hasten to add because of doubt that it could fly but because of its low priority in the experimental shop at Hursley. This was built to a Naval specification and was intended as a torpedo bomber. The unique feature was a variable incidence monoplane wing, incorporating all the latest high lift flaps, mounted on top of the fuselage. The device was arranged to pivot about the centre of lift and interconnect with the flaps to give high lift to allow a low approach speed and good view forward for deck landing.

Jeffrey made the first flight while I watched with a little group consisting of Joe Smith, Clifton and Mansbridge, the design team. The first flight of an entirely new aircraft is still an anxious moment and their evident relief when it landed safely was apparent, as also was Jeffrey's. The aircraft looked very strange coming in to land as its tail was well up high in the air with the nose pointing at the ground.

The Vickers-Supermarine Type 322 S24/37 (Merlin), nicknamed 'Dumbo' or 'Mayfly', had a unique variable incidence wing, which folded. (Vickers-Armstrong)

Later I had a go but my own assessment was blurred by events. On taking off, the detachable hatch above my head lifted a couple of inches off the windscreen. The forward catch was not fully home although the aft end was properly located. It created a tremendous draught but for the first few minutes I was busy trimming the aircraft and gaining a safe height. On closer inspection I thought that I could pull the hatch down and fasten it, but on touching it, it flew off taking my hand back, hitting the rear edge of the cockpit very hard. It cut one finger to the bone so I decided to land. Jeffrey had had a good grumble about the hand wheel which needed 120 turns to apply the wing incidence and flaps but it was then that I really took his point. Winding on incidence merely raised the tail as one instinctively kept up a steady approach speed. Before the flaps were reasonably far down for a landing, one was sitting looking at the ground, being held back by one's straps to prevent sliding off the seat. Meanwhile in turning the handle I had spread blood all over the place as the injured finger was on that side. As it turned out the cut was deep but not serious, although it took a long time to heal. This may not have been helped by the coldness of a Spitfire's cockpit at height, for I had had a rather similar experience years before flying in winter in Northern Canada.

The main production of the standard Spitfire was in a very large factory at Castle Bromwich near Birmingham. I was sent up there to help George Lowdell while Alex Henshaw, who was in charge of the testing, was away attending a funeral. As about twenty-five aircraft were coming off the assembly line daily, waiting to be flight tested, any delay caused a backlog. The weather deteriorated just after my arrival. Visibility was about a mile but the whole area was thick with balloons and flying was impossible, at least I thought so. However, the local test pilots were so accustomed to the smoky industrial murk, that after a couple of days they decided to try to clear a few aircraft. There was a narrow passage through the balloons in an easterly direction to the big power station at Hams Hall; from there they turned north and went up through it to 20,000 feet, returning on a reciprocal course to complete a dive to maximum air speed. They had no radio for direction finding and navigated by flying accurate courses and using the balloons and smoke from the power station as reference points. They made flying in these conditions sound easy, but I did not enjoy them, and I was very glad when Henshaw returned. They did a tremendous job clearing all those aircraft pouring out of the factory. It was a tiring, monotonous and highly dangerous task, for which they received little thanks.

Back at Eastleigh aerodrome itself, Supermarine did a small amount of production testing. Although there were balloons all round, there was no industrial smoke, and the area was familiar. All the ferry hacks were kept there, however,

as officially it was our office, and, knowing the route from Worthy Down so well, Jeffrey and I would fly in and out regardless of balloons and almost of weather. The railway lines provided the guide, and the site of the winches was well known, so if one flew at about 150 feet along one side or the other of the railway tracks to allow for sag in the wires according to whichever direction the wind was blowing, one was quite safe. I liked the Hawker Tomtit or the Monospar best as both of them could be turned within the boundaries of the aerodrome to line up for a landing into wind. They say an old horse can find its way home blindfold and I suppose this procedure was about the flying equivalent.

With the high flying Spitfires we were running into trouble with both oil overheating and petrol boiling, a strange mixture. The extreme cold at 35,000 to 40,000 feet was causing the oil to congeal on the inner surface of the oilpipes and oil coolers, leaving only a small core for the hot oil to flow through. The symptom was a sudden rise in oil temperature to unacceptable figures. The petrol boiling was simply due to the low pressure of the atmosphere near the ceiling of the Mark IX and XXI. The engine would start to misfire and on one occasion I had it cut out completely at 38,000 feet. On reaching lower altitude it picked up and behaved normally. The addition of a petrol cooler cured the trouble.

The Spitfire was an interceptor fighter designed to defend the home bases against enemy attack. As the war continued it became apparent that aircraft with longer range would be required not only to accompany bombers but for reinforcement of overseas bases, such as Malta. A programme for the development of long-range tanks was started with slipper tanks of 30, 60 or 90 gallons attached below the fuselage. These tanks could be jettisoned by pulling a lever in the cockpit and were not intended to be used in action. The effect of these on the handling characteristics in normal flight was small but the petrol feed connection was not very reliable and they could not be used for take-off and not infrequently failed on the changeover when in flight. A flight test was essential after fitting, although on operations an engine run-up check was acceptable. Later, a streamlined pear-drop 90 gallon tank was designed which overcame the feed difficulty experienced with the slipper tanks.

By the early spring of 1943, I put in a request to the Admiralty to rejoin the Navy as, by then, the Seafire was in full production and I hoped that I might be given a fighter squadron. On visiting the Appointments Board it was made clear to me that at the age of 35 my experience as a test pilot was of more use than my ability as a fighter pilot, and they had arranged for me to be appointed to the Aircraft and Armament Experimental Establishment at the Royal Air Force Station, Boscombe Down. I was very disappointed at the time at not getting a squadron.

Spitfire Mk IX with an experimental 90 gallon long range drop-tank at Worthy Down, August 1942.

I remember well one of my last flights before leaving Supermarines. As previously mentioned, the Spitfire Mk IX had a Merlin with an intercooler. We had noticed how difficult it was to obtain a steady indicated air speed when doing level speeds to measure its performance, but it was only on adding an inlet charge temperature gauge to the inlet manifold that the reason became obvious. The temperature rose gradually when at full throttle as the water in the intercooling system tried to cope with all the extra heat from compressing the charge. As the charge temperature rose, the power fell off and so, of course, did the speed of the aircraft.

I had adopted the habit, between each measurement of speed, of cooling off thoroughly by closing the throttle to about a quarter and putting the propeller pitch into full coarse to reduce the revs. On this occasion while doing some level speeds I adopted the usual procedure of selecting fully coarse pitch in order to cool off between each run. On opening up again and fining off pitch there was no response, the engine just spluttered and would not take more throttle. My first reaction was that there was a lack of fuel or a choked main jet, but looking at the slowly revolving propeller it became clear that the blades were feathered and that it was not turning fast enough for the engine-driven oil pump to unfeather it. From 20,000 feet over the Wiltshire Downs I could see some runways in the Swindon direction and made for an unknown aerodrome there. The undercarriage and

flaps went down normally and with the engine still idling I landed safely.

It was, of course, not possible to taxi so I had to wait patiently for help in getting off the runway. Eventually a Hillman Minx pick-up arrived, but the driver looked blank when I told him that the aircraft could not be taxied but needed a tow and he disappeared, saying he was going to tell his boss. The aerodrome was Wroughton, a maintenance or supply base under the control of civilians, but after a lot of delay we got the aircraft to a hangar.

My replacement at Supermarine, Lieutenant Commander Frank Furlong, who as an amateur jockey had won the Grand National on Reynoldstown, kindly came over to Wroughton to pick me up in the Miles Falcon. (A year later, Furlong was killed at High Port near Salisbury, caused, I heard, by a jammed aileron while testing a production aircraft.) It turned out that in the assembly of the propeller someone had forgotten to fit the coarse pitch stop: whether it was our own fitters' fault or those of Dowty never came to light. In the end no harm came of it and it was a million to one chance that the combination of events would occur again.

The nine months which I had spent as a civilian pilot flying for Supermarines had taken me away from my old love, the sea, but it was a job after my own heart to be lending a hand and learning about the process of developing the Spitfire. On receiving my orders from the Navy, it was ironic to think that I should find myself at Boscombe Down in the middle of Salisbury Plain doing much the same work but with a far greater variety of modern fighters, dressed up in naval uniform but even further from the sea.

First solo: Avro 548, Brooklands, August 1928

Sports flying: D.R.R., Tipsy and Richard Muspratt, Lympne, 1946

"Tipsy"

Supermarine test pilot: Sea Otter, 1942

PART III

BOSCOMBE DOWN

Supermarine test pilot: Spitfire Mk XXI and XII prototypes, 1942

Naval fighter pilot: Fulmar, 1940–42

Naval pilot: D.R.R. and Sea Gladiator, 1941

18 Naval test pilot

The Royal Air Force station at Boscombe Down, or, to give its full name, the Aeroplane and Armament Experimental Establishment (A&AEE), had been moved from Martlesham Heath at the beginning of the war. The new location in the middle of Salisbury Plain was considered to be less vulnerable but, although it frequently had up to 150 aircraft on the aerodrome, most of which were either prototypes of new aircraft or at least developing new weapons, during my time there it was never bombed nor, to my knowledge, was it ever seriously attacked by low-flying enemy aircraft, although the odd single enemy aircraft unable to find its objective did unload in the vicinity.

The station employed a large number of civilians, and was concerned primarily to test, report on and accept new and modified versions of aircraft for use in the Armed Forces, including the Royal Navy. Later, civilian aircraft were also tested there. Although under the functional control of the Ministry of Aircraft Production, it was administered by the Royal Air Force, No. 23 Group, Technical Training Command running the station and flying. The technical office was manned by senior technical officers from the Civil Service who issued the instructions on what tests were to be undertaken, and subsequently made the reports to the Ministry in London and so to the Chief of Staff.

I was sent to Boscombe as a Lieutenant (A) RNVR, seconded from the Fleet Air Arm headquarters at Lee-on-Solent. The only other Naval officer there was Lieutenant Commander Torrens-Spence RN, a regular, also on secondment who had preceded my own arrival in April 1943 by a year. 'T.S.' as everyone called him was one of the few experienced officers in the Navy who really understood the capabilities and limitations of aircraft and had made a deep study of their application to naval warfare. His interest lay in the tactical and strategic use of this new weapon, and with his knowledge I always expected to see him rise to the top. In pre-war days the senior jobs in the Navy tended to go to the experts in guns and armour, and not the flying side, which was still regarded as a backwater where the 'playboys' and other less serious types could be moved sideways! T.S. was different, but he retired relatively soon after the war.

On arrival at Boscombe Down, I was sent to 'A' Flight Performance Testing Squadron (known as 'A' per T) under Squadron Leader Sammy Wroath, a great piece of luck for me. Sammy had a strong personality, was very popular, and already probably the most experienced active test pilot in the RAF. Like Quill, he had a very sharp sense of observation, a gift for explanation in detail and was a brilliant natural pilot.

Every aircraft that came to Boscombe Down had a programme of trials to assess its suitability for service use and to measure its performance.

The organisation was split into halves, performance testing and armament testing, each division having its own offices and personnel. My own flight, 'A' per T, was primarily concerned with fighters and other single-engined aircraft, and 'B' Flight dealt with the bombers. Some of the armament trials affected the flying qualities of an aircraft and in that case we would be called in to make our own reports.

The programme for any entirely new type was extensive, but under the extreme pressure of war and the practice of laying down a production line before the aircraft had been accepted, we were called upon to produce results in as short a time as possible. We worked a seven-day week taking odd days off when the weather was unsuitable for flying. There was a graded system of priority with a constant call for interim reports, but inevitably a backlog of work accumulated and, although a considerable portion of the trials resulted in figures to be passed to the technical office, there were also the handling reports to be considered and written. On some days one might fly half a dozen different types or have to make several flights above 30,000 feet; variety, they say, is the spice of life, and I liked it. Sammy was very fair in his doling out of jobs, and I got my share of the 'plums'!

The trials of new types went whenever possible through a logical sequence. On arrival the aircraft would be loaded with full operational equipment, the weight would be measured, the centre of gravity position checked against datum, all the flight instruments would be removed and replaced by specially calibrated ones, and any special instrumentation added. Before any serious flight testing was carried out, the cockpit was checked on the ground and in flight for carbon monoxide contamination. From then on handling at low levels, level speeds, partial climbs, climb to ceiling, dives and all the handling qualities observed or measured until the whole spectrum of performance had been covered. This could well take three months or more depending on any faults which arose.

Throughout preliminary trials, representatives of the various aircraft and engine manufacturers would be present, partly to advise on maintenance and no doubt partly to advise their companies of progress, and the likelihood of acceptability. For the same reason, we ourselves received many invitations to visit the various factories and meet the senior people involved. Having been attached to Supermarine for nine months, I myself knew then all well

The Aeroplane and Armament Experimental Establishment, November 1944. The author is at the right, in Naval uniform.

there, but I also got to know Hawkers at Langley, de Havillands at Hatfield and Faireys at Heathrow. The old natural secrecy among different companies went overboard completely during the war and, in fact, all the senior test pilots were welcome to fly any aircraft we had at Boscombe Down and many made a point of flying rivals' latest types.

Although a Royal Air Force station, Boscombe Down must have been very difficult to run from the service point of view. There were hundreds of civilians, a large aerodrome without a full perimeter fence, 150 very valuable aircraft dispersed around the perimeter and over all a flying programme of enormous variety. It was no wonder that normal service discipline was practically non-existent, with no duties or parades! In addition, there was insufficient housing accommodation, and a large number of officers and men lived out, as did Ella and I. The best time and almost the only time one met other officers and technical staff was in the mess over a drink before lunch. It was rather like a man's club. In the course of time nearly everyone connected with aviation seemed to find their way there and it was a good time to make contacts and also to get instant decisions.

The permanent test pilots in 'A' per T consisted of Sammy Wroath, Flight Lieutenant Brunner, and a Polish Officer, Flight Lieutenant Kulczyski, and myself. This number was supplemented from time to time by other pilots having a 'rest' from operational tours or by borrowing officers from the other Flights. Apart from Kulczyski, who was also a very knowledgeable expert on missiles, there were a number of Poles at Boscombe Down, all of whom I got to know well. They had all escaped when their country was overrun by the Germans, leaving their homes and families behind to survive as best they could. Consequently, they all had an intense hatred of our mutual enemy, and they were waiting and longing to be posted to operational squadrons.

When I arrived at Boscombe Down in April 1943, the war was not going well for us, but the country had recovered from the loss of all our equipment at Dunkirk and the mass production of weapons was surging ahead. However, the losses at sea were enormous as were our losses in the very large night bomber raids. The Germans were well dug in and a menace just across the Channel. As for the war in the air, the new Focke-Wulf Fw 190 was beginning to appear to challenge the air superiority in the west, which we had established while the Germans were fighting in Russia. It was no time for complacency and we expected the renewal of heavy bombing attacks on our cities and factories. All these pressures were reflected in the priority and urgency of the trials we were undertaking.

Looking back to that period of the war, it is interesting to note how the work load shifted to the carrying of external stores (bombs, rockets and other tactical weapons), obviously to support an army in Europe, and later to modifications to meet the requirements for tropical conditions in the Far East and the Pacific. By 1944, the urgent demand was for longer range by extending the fuel load of our fighters, which basically were intended for interception or defence of the United Kingdom, rather than in the support of day bombers or advancing armies. Put in another way, it is apparent that the Boscombe establishment was used by the Air Staff to meet their future needs not only strategically but also tactically. The Admiralty also had their own requirements so far as aviation was concerned and aircraft such as the Barracuda, Firebrand and the Wyvern were the result. I was going to say the disastrous result, but perhaps the inevitable result would be more appropriate: it was the price the Fleet Air Arm had to pay for the political battles between the wars.

A Blackburn Firebrand with flaps extended which increased the wing area and adversely changed trim.

Boscombe Down and the Royal Aircraft Establishment Farnborough are in many respects complementary. The general public are probably more aware of Farnborough as an aircraft testing centre but the work there is of a scientific research nature concerned with aerodynamics and the future. They are also equipped for testing structures, electronics and other components connected with aviation. If any manufacturer was in trouble with a new type of aircraft, they would go to Farnborough for advice. Another division was devoted to naval problems such as catapults and other methods of short take-off and arresting aircraft on the deck. At Boscombe Down we had no facilities for testing these features and we frequently visited Farnborough delivering or collecting an aircraft for some special trial.

As a Service test pilot, one was of course bound by King's Regulations and Admiralty Instructions not to impart information, but there was in addition the Official Secrets Act covering Boscombe Down's activities. Inevitably, a great deal of information about existing aircraft, shortcomings in new aircraft, new weapons and other developments came our way, and in our Flight we would naturally talk about these things among ourselves.

I very soon learned to stick strictly to facts and not to give any opinion, unless this was specifically called for in a report. Obviously, a large proportion of the test procedures involved the obtaining of figures, such as speeds, rate of climb, temperatures and so on, but in reporting on the handling qualities of an aircraft great care was needed to describe the response and wherever possible to give facts. For instance, one would not write that 'the aircraft was unstable because it tightened up in turns', but 'the aircraft was trimmed in level flight at x miles an hour; on entering a turn to port the aircraft increased its rate of turn, and a forward pressure of 10 lbs on the top of the control column was necessary to prevent the acceleration exceeding 5G.' By describing the aircraft's behaviour in this way, the same fact can be checked by others.

One of the reasons for writing a report in this form is that an aircraft which tightens in turns is unacceptable. If it was a new type the Ministry may already have committed itself to a substantial order, a whole factory may be committed to its production, thousands of men and women earning their living working on it, and any serious delay could have political implications. As pilots of the aircraft we had pretty shrewd ideas as to whether it could ever reach operational service, but for the civil servants concerned, the decision to cancel was more difficult; it was easier to carry on while calling for modifications. For the manufacturer, the mere thought of the cancellation of an order probably meant the loss of millions of pounds, hence their intense interest in the progress of the acceptance testing.

While aircraft were at Boscombe Down they were maintained by Royal Air Force personnel, although in the case of prototypes the company usually sent their own engineering representative to act in an advisory capacity. The large engine companies, Rolls-Royce, Bristol and Napier had permanent staff as did Dunlop, Dowty and de Havilland propellers. Our own Flight engineer officer, Flight Sergeant and airmen were picked men. They had a difficult task in having to deal with so many different types and inevitably were always under pressure to keep prototypes serviceable.

19 Fireflies and other troubles

An entirely separate intensive flying flight was created in 1943. Before any new type of aircraft was issued for squadron service, a sample from the production line came to Boscombe Down where it was flown from morning to night seven days a week for a period of three months. The Engineering staff were responsible for the trial while a complete record was kept of its reliability, maintenance times, spares requirements and all details of any faults which developed, thus providing a source of information which had been sadly lacking in the past and no doubt was extremely valuable.

Before being sent to Supermarines, I had never flown much higher than 25,000 to 30,000 feet but, while doing development work on various high flying versions of the Spitfire, I gradually acquired a taste for it. This was partly a kind of competitive urge to get higher and higher but I found there was also a feeling of isolation and even solitude at great heights. It was very rare to see another aircraft above 10,000 feet, the sky is so vast, and although while climbing one would be concentrating on the test in hand, maintaining the best rate of climb, and recording what one was doing, the long slide down to earth was pleasant and relaxing. Similarly, when doing level speeds at altitude intense concentration was required to obtain good figures, as the engine power varies with the forward speed due to ram pressure, but in a way one was living at least temporarily in a world of one's own.

During part of my time at Boscombe Down 'A' per T Flight was also responsible for the daily weather flight. This was not done for meteorological or weather forecasting but solely to measure the air temperature at all altitudes for use by the technical office in calculating the true air speeds from figures obtained in performance testing. I enjoyed doing these climbs, but rather to my surprise some people did not. None of the aircraft we used for measuring air temperatures was pressurised, and certainly if one was a bit off colour it was an effort to go high.

One day while measuring speed at about 35,000 feet, the Spitfire I was flying started to shake just as if it were a car going over cobblestones or over a bad stretch of road. It was something I had not experienced before as normally the air at altitude is smooth, but others had also reported this. It was possibly due to the meeting of two horizontal air streams rather similar to the conditions which sometimes occur on the surface of the water when a tidal stream meets the current from a river.

On another occasion I was flying a Spitfire and on completing a climb to altitude, noticed a large thundercloud. I thought it would be interesting to fly through part of it, so

headed towards the top. I soon wished I had not, as it was extremely turbulent with violent bumps making it difficult to maintain any sort of heading on the instruments. Fine snow was blown through tiny gaps around the perspex hood and at one moment I noticed that the rate of climb was off the clock at over 4,000 feet per minute! One lives and learns, and I was glad to shoot out of the far side into clean air, but I could not resist clipping round the edge of the enormous and magnificent mountains of cloud!

The affection which so many fighter pilots had for the Spitfire was, I believe, the feeling on entering the cockpit, of strapping on a pair of wings, sitting behind a powerful and responsive engine and putting the guns to one's shoulder. To me, who never fired the guns in anger, it represented putting on an old glove, it fitted! It responded to the slightest touch, it gave an outstanding rate of climb to cheat that old airman's enemy, gravity. But above all, was the feeling of mastery of the third dimension — climb, dive, quick turns, hanging on the prop, or in another mood creeping quietly through the upper sky with a wisp of power, or listening to the gentle lapping of the air past the cockpit in a glide, appreciating the beautiful curvature of the wings silhouetted against a cloud, or reflecting glints from the sun as one banked and turned. These things to a Spitfire pilot must be what a painter feels when contemplating a work of art, a sculptor the sight of a beautiful figure, or a musician listening to music, a sheer *joie de vivre*.

After the Battle of Britain, the Defence Staff had expected any future attack on the United Kingdom to be from high altitude. The aircraft intended to deal with this expectation were the Spitfire Mk XXI (later changed from Roman to Arabic figures, i.e. 21) and the Westland Welkin, both of which were undergoing trials. I had already done a lot of flying in the prototype Mark XXI, while attached to Supermarine, so it was an old friend but the Welkin, built by Westlands, was rather different. A twin-engined single-seater with a 70-foot wingspan, it had the two-speed, two-stage intercooled Merlin to give the power at height, a modern pressurised cockpit and electric trimmers. Fortunately, it was an easy aircraft to fly as I had had practically no experience of twins, certainly not of this power, but the two engines seemed to give one a sense of security and the cockpit was comfortable compared with other fighters. However, there was a serious failing in its performance, namely a loss of control in a dive at high altitude.

At the time nothing was known about the phenomenon and the word 'compressibility' trouble began to be used. There

Westland Welkin, Boscombe Down, April 1943. Developed as a high altitude fighter with pressure cabin, it was in serious trouble from compressibility, or the sound barrier. (Charles E. Brown).

were reports that the American Lockheed Lightning fighter was also in similar trouble. The Welkin would climb up to 40,000 feet at about the same rate as a Spitfire Mk IX but on putting it into a dive, even of only 15°, it would start to pitch fore and aft with a frequency which could not be checked by use of the elevator control. There was clearly a breakdown or substantial change in the airflow over the wings.

To achieve the high rate of climb and speed at height the designer, Mr Petter, had chosen a very high aspect-ratio wing layout but to meet the strength required he had had to use a thick wing section and it was this which caused the 'compressibility' trouble. It was interesting that, many years

later, the same designer was responsible for the Canberra bomber which had a short span and very thin wing. This has proved to be one of, if not the most successful of post war designs, large numbers being built for both the Royal Air Force and the United States Air Force.

Brunner, who had recently had to bale out of a Miles Master when the wings came off in a dive and had been badly shaken by his passenger flatly refusing to get out, was shortly afterwards flying the Welkin when an engine caught fire. He soon found he had no lateral control. In fact, the push pull tube to the aileron had been burnt through allowing the aileron to fly upwards to its maximum travel, but after a series of uncontrolled swoops and stalls he managed to regain control from the top of one swoop by using full opposite rudder and some power from the good engine. Somehow he then managed to land it at Upavon, really an amazing feat of airmanship; he was very shaken especially coming so soon after his other recent experience.

Richard Muspratt riding a Mustang, not a wild horse, but an American thoroughbred. It carries two duplex rockets under each wing, which proved a devastating weapon against tanks.

One day Philip Lucas, the chief test pilot of Hawkers, asked to fly the Welkin. He turned up in a light check suit looking very smart, and while filling him in with details of the aircraft we told him of our new name for it, 'The Japanese firecracker model', for by then we had had two Welkins catch fire in flight. Off he went, but as it was a wet afternoon with low cloud we were not flying ourselves but making up reports and chatting. About an hour later a strange car arrived and through the door walked Philip, wet to the skin, mud up to the knees and looking rather pale and shaken, to be greeted by an unkind roar of laughter! He had had another fire but had managed to set it down in a ploughed field without turning it over. By now the aircraft's reputation was not good, and rumour had it that as fast as they came off the production line at Yeovil they were flown to Scotland, the two slave engines removed and reinstalled in the next one at Yeovil! Production continued for some time but I believe no aircraft ever saw active service.

I was detailed off to do the terminal dives of the Welkin at low altitudes. Starting at maximum speed at 10,000 feet, I did a series of dives at increasingly steep angles, so that I reached the maximum permitted indicated air speed step by step. On about the fourth dive with an ASI of about 400 mph there was a sudden thump followed by the nose dropping to a steeper angle. It is surprising how quickly one reacts in an emergency and thinking the wings had come off I instinctively reached for the quick release on the hood in order to bale out, but it was only then that I realised that the hood itself had torn off and that the wings were still there! It would

be interesting to know how much lift the curvature of a hood can give but it certainly made a big difference to the longitudinal trim of the Welkin. A kind spectator of the incident returned the hood to Westlands and I still have a part of it which I use as a ruler on my desk.

Of all the American fighter aircraft, the various versions of the Mustang were nearest to the British idea of a fighter. It was fast, handled well, carried plenty of fuel and was very well finished, in fact an ideal long-range fighter for daylight bomber support. The Mark V (P-51H) version of the Mustang was almost a new design but the first one did not arrive at Boscombe Down until 1945, too late for operational use, when it made a very good impression. One of its good features, way before its time, was the fitting of disc brakes; most of our aerodromes were still grass whereas I suspect that most of the American air bases were already built with concrete runways where brakes become more important for a fast-landing aircraft like the Mustang.

We also had a P-40 Kittyhawk and a P-47 Thunderbolt for performance measurement. Both were disappointing and the Kittyhawk, which was a pre-war design, could only be used in secondary operational areas. The Thunderbolt had several big disadvantages for pilots trained on British aircraft, the climb performance was very poor and the big air-cooled

The Republic P-47 Thunderbolt was claimed to be the heaviest Allied single-seat fighter. It certainly was, with a resulting performance to match.

The Curtiss P-40N Warhawk (Allison engine), designated Kittyhawk Mk IV in RAF service. The P-40 was basically a pre-war design, and was uncompetitive in Europe.

engine, a Double Wasp, had a turbo-charger which required an extra lever to control the power. British engines were all fitted with an automatic boost control to prevent the engine being overboosted at low altitudes; this device automatically opened the throttles to maintain the chosen setting of boost as the aircraft climbed or dived. The turbo-charger of the Thunderbolt had a waste gate which simply opened a valve to release the exhaust to atmosphere in order to prevent overspeeding the supercharger at altitude. In any combat manoeuvre one constantly had to glance at the boost gauge and alter the turbo-charger control lever; in the excitement of the moment some pilots could hardly remember their propeller pitch which controlled the engine rpm let alone the boost pressure. The aircraft was really more suitable as a tactical bomber than as a fighter; like an American car, its sheer weight gave it the comfortable boulevard ride but it lacked the nimbleness of a good sports car.

The Fairey Firefly, the successor to the Naval Fulmar two-seater fighter, arrived at Boscombe early in 1943, but it was in trouble. The company's chief test pilot, Stanilland had just been killed while doing stability trials. There did not seem to be any explainable reason for the accident, although the spinning trials of a model in the Farnborough vertical wind tunnel indicated a possible reluctance to recover when the flaps were extended. I did endless dives at increasing speeds and it was obvious that the very big change of longitudinal trim with speed was quite unacceptable. If trimmed for level flight, it was not possible to hold it in a dive, for on releasing the stick, recovery produced a lot of G. Alternatively, if trimmed into the dive, it required about five turns of the trimmer wheel and it then became difficult to pull out as the speed fell off.

Mr Dickenson from the technical office at Boscombe,

asked for more and more figures, and then announced that from an examination of the figures the trouble was caused by an unexplained relationship between coefficient 'A' and coefficient 'B'! This meant in laymen's language, that from the figures given to him, there must be a bending of the structure. So it proved, for when an all metal elevator was produced by Faireys, the aircraft behaved normally. The original elevator had been fabric covered and this must have been distorting at speed. This analysis and cure of the trouble by the 'boffins' was to me most interesting, as none of them could fly and their deductions were entirely mathematical.

As the Firefly was designed for deck landing it had a special high-lift wing. This was also designed to fold to enable the aircraft to be 'struck down', that is, sent by lift to the lower deck for stowage in the hangar. The Youngman type flap extended on rails to a position well aft of the trailing edge to increase the wing area and it could then be set at various angles of incidence for extra lift and drag. It was very successful and effective but there were doubts about its possible blanking of the tailplane, thus preventing recovery from a spin. Starting gingerly with a forward centre of gravity and one turn only, Sammy Wroath, our CO gradually covered the whole CG range step by step, both at low and at high altitude. There was no tendency to spin 'flat' or difficulty in recovery much to everyone's relief.

When the aircraft entered service it was popular but there were requests from the squadrons for a higher rate of roll. By this time spring-tab ailerons, a method of self-powered or servo-assisted control, were being tried on a number of different aircraft and the ailerons of the Firefly were modified accordingly. Rate of roll was measured, relatively crudely, using a stop-watch while the aircraft was rolled through 180°; in other words, one finished the manoeuvre inverted.

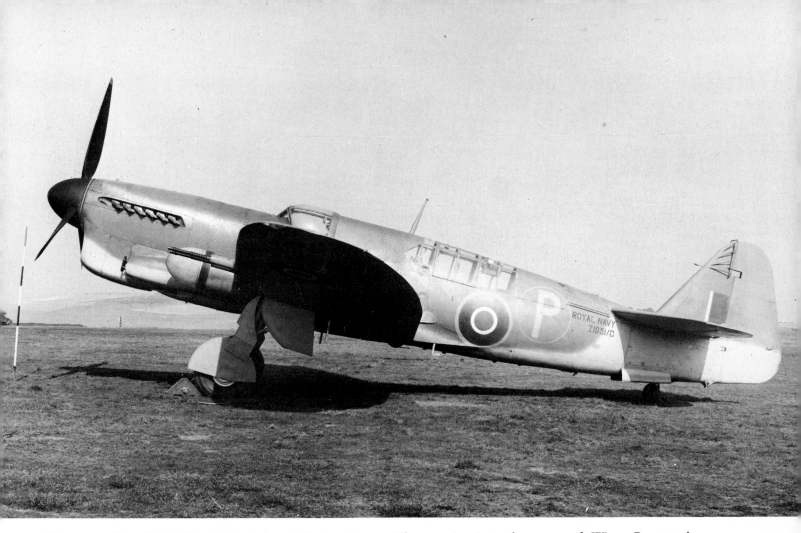

The prototype Fairey Firefly, Z1831/G (single-stage Griffon low altitude engine) with an AIX radar on the port wing root. After development on both elevator and aileron controls, the aircraft proved very manoeuvrable and was a highly effective Naval weapon. The anti-spin parachute fairing panels on the rear fuselage top deck and the parachute guard on the fin can be seen clearly.

When the instructions for doing this trial were received the technical office asked for it to cover the complete speed range. We queried this as it is clearly unusual to roll inverted at maximum diving speed, but the instructions were not amended. I did some of the trials and it was clear that the spring tabs were giving a very considerable improvement. Wing Commander Webster DSO, on loan to us after completing two tours of duty in bombers, undertook the completion of these trials. The aircraft was seen to dive into the ground inverted; whether the wings came off or what went wrong never came to light. This accident was a great shock to all of us at 'A' per T and a sad waste of one of our top bomber pilots. It was a cold bleak day when the little party set off to bury him in the cemetery near Tidworth.

The enquiry into the cause of Wing Commander Webster's accident was the responsibility of Mr E. T. Jones, the Chief Technical officer, and his assistant Mr Scott-Hall. They were both rather distant figures, locked away in their backrooms and, although permanent residents at Boscombe, our paths normally never crossed. Having in the past had so many frustrations over obtaining my flying licence from the Air Ministry on my return from Canada, I was prejudiced against civil servants, but I came to know, like and respect these two men. Since I had been the last pilot to fly the aircraft, and had given the pre-flight briefing as to how to measure the rate of roll, I was much involved and was called to give evidence.

Accidents in wartime are such frequent occurrences that not much time could be spent investigating them, but in this particular case I was satisfied that every possible cause was taken into consideration, and that it was not just put down to pilot's error. Somehow it often seems to take an emergency or crisis to break through a person's normal reserve, and one can then get a glimpse of the human spirit behind it. Certainly it proved true for me with Jones and Scott-Hall.

20 High-speed passes

Known to us at Boscombe as the 'blunder bus', the Typhoon came from the Hawker stable, but it did not seem possible that it had come from the drawing board of Sydney Camm, the designer of that elegant line of pre-war biplane fighters, such as the Fury and the Nimrod. It was a low-level, high-speed ground attack aircraft. The Napier Sabre engine of 2,200 hp had two crankshafts geared together, twenty-four cylinders and sleeve valves, all of which made it very compact but complicated. The aircraft had a relatively thick wing section and was heavy, making it more suitable for carrying stores (external weapons) than for interception and dog-fighting, for which it had been designed. Having been attached to Vickers Supermarine for nine months, I was perhaps prejudiced in favour of Spitfires and could not help regarding the Typhoon as somewhat lacking in finesse as an aircraft, but as a weapon it was an effective blunt instrument backed by brute force.

For dropping stores, bombs or rockets, we had the use of three alternative bombing ranges: Lyme Bay, Crichel Down or Porton. This latter was really for use in experiments in bacteriological warfare, although my first job on a Typhoon was to drop some standard 45-gallon oil drums there. The drop was to be from 150 feet above ground at a medium speed in order to see if there was any likelihood of them rebounding on hitting the ground and striking the aircraft! They certainly bounced quite high but were well clear of the tail of the aircraft; I am not quite so sure that we should have given them such a clean report if we had known that the intention was to use the drums for napalm. At the time we had not even heard of this terrible weapon which I believe was never used in Europe.

The Sabre engine was not proving a reliable engine in service but we were sent a fully modified version which the makers absolutely guaranteed. It also had a special radiator with a mixed matrix. This incorporated an oil cooler and water radiator combined and was intended for use in the tropics as well as for overcoming oil coring problems due to extreme cold. In order to monitor the oil circulation throughout the system, an automatic recorder was installed in the fuselage behind the cockpit which took photographs every thirty seconds of about twelve thermometer dials mounted in a lightproof box.

Intending to do a full power climb to measure the oil temperatures, I started the automatic recorder before take-off and also had prepared my kneepad for other readings. There was a layer of five-tenths cloud at 10,000 feet with a north westerly wind. My usual practice when flying high was to fly

upwind of the aerodrome as, in case of having to bale out, I did not wish to be deposited in the sea, but also navigation was easier as, on taking a reciprocal course, one could recognise any special local features with height in hand. On reaching 30,000 feet I noticed a faint blue haze near my feet lit up by a shaft of sunlight from over my shoulder. Oil temperature seemed all right, but there was a slight drop in oil pressure, both of which I had been recording every 2,000 feet.

As the oil pressure continued to drop I throttled back and with reducing rpm the pressure dropped abruptly. Turning round to return to base in a long glide I thought that with luck there might still be some pressure to allow me to use the engine for landing. However, through a small gap in the high clouds I saw a straight white line indicating an aerodrome runway and decided to glide down there. Unfortunately, there was some more broken cloud at about 3,000 feet but from odd glimpses the runway was still there.

The decision to land was made at about 8,000 feet when the undercarriage was lowered and locked down. The engine was idling and responded to a touch of throttle but I left the flaps until later. Finally, on breaking through the lower cloud layer in a reasonable position, I selected flaps down. A few seconds later the propeller stopped turning with a thump as the engine seized. By now oil spray was being sucked up onto the inside of the windscreen as I had opened the small side window and from my limited view I saw that there was a steam roller working on the runway so it would have to be the grass to one side. The Typhoon with a dead engine and wheels down has about the gliding angle of a brick and wanting enough speed to make the flare out I crossed the boundary at about 160 mph.

The landing hold off seemed very prolonged and as the aircraft still had not lost flying speed I eased it forward onto the wheels and got busy on the brakes. Eventually the tail came down and having crossed the perimeter track the aircraft finally came to rest only 50 yards from a wire fence at the edge of a railway cutting! Jumping out and getting clear by 30 yards or so I lay stretched out on my back. Everything was still and very quiet, the sun had broken through, even the blades of coarse grass looked green and there were some low hills in the distance but the best thing of all was the good earth, never before had it seemed so solid and peaceful. Glancing up I thought the aircraft looked undamaged although there were brown streaks of oil all along the fuselage. These were trickling down vertically to join and form a steady stream along the belly of the aircraft running towards the tail where it dripped off, forming a large pool. At least the aircraft and engine were saved and the investigation would show the cause of the engine failure. I suddenly noticed that the flaps were only 30° down, which had obviously lengthened the landing. Then I remembered that the engine had stopped shortly after selecting flaps down and without the hydraulic pump working the operation had, therefore, not been completed.

As I lay, seemingly for some time, enjoying the warm sun shining through a gap in the clouds, listening to the larks singing and the joys of spring, I could hear the ringing of the fire-engine bell and approaching vehicles. It appeared that the aerodrome was Defford, an experimental radar establishment, requiring prior permission to land, it was under repair and notice had been circulated to all RAF stations, etc., etc. I thought the Commanding Officer was going to burst a boiler especially as I was not wearing RAF uniform. In fact, I had on Naval trousers, a white submariner's sweater, RAF flying boots and over the lot an old brown overall which I used for working on my car in the days before the war, and in addition I was looking scruffy as I was covered in oil from head to foot. Having explained Newton's law on the force of gravity, it seemed that Rules and Regulations had priority! In any case, I was not in the mood to argue and although not actually arrested was persuaded to wait quietly in the Watch Tower until my story was confirmed. Brunner arrived later in our communication hack, a Miles Mentor, to pick me up.

The Typhoon was dismantled and taken back to Boscombe on a trailer. The investigation showed that one of the special thermometers installed in the engine oil system for the automatic recorder had not been properly locked. It had unscrewed with vibration and all the oil had been pumped out; in other words, our own fault, not a true failure in the engine itself!

All Typhoons suffered from a lot of high-frequency vibration apparently coming from the engine and in fact the operational squadrons had complained bitterly that it made the pilots impotent! We received a new modified seat with springs set across the frame, like certain types of armchairs, to try on our own aircraft. On this special occasion the technical office only asked for opinions but waived practical tests! History does not record the squadron pilots' reaction.

Boscombe seemed to collect a number of odd aircraft rather like a home for lost dogs. Most had been sent for some specific trial and on completion had been forgotten by the sender. The Commanding Officer's Performance Testing Squadron had a spare Hurricane which could be borrowed for odd jobs, in 'A' per T we had a B-17 and a B-25 Mitchell twin-engined bomber parked on us. It was too good an invitation not to get multi-engined experience, so with a bit of study we sorted out the taps and flew them. It was, after all, our job to keep the aircraft serviceable!

The B-17, popularly known as the Flying Fortress, was rather like a large four-engined Anson to fly. It was, of course, without any load and with a large wing area it floated round the sky. There was plenty of room in the well up-holstered cockpit, chromium-plated switches for all services such as undercarriage and flaps, and all I needed was an airline captain's cap and a large cigar to relax in complete comfort. It was with some surprise that on reaching the dispersal area the lower hatch opened and five of our own airmen got out. They had stowed away in the bomb aimer's compartment and come for the ride without bothering to let me know.

The Mitchell was a different kettle of fish. Lots of power, not much wing area and a very complex fuel system. It was also the first aircraft that I ever flew with a tricycle undercarriage, not very suitable for the grass aerodrome at Boscombe but very welcome nevertheless. Placing the main wheels carrying the weight behind the centre of gravity effectively simplified landing and take-off because the aircraft had no inherent tendency to swing or to bounce. Some would say it took a lot of the skill out of flying but it was a big safety factor soon to be incorporated in all future aircraft.

As very few of the single-seaters under trial at the A & AEE had radio fitted there was practically no flying control of the aerodrome. One might notify the Watch Tower before doing measured take-offs or before a cross country flight, but normally, being a grass field, one took one's own precautions. There was, however, one particular test which always seemed rather dangerous, namely measuring Position Error (PE). This involved flying an aircraft at a known height, such as the top of a hangar, at a steady speed in a series of passes between its maximum and its minimum. Any other aircraft using the aerodrome, unless familiar with the procedure, might not see the aircraft under test approaching at 50 feet at maximum speed, or alternatively it could be a hazard to the aircraft approaching just above the stall.

The Position Error correction is essential in calculating an aircraft's speed as it measures the error in the Indicated Air Speed instrument as well as that of the altimeter. There is always a difficulty in finding a position on the surface of an aircraft where the true outside atmospheric pressure is not disturbed by the passing flow of air. Finding a static vent position to give the minimum error involved endless PE flights.

The true height during each pass was found by an observer located on top of a hangar taking a photograph and later analysing the fuselage height in relation to the horizon. At the same time the pilot pressed a switch which took a photograph of a very sensitive altimeter connected to the vent. The resulting figures were of vital importance, both in measuring performance and obtaining the necessary accuracy in bombing and gun sighting. Before starting this particular exercise we used to inform the Watch Office who

119

would do their best to warn other aircraft and keep them clear. On one particular occasion there was an engineer working on an engine of a Mosquito right in my line of flight; after about a dozen passes at ever increasing speed he finally gave up in evident disgust. He must have thought I was deliberately trying to tip him off his ladder, but it did require consistency and extreme accuracy of flight.

One morning in October 1943 while measuring the performance of the Spitfire Mk XXI, I did a level speed at 43,000 feet and, for interest sake, pulled up into a climb until I saw 44,500 feet; not bad with a full load of guns and ammunition. This altitude is getting near the limit for a pilot without a pressure cabin as it is only about 25% of sea-level pressure. I did feel a bit light-headed walking back afterwards to the mess for lunch but otherwise had no ill effects. Plenty of neat oxygen is a help but even so, at low pressures, the lungs are hardly getting enough. When flying high-altitude aircraft an additional emergency supply of oxygen was attached to the parachute harness to sustain life until thicker air was reached during the descent in the event of having to bale out.

A few weeks later I was flying towards the east at about 16,000 feet measuring speeds in level flight. It was still early morning with the low sun reflected by the River Thames winding its way through London to the widening estuary. Trying to maintain an accurate height on the sensitive altimeter and reading the speed, engine rpm, boost pressure and intercooler temperature keeps one busy, but out of the corner of my eye I thought I saw a fly on the windscreen. It was not, but turned out to be a squadron of B-17s in formation gaining altitude, presumably for a daylight raid on Germany. They were flying on a reciprocal course to me and I just missed the aircraft on the leader's starboard wing by passing close under him. Hardly had I had time to realise how lucky I was when I met another squadron this time slightly lower so that they went underneath me again missing by probably 50 feet. My speed was about 400 mph and their's was probably about 150 so that the total converging speed was around 550 miles an hour, not much time to take avoiding action. It was very rare that one ever saw another aircraft above 10,000 feet and one flew there in a world of one's own, but this incident shook me as it is not possible to take accurate readings for test purposes and look where you are going all the time. The B-17 pilots also were probably not looking and in any case, being in close formation, could have taken no action anyway. It was just lucky that the second formation was staggered well downwards, obviously avoiding the slipstream of the lead squadron.

Occasionally there was a call for an assessment of an aircraft's manoeuvrability in comparison either with one of our own or alternatively an enemy aircraft, although these latter comparisons were usually made by pilots with recent operational experience in, for instance, the RAF Air Fighting Development Unit at Duxford. A Spitfire could turn inside a Mustang in a dogfight, whereas a Firefly could, in a continuous turn, keep its sights on a Spitfire. This was largely a function of wing-loading or, in the case of the Firefly, the high-lift flaps.

During one of these exercises I was flying a Spitfire and Zurakowski*, a Polish officer, was flying a Mustang. I should not like to meet him in action as he could pull every trick out of the bag and knew instinctively how to get the maximum out of the aircraft to his own advantage. One of his manoeuvres which completely defeated me was to go into a diving spiral turn at full power pulling a lot of G. As the speed increased the radius of the spiral increased so that the path of the aircraft was like a cone. With 5 to 6G it was not easy to see where he was, as I was on the threshold of blacking out. Then, unexpectedly, he would turn the diving turn into a steep climbing turn still maintaining high G. This upward spiral finally finished with a kind of upward flick roll where he had no speed but sufficient control to get round on to your tail!

I have always been amazed how the human body can, without any training or adaptation, suddenly be subjected to all the stresses and strains that occur when flying military aircraft without coming to any harm. A 5G turn for instance, means that everything becomes five times its normal weight. The only obvious effect is that the blood is drained from the back of the eyes and vision is lost, i.e. blackout, but it can easily be recovered by easing the turn. In a simulated dogfight, one can be fully conscious and yet be unable to see the other aircraft which one knows to be 50 yards ahead.

It is also the case that no damage seems to occur from a drastic lowering of pressure and density. At 40,000 feet with the pressure only about a quarter of sea-level pressure, one's body does not seem to swell, although I did find it more comfortable to undo my belt and top trouser button. However, there comes a point when lack of oxygen to the lungs through the reduction in density becomes dangerous, so that at 40,000 to 45,000 feet, if the oxygen is cut off for any reason, one's life expectancy is under one minute.

Undoubtedly, the greatest strain is on the nerves. The noise, vibration, cold and anxiety, all contribute to this, as does the fact that at the back of one's mind is the thought that fuel and, therefore, time may be running out, which will make a landing inevitable. As my friend Monkey Sherlock used to say, 'the worst part of flying is the space between you and the ground.'

---

* Zurakowski made a name for himself after the war when he demonstrated the twin-engined Meteor at Farnborough. He invented a new aerobatic manoeuvre by turning it into a kind of catherine wheel by throttling back one engine in a vertical climb.

The officer commanding the Performance Testing Squadron was Group Captain 'Bruin' Purvis, popular throughout the RAF, and probably the oldest and most experienced test pilot in the Service. I was detailed to fly one mark of Spitfire while he flew another with the object of comparing their manoeuvrability at 35,000 feet. We went up together and having no radio I kept in close formation until we started our dogfight. After a hectic tear round the sky, he throttled back and seemed to lose interest; thinking that he was satisfied with the trial I attempted to take up formation on his port wing but overshot hopelessly. Thinking it was the altitude affecting my speed as we were above 30,000 feet, I made another attempt, coming in slowly and carefully; again

a bad overshoot. The third time I was determined to make it, so came in throttled right back and very low so as to be able to pull up and lose even more speed. Finally, I made it successfully only to be greeted by Purves waving me away; my first thought was that I had put up some black but it turned out that he had burst his engine and was making a forced landing.

Bruin Purvis was the most calm and collected pilot; he was so completely at home and at ease in the air that going on a cross-country flight with him was rather like going for a country walk — any point of interest en route, such as a cricket match or a picnic party, was worthy of a diversion to have a look.

21 Firebrands and rockets

Boscombe Down's armament squadron had its own pilots but in some ways our trials overlapped. For instance, the equipment of fighter aircraft with rocket projectiles (RPs) involved measuring the attitude of the aircraft, or wing incidence at different speeds because the flight of the rocket would not be true if it was fired with any 'skid'. This new weapon was extremely important to the Allies as it would knock out a well-armoured tank much more effectively than any fighter-bomber.

Firing a rocket projectile takes time to perfect as its trajectory is quite different from that of a shell from a gun which leaves the barrel at its maximum velocity. The rocket continually gains speed in flight but leaves the aircraft relatively slowly. To get accuracy with the RP it was necessary to fly the aircraft at a predetermined speed, to dive on the target at a fixed angle, and, of course, to fire the rocket at the correct range. All this required great skill on the part of the pilot. In order to broaden the chance of a hit a number of RPs were carried on racks under the wing. A Typhoon was equipped with eight duplex RP i.e. sixteen rockets. These could be fired singly, in pairs simultaneously, in a trickle by a timing device known as a Mickey Mouse, or finally as a salvo.

Having done a lot of the measurement of attitudes at varying speeds in level flight in the Typhoon, I was given the job of assessing the handling characteristics, and in particular to determine the maximum speed for release in a dive. Our bombing range for this type of trial was Lyme Bay off the Dorset Coast. After a search round for any fishing boats I climbed up to 10,000 and dived, reaching a speed of 380 mph. On firing the salvo of sixteen RPs there was a fine firework display around the aircraft followed by a lot of flames disappearing into the distance. Then a number of splashes appeared in the sea roughly in a circle of about 100-ft diameter. The aircraft had been trimmed into the dive and after releasing the load, recovered normally. Talking to the armament experts afterwards they told me that the salvo was the equivalent of a broadside from a cruiser. In fact, the RP head was a 60-lb 6-inch diameter naval shell with a tube attached carrying a solid propellant.

There is a streak in human nature which makes us like to play with fire, and guns have the same attraction. Some people are even prepared to spend their life perfecting them and their use. I had not recognised this until the war but firing a salvo of rockets was, I must admit, very satisfying!

Another weapon-proving trial which required the use of Lyme Bay involved the guns of the Spitfire and all the other fighters. Starting with a full load of ammunition the object was to investigate any stoppages while firing under heavy G in a turn. Again it was up to the pilot to ensure that the firing area was clear. Having climbed to 10,000 feet and while maintaining a steady 4G in a full-power turn, all guns were fired and kept firing until they stopped or the ammunition ran out. On returning to Boscombe the reason for any stoppage was investigated. The belts of .303 cartridges lay on top of each other so that when subjected to 'G' the upper layer of cartridges dropped into the gaps of the lower layer causing an added resistance to their movement and so to the breech blocks feeding the machine-guns. The Browning could usually cope with this but the 20-mm Hispano cannon often stopped until someone invented a spring-loaded sprocket feed which overcame the difficulty.

Spraying out bullets and shells like this while circling seemed hazardous to me but I was assured that the lateral distance never exceeded a mile before all the energy had been dissipated and they fell harmlessly under the force of gravity.

Boscombe Down had no concrete runway until the end of 1944 so that for trials involving bombs we flew over to Thruxton to load up for take-off on the long runway there. The bombs were always dummies and merely represented the true shape and weight. These were dropped on the range at Crichel Down, a place which received some political notoriety after the war when the Ministry proposed selling the commandeered property to a new buyer but not to the previous owner! These bombs were mounted on external racks under the wings and our trials consisted of releasing them at increasing speeds in dives. Occasionally a bomb would be deflected by the airflow and knock its detachable tail fin off on the underside of a wing, sometimes causing damage; it would then 'tumble' end over end and undershoot the target. Another difficulty could be a 'hang-up', in other words, a failure to release. This could be embarrassing as on fighters the bombs are hidden by the wings when in flight and one did not know whether it was a mechanical fault, in which case it might fall off at any moment or whether it was only electrical trouble. We also had to deliberately drop one of two 1,000 lb bombs to make an assessment of the handling characteristics with the unbalanced weight and drag, in particular whether it was feasible to attempt a landing or whether with a 'hang-up' a pilot should be ordered to bale out.

From top, the prototypes of the Blackburn Firebrand Mks I, II and III, at Boscombe Down, 1943, and all in trouble from the start.

Another armament test with which 'A' per T Flight was involved was a comparison of the effectiveness of an attack on dispersed aircraft with fighter aircraft guns as compared with low flying aircraft carrying bombs. About twenty-five different aircraft, which were serviceable but becoming obsolete, were parked haphazardly around Stoney Cross aerodrome in the New Forest. Our orders were to make a live ammunition attack from a low level simulating an attack by the enemy. All the pilots concerned went over by road to inspect the site after being briefed on the direction of attack and where the spectators were to be. It seemed a pity to ruin so many good aircraft, but after our visit I regret to say that some of the hard to get spares and instruments mysteriously disappeared before the onslaught! After every attack a party of engineers searched each aircraft for damage to vital parts such as the electrics, the hydraulics, the fuel system, and marked each bullethole with a different coloured paint so that the damage done in each attack could be assessed. We never saw the final report but it was an expensive trial much enjoyed by all! A brother officer in No. 807 Squadron capped it though when he told us about the time he put a torpedo into the French battleship *Richelieu* in Dakar harbour when the Vichy French refused to join our side. She sank alongside the quay. He reckoned he had done a few million pounds worth of damage that afternoon.

The same aerodrome was also used for the trials of the 'dambusters' weapon which, at the time, was highly secret. Another secret weapon tested there was the Grand Slam. This was a 22,000-lb bomb in a streamlined casing with four tail fins set to make it rotate in flight like a bullet from a rifle. Several of us, not directly concerned, went over to witness the first release. It was to be dropped from a Lancaster at

18,000 feet which it was calculated would allow it to gain supersonic speed.

All the top brass having assembled, the Lancaster started its dummy run and dropped a 12-lb marker to check their allowance for wind. A loudspeaker had been installed so that the bomb aimer's instructions to the pilot could be heard on the ground. In the briefing we had been warned that there would be a delay of about 25 seconds while the bomb fell and there was an eight second delayed fuse in the bomb itself. The big moment arrived: 'Left, left, right, steady, steady, steady, bomb away.' With considerable tension and a hushed silence everyone waited for what was thought to be the biggest explosion ever. However, some wit from 'B' Squadron let off a firework just behind us. I nearly jumped out of my skin and so did a lot of others. Practical jokers can be a menace and this time it was not very funny. I then saw a splash of earth being thrown up at the designated target followed shortly afterwards by a supersonic bang and then what seemed an interminable delay. Suddenly, there was a deep thud and chunks of earth half as big as a railway carriage flew up into the air to several hundred feet and fell pitter patter for seconds afterwards. The crater was about 60 feet across. These bombs subsequently penetrated 6 feet of concrete covering the submarine pens at Brest.

Two new purely naval aircraft designed to meet Admiralty requirements came to Boscombe Down for trials, the Firebrand, a large single-seater able to carry a torpedo or a variety of stores under its wings produced by Blackburns of Brough, and the Fairey Barracuda, a two-seater with a similar capability. Both of these aircraft had many technical and handling troubles. The Firebrand even reached the Mark V version before reaching training squadrons and was too late for operational service, and the Barracuda, although reaching squadrons in 1944, was not exactly a popular aircraft. About the same time a flood of different US Navy aircraft also arrived for assessment, including the Corsair, Wildcat, Avenger, Hellcat, Dauntless, and a big twin-engined fighter, the Tiger Cat. All these were built to a different set of requirements, presumably with the Pacific in mind where long range and tropical conditions prevailed. Fundamentally, they were good aircraft adapted to carry weapons into action whereas ours were weapons which needed an aircraft to carry them into action.

The Firebrand was a well engineered aircraft, that is to say the systems, electrical, hydraulic, air pressure and fuel were easily accessible and servicing was simple. The troubles lay in its aerodynamic qualities, basically those of the wing, which could be folded. It was a high lift wing with big flaps, but when the flaps were extended for deck landing there was a serious nose down change of trim. This was checked by an equally large up movement of the elevator so that perhaps half the extra lift from the high lift wing was countered by a

The US Navy Curtiss Seamew (Ranger engine) was quietly relegated to training. This example combines RAF tail flashes, serial and camouflage with US stars.

Grumman TBM Avenger, a US Navy carrier-based torpedo-bomber adopted by the Royal Navy. (Charles E. Brown)

large downward force on the tail. The Marks I and II had a Napier Sabre engine but as more and more power was required for the take-off from a deck a Bristol Centaurus was fitted to the Mark IV. The torque of this could not then be held on the rudder at take-off power and this had to be increased, producing the Mark V. All these difficulties arose while the production line was rolling and some fairly heated meetings took place. The Navy urgently wanted the aircraft and contracts worth millions of pounds were involved. It is on such occasions as this that a test pilot must base all his reports on facts which can, of course, be verified by being repeated and avoid giving his own opinion. This applies

The Douglas SBD Dauntless (Cyclone) behaved as it looked — unexciting.

The Fairey Barracuda met all the Naval requirements for a general purpose torpedo spotter and reconnaissance aircraft. The trailing edge outrigger flaps gave both lift for landing and drag (as shown) for torpedo attack. (Charles E. Brown).

particularly to permanent Service officers who naturally have to consider their future. The wartime only officers were in some respects able to be more outspoken, rather like a non-executive director of a company.

I had an unfortunate experience taxiing out a Firebrand one day. A couple of hundred yards from the tarmac the undercarriage started to collapse, the legs splaying apart like a giraffe lying down. Those who saw the accident said they thought I was trying to lay an egg. Fortunately, the torpedo had just been removed or the remarks might have been ruder.

The Barracuda met all their Lordships' requirements. It had a hook, folding wings, retractable undercarriage, dive brakes, high lift flaps, catapulting hooks, tropical radiator, and a cabin for the observer and was equipped to carry a torpedo, bombs, RPs, radar and, of course, radio. In fact it was a versatile aircraft, all singing all dancing! The difficulty arose over getting all this weight off the deck and again, as with the Firebrand, more and more power was required. The final mark had a low altitude rated Griffon but this reduced the range and consequently the aircraft's usefulness.

The American Corsair became, during the latter part of the war, the main fighter for the Royal Navy. It was a tough, no-nonsense aircraft which did yeoman service. Our trials at Boscombe were not extensive but were confined to measuring carbon monoxide contamination, lengthening the control column to British standards, and measuring flame damping and take-off distance with varying loads. The aircraft, in common with all American fighters, had an enormous cockpit by our standards. If one dropped something like a pencil it would disappear into the depths and require a proper expedition to find it. American seat belts were lap straps only and their requirement was for the instrument panel to be clear of the pilot's head when leaning fully forward. Our own version called for standard British Sutton harness and this modification nearly got me into serious trouble. During the flame tests at night I inadvertently switched off the cockpit instruments. These were lit by 'black' light which illuminated the instruments only, but I could not find the variable resistance knob which was almost out of reach and in total darkness. To add to my troubles the wind changed and the glim lights marking the landing strip took some time to be repositioned. In the blackout with no horizon I was powerfully worried, expecially as my experience at night

The Grumman F6F Hellcat, a well developed aircraft based on experience, was the main US Navy carrier-based fighter of the Pacific.

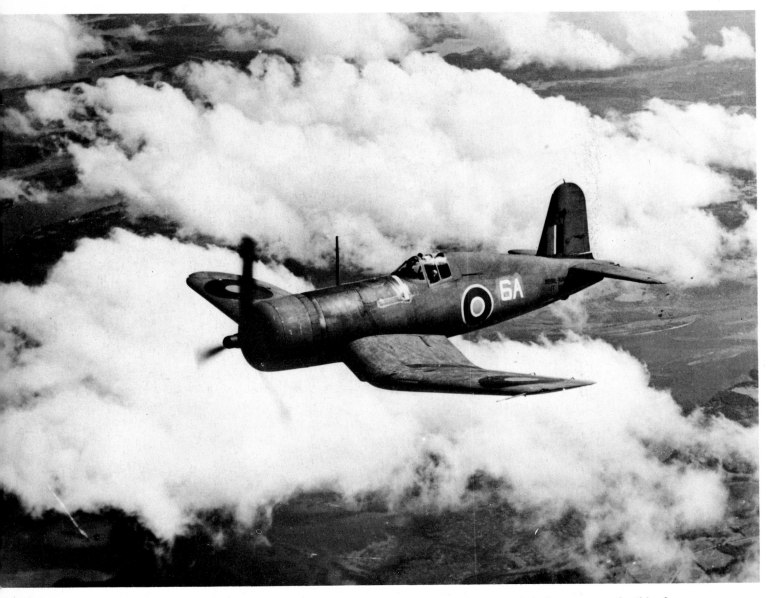

The US Navy gave the Chance Vought F4U Corsair second choice but the Royal Navy liked it and found it a tough and reliable fighter.

was virtually nil. At least I never flew again at night without a hand torch!

There were two Naval aircraft which, in their different ways, were outstanding; both were conversions of Royal Air Force fighters. The Seafire Mk XV had a Rolls-Royce Griffon engine rated to give maximum power at low altitude which gave it an exceptional rate and angle of climb; in fact, although few realised it, the thrust from the propeller was about equal to its all-up weight and theoretically it could have climbed vertically like a rocket without wings thus beating the 'Flying Bedstead' by many years. In fact, of

course, vertical flight was not feasible for many reasons connected with control and engine lubrication, but it was quite an aircraft with its power or thrust to weight ratio of one to one.

When Sidney Camm, the chief designer of the Hawker Aircraft Company, replaced the Typhoon, he chose a laminar flow wing, with the thickest part about half way back on the chord for the F2/43. Called the Tempest, the Mark I, which did not enter service, and the Marks V and VI, which gave excellent operational service, had the Napier Sabre, like the Typhoon. However, the last production model, confusingly designated Mark II, had the Centaurus, which with a new fuselage but the same wing, became the Fury for the RAF, but also did not enter service. The Naval version of the Fury, the Sea Fury, had a redesigned fuselage with a raised

The Grumman F7F Tigercat was the US Navy's equivalent of the Sea Hornet. It was the first fighter with a powered control, the rudder.

cockpit to improve the view over the nose for deck landing. Although the aircraft had a high wing loading and stalled at about 90 knots, it was easy to deck land. The propeller diameter was large and the slipstream covered a fair proportion of the wing so that on cutting the throttle it just fell out of the sky on to the deck without any 'float'.

Compared with the Seafire Mk XV, the Sea Fury was rather underpowered, although it handled very well, being just positively stable in all axis with light, crisp and powerful controls. It also had a very high cruising speed and plenty of fuel. Although it did not reach the squadrons until after the war, I personally felt at the time that at last the Navy was going to get the fighter it deserved. Ultimately, it did see active service in the Korean war when its outstanding qualities were appreciated. It was the last piston-engined fighter before the arrival of jets.

In spite of its early handling troubles, the Firefly had, by the end of the war, established itself as a tough, reliable, long range, highly manoeuvrable aircraft. With its formidable armament of four 20 mm Hispano cannons and carrying rockets or 1,000 lb bombs it was highly regarded by the US Navy and in the hands of the pilots of No. 1772 Squadron from HMS *Indefatigable* was the first British aircraft to fly over the Japanese mainland and Tokio.

22 Rogues and failures

The routine measurement of performance called for full engine power both in the climb and during level speeds. In normal use full power is, of course, used at take-off but rarely at other times, so occasional failures were understandable in test flying. Having made a forced landing in a Typhoon and knowing the reputation of the Sabre engine, from that time onwards when flying any Sabre-engined aircraft I made a habit of doing all level speeds above the aerodrome or at least upwind and within gliding distance. Although the previous failure had not been due to any engine fault, within weeks I had a genuine one. With a bang and a gush of steam and oil a cylinder head came off very quickly followed by a complete stop. From 10,000 feet I could see Boscombe Down lying conveniently on my port bow so was able to glide down and make a normal landing. With a sleeve-valve engine the sleeve slides up into a circular slot in the cylinder head, and it was suspected that oil trapped in this slot had caused an hydraulic lock. Whatever it was, this failure did not increase my faith in the Sabre.

The Bristol engine company had put their faith and reputation into backing and developing the sleeve valve, and produced a string of successful engines based on that principle. In earlier days many great engineers had also pursued the same valve mechanism in motor cars. It was smooth and silent as well as being totally enclosed. The famous Daimlers used by the Royal family all had sleeve valves. Unfortunately, the lubricating oil of the period lacked present day qualities, and every sleeve-valve engine's exhaust left a trail of blue smoke. In addition there was also a lot of viscous drag from the sleeves and in cold weather this, in the case of the 24-cylinder Napier Sabre, became excessive. In the months before D-Day, we received orders to warm up all Sabre-engined aircraft every four hours throughout the day, so as to ensure an easy and certain start. It had been found that even with the correct mixture they became almost impossible to start from cold if parked in the open. The engine would fire correctly but each single cylinder lacked the power to overcome the viscous drag and it would gradually peter out. What this order entailed in increased maintenance and ignition troubles can be imagined, but ultimately the object of the order became clear — the aircraft were at immediate readiness for the landing of our armies in France.

Another serious failure occurred with a Rolls-Royce Griffon in a Spitfire Mk XIV while doing partial climbs. This involved climbing at full power at different indicated air speeds. At low forward speed the angle of climb of the Mark XIV was very steep, probably about 45° from the horizontal.

The first sign of trouble was a puff followed by a stream of blue smoke from the port bank. The engine was still alive but I dared not use any power, but crept back and landed. The forward piston had failed. About a week later repeating the trial with a new engine, exactly the same symptoms developed followed immediately by total failure. I had taken off from Boscombe Down and was near Warminster about ten miles away. There was 9/10ths cloud cover at 1,500 feet over Boscombe extending to a line just along the river Avon with clear skies to the west. Knowing the area well, I decided to go for a landing wheels down, approaching through the 500 feet layer of cloud. Using Stonehenge as a point of reference my navigation proved about right as on breaking cloud the aerodrome was within comfortable gliding distance. It seemed clear to me that there was some shortcoming in the Griffon's lubrication or cooling system, which would not cope with high power when running at a steep angle, but Rolls-Royce as was their habit, insisted that it was due to incorrect installation or mishandling but not their engine!

The acceptance of new fighter aircraft involved spins both at low altitude and near its ceiling. These tests were about the last to be undertaken just in case the aircraft should fail to come out, although new types always had tail parachutes to assist recovery in the event of the spin becoming 'flat'. The requirement was to complete two turns in both directions before taking recovery action. The main warning of danger is when the spin becomes flat and quiet; the more the aircraft pitches the better. In recovery whatever action one takes with stick and throttle, full opposite rudder must never be taken off.

Jeffrey Quill had a nasty experience with an anti-spin parachute. Later versions of Seafire had what became known as a 'sting' type hook, instead of the more usual A-frame type which retracted into a recess in the bottom of the aft fuselage. The sting type projected beyond the rudder and was attached to the rudder post, which meant that the bottom of the rudder was cut back, losing a small amount of area. More or less as a formality to cover the regulations, he decided to do a check spin. The aircraft failed to recover so Jeffrey pulled the plug. The parachute streamed all right but its cable somehow got round the outside of the rudder which was fully over. This flicked the rudder and rudder pedals over so violently that it broke Jeffrey's ankle but it did stop the spin and he landed the aircraft safely.

It fell to my lot to do the spinning of the Tempest Mk I, the Sabre-engined version. This was a relatively heavy aircraft with a laminar flow wing, a new development at that time.

Tempest Mk I (Napier Sabre engine) with long range tanks at Boscombe Down in 1943 with the author at the controls.

At 30,000 feet it behaved impeccably rather to my surprise and relief, but on the recovery I noticed blue smoke coming from the exhaust stubs. On the next spin I glanced at the engine revs which indicated 4,200 with the throttle fully closed! The maximum permitted at full power was only 3,600 rpm. It was clear that the propeller pitch and constant speed control mechanism could not cope with the rapid increase of windmilling speed during the spin recovery. The over-speeding of a big engine like the Sabre, particularly with closed throttle, meant an engine change.

The Centaurus-engined Tempest Mk II completed its trials almost without fault although the Mark I had run into the problem of a change of trim in a dive with high G on re-covery. There was, in fact, some doubt about its acceptability for service use but what I found interesting was the report from the technical office for the Ministry in London. The cautious civil service approach, not wishing to upset the powerful Hawker Aircraft Company by turning their pro-duct down stated that the Tempest Mk I was 'not unaccept-able'. This double negative meant to imply that they did not like to accept it as it did not quite meet the requirements laid down in the rule book but that it was a marginal case and under the exigencies of war they would accept it. To them a double negative had a subtly different meaning to a positive!

As a light relief we had two very unusual aircraft sent to us in 1943 at 'A' per T. One was the Boulton and Paul P92, a light twin Gipsy-engined aircraft with a large saucer-shaped centre section. It was a half-scale model of a project, which we thought at the time was a flying radar scanner, although its purpose was top secret, but it turned out later to be for mounting a 40 mm gun in a revolving turret. Its flying characteristics were very good, the back to back saucer-shaped housing for the gun producing considerable lift. The

The Short Stirling half-scale model with four Pobjoy engines was used for assessing the handling qualities of the Stirling bomber but not the undercarriage structure which collapsed on the first landing of the full-scale prototype.

second unusual aircraft was a half-scale model of the four-engined Short Stirling bomber fitted with four Pobjoy radial engines. Well before the war Short Brothers of Rochester were in full production of the Sunderland flying boat with the wings and tail well proven, and by designing a suitable fuselage and undercarriage it was hoped to build a heavy bomber with the minimum expenditure of time and money. How successful Stirlings were in service I do not know but a rehash of something built for a different purpose is a doubtful policy to follow. The half-scale Stirling was another type for one's log book but left no lasting impression.

Apart from the designer's own stamp on the actual design of any aircraft, I always think that the manufacturer also put a family image on his product. This characteristic up to 1939, which has now faded out, was a survival from the early days of aviation when the pioneers were not only the designers and test pilots, but were even responsible for the formation, finance and running of their own company. The names of Sopwith, Hawker, de Havilland, Blackburn come to mind, but there were also other companies such as Bristol, Fairey, Gloster, Handley Page, Armstrong Whitworth, Westland, Vickers, and a number of others which came into existence during War World I which had their own characteristics.

All these companies were deliberately kept in business by the Government of the day, so as to have an industry which, if called upon, could be rapidly expanded in the event of another war. All the respective design teams were kept busy, and endless prototypes appeared, but the factories were kept alive by sharing out orders for limited numbers of the best aircraft in their particular range whether designed by them or not. This policy gave great flexibility of choice to the Air Staff and incidentally led to the Supermarine company designing the Spitfire, but it could be argued that it left the country in a vulnerable position in 1938 at the time of Munich, as our factories were not capable of mass production.

The different manufacturer's construction methods and cockpit layouts were still evident to older pilots. If one had somehow been placed in a cockpit not knowing which aircraft it was, it would often have been possible to tell the manufacturer; Hawkers with their tube and socket type structure; Supermarines could be recognised by their use of stressed skin construction and cocks and pumps made by Vickers, their parent company; Faireys were different from other aircraft in that the various controls were made in their own factory, the Naval connection being apparent by the strange boxes, switches and other gadgets; Blackburns were more formal in their cockpit layout, everything neat and tidy, all the pipes and wires clipped in parallel lines, the controls logically laid out and marked, rather like a robot, not untidy like a Spitfire which had had many additions over the years.

American aircraft were always recognisable as they had extremely large cockpits by our standards. This was partly because of the specification called for by their Service Chiefs, but I suspect that, as they had no powerful in-line water-cooled engines, the natural streamline behind their large radial air-cooled engines led to a fat teardrop shape. As they used electricity for operating their auxiliary services, such as undercarriage, flaps and cooling gills, the appropriate switches were arranged conveniently in neat rows, often on a shelf beside the pilot. On their fighters, the control column was much lower than on our aircraft and the firing button and safety catch were mounted in a straight moulded plastic handle on the top. Our own guns were fired pneumatically and the firing button with its safety lock was incorporated in a circular ring type handle which in some cases was hinged at knee height to allow unobstructive movement of the lateral control.

British aircraft still retained one vestigial relic of the early days. The dual ignition switches were still an aircraft version of the ordinary domestic light switch which is pressed down to turn a light on, but in an aircraft this switches the engine off. The down position earths the contact breaker of the magneto and prevents a spark. How many men have been killed or injured by not understanding this, will never be known. The Americans, however, were more sensible as all their aircraft were fitted with a swinging lever switch with the various positions unmistakably marked.

One day a signal arrived at Boscombe for me to report to Air Commodore Jones at the Ministry of Aircraft Production at Millbank. Intrigued, I flew up to Fairey's private grass aerodrome at Heathrow and parked my Firefly there. Dixon, the chief test pilot, kindly drove me as far as Osterley Park to catch the tube into London. On reporting to the Air Commodore we immediately, without explanation, set off by car for Heston where I used to fly in prewar days. To my astonishment he then asked me if I considered the grass aerodrome there as being large enough for use by Naval aircraft, which it obviously was. It was only later that it became known that Fairey's Heathrow aerodrome had been commandeered under wartime legislation for conversion into a 'bomber' station! My little visit had been a yardarm clearing operation in case the Navy objected to Fairey's, the chief contractor of naval aircraft, being moved out. As is well known Faireys fought for fifteen years or so for compensation, finally receiving a pitiful sum for their valuable land. Vast sums were involved in turning the grass field into the present airport, including the cost of filling a very large gravel pit where the approach tunnel is now.

While standing on the tarmac at Heston a US Army B-17 landed and taxied in. They were returning from a daylight raid on Germany and were lost and obviously exhausted. I remember in particular one young gunner who could not have been more than about 19, who came up to our little party. He was very excited and had to tell us all about it. He said he saw the enemy fighter coming in to the attack over and over again. He could see it firing, it was actually aiming at him, he was sure because it came so close he could see the pilot who was trying to kill him! It was his first time in action. I went over to look at the aircraft which was riddled with bullet holes and the side gunner's blister had certainly seen some use — the bottom of the fuselage was six inches deep in empty .5 inch shell cases.

From time to time 'rogue' aircraft were reported as being unacceptable by squadrons. For various reasons these particular aircraft misbehaved, or at least got a bad name for handling qualities and whenever possible, were quietly returned either to the main maintenance depot or passed on to another squadron, which was not popular with higher authority. A scheme was put in hand by which independent assessors flew these aircraft and if possible put them right on the spot. I was sent up to Castletown on the north coast of Sunderland to deal with a rogue Spitfire. For this sort of

The author flying the Hawker Tempest Mk II prototype, LA602, (Bristol Centaurus), Boscombe Down, 3 May 1944. Intended to replace the Typhoon, the Tempest had a greatly improved laminar flow wing. Relatively free of development problems, it had great potential as a weapon carrier.

journey a Firefly provided ideal transport as it was reasonably fast, had plenty of fuel and would land in a short space if required. On my arrival at Castletown the local RAF fighter squadron was, I think, a little surprised to see someone in Naval uniform appear but they could not have been more polite and made me very welcome in their mess. It happened to be the week of Christmas in 1943. The offending Spitfire was flying very right wing low and the wing could not be held up in a dive, a not unusual fault on a new aircraft coming off the production line, but which certainly should have been rectified before being issued to the squadron. It may well have had a damaged aileron replaced while in a maintenance unit but had not been subsequently test flown. They changed the starboard aileron which made a big improvement and with a bit of reflexing of the trailing edge, it flew well and was accepted by the Commanding Officer.

Returning south via the Western Highlands and Machrihanish on the Mull of Kintyre I had a superb view of this lovely mountainous country. It was a change from flying over the southern half of England with which I had become very familiar. Although occasionally a radio was fitted, frequently it was not, and as a lot of our flying was at altitude quick recognition of one's locality was important. On breaking cloud, the plains to the north of Salisbury, the flat area of Somerset with its drainage dykes, the Cotswolds with yellow limestone houses, the sandy pine tree area around Aldershot,

often only a glance was enough to give a clue as to one's whereabouts. Strangely enough I found it was often more difficult to recognise one's position when flying low, the contours of hills and other landmarks appearing different to the view from above. In a way the sky became one's habitat, one lived in it and became part of it.

During 1944, Air Commodore Boothman (later Sir John Boothman KCB, KBE, DFC AFC) took command of Boscombe Down. He was well known as the outright winner of the Schneider Trophy in 1931. He was a popular commanding officer, and much liked throughout the Air Force. He and his wife entertained a good bit, giving a number of small dinner parties. Ella and I got to know them well, Ella particularly getting on with Mrs Boothman, as she was then. She used to drop in to our small bungalow quite often, and I think enjoyed not having to be formal, as she had to be with regular RAF wives.

Sammy Wroath left 'A' per T in the spring of 1943 to set up and command the Empire Test Pilots School (ETPS) whose main object was to train test pilots for the future and to raise the standard. Whereas in the past pilots had been picked for these jobs largely for their skill in flying, now with the latest aircraft, the testing was becoming more sophisticated, and much more technical. A greater knowledge of engineering and science in all its aspects was of far greater value than an ability to give a good demonstration of aerobatics. The ETPS was set up to emphasise this and was a turning point in the type of pilot specialising in test work. Candidates were not only from the Empire, but included Americans, Canadians and eventually men from the Armed Services of nearly every country in the world. It had the intended effect of standardising performance measurement, handling and all other aspects of an aircraft's behaviour worldwide and unquestionably raised immensely the professional test pilots' status in the aviation industry.

Group Captain McKenna took over the second course at the ETPS in 1944. As he had not flown a Mustang, he came over to 'A' per T one afternoon to borrow one of ours. It was a standard Mark IV in which I had been measuring the stick forces in turns. On my last flight I noticed that a panel over the ammunition tank on the starboard wing had started to lift at the aft edge when pulling about 4G. On landing to investigate, it appeared to be fastened down normally but it was reported to the engineering staff who examined it and were satisfied that it was fastened securely. The quick release fastenings were an American type with two lots of slots for a screwdriver, the alignment of which confirmed that it was locked down properly. I showed McKenna the taps and off he went. Half an hour later an aircraft was reported to have crashed somewhere near Salisbury. It was seen to be diving when it rolled over and crashed into the ground. McKenna's death was a great loss as he was one of our older and most

respected test pilots. His name lives on, as the much sought after McKenna Trophy is presented each year to the test pilot who has done best in the course.

This was followed by a spate of other accidents. 'B' Squadron were investigating a series of losses in Halifax squadrons which I was told were occurring during take-offs at night. Take-off conditions were being simulated at 10,000 feet when the aircraft under investigation was seen to spin and crash killing the whole crew. The particular trial they were carrying out was to switch off one of the outer engines as if an engine had failed. The final investigation showed that the pilot had no positive indication of which engine had failed as the offending engine was still showing some boost and rpm because it was being turned over by the wind-milling propeller which had of course not been feathered. Attempting to hold the aircraft straight while in the climb led to a fully stalled fin and rudder followed by a spin. As a result of these trials most multi-engined aircraft were fitted with torquemeters which gave a positive and immediate indication of which engine was failing or had failed.

Another Halifax accident which had a happier ending occurred one evening when we in 'A' per T had finished for the day and were walking back to the officers' mess along the perimeter road. There is a big dip in the road in front of the mess and we saw on the other side of the aerodrome a Halifax approaching to land. The sun was low and the aircraft dipped out of sight to make the touch down. To our surprise instead of the aircraft appearing over the brow the first thing to appear was a very large rubber tyred wheel which came bounding over the hill in our direction. It turned out that this was Al Truran's first flight in a four-engined bomber. A very popular Canadian Wing Commander, he was really an armament expert and had borrowed the aircraft from 'B' Squadron. He and the crew were unhurt but in spite of a lot of talk about 'sun in his eyes' he had his leg well pulled and was not allowed to forget it in a hurry!

One terrible accident, which should never have occurred, involved a Liberator that took off with locked controls, killing everyone on board. American aircraft had a different method of operating the brakes from the British system. On our own aircraft the differential use of the brakes for manoeuvring on the ground was controlled by movement of the rudder bar, and the application of the amount of braking by a hand-lever on the control column. The Liberator had hinged pedals on the rudder control, their brakes being activated by pivoting one's foot from the ankle using the ball of the foot to apply the appropriate brake. It was not easy to apply heavy pressure as in a turn one's leg was nearly fully extended, so it was easier to taxi with the rudders locked central. I never heard the result of the final investigation of this accident, but confusion could well have been the cause.

One afternoon when we were grounded by low cloud and

The author flying the Tempest Mk I at Boscombe Down, 1943.

unable to do any test flying, a friend of Wing Commander Lamb's, who was then commanding the flight, flew over to see him. He had come from an operational Spitfire squadron in Southern England. We sat around chatting and after a cup of tea he decided the weather was just passable and that it was time for him to return to his base. Peter and I helped strap him in and pulled an accumulator trolley over, plugged in and he got a start.

As he taxied to the far end of the aerodrome we set off on foot for the Officers' mess. As he took off we glanced up and saw him immediately make a left hand climbing turn. This became a vertical bank and it was clear he was evidently stalling out of control. The aircraft hit the ground with full power and burst into flames amid a cloud of black smoke. It was clear that there was nothing we could do. The accident was like a bad dream and my mind went over it again and again rather like a slow motion action replay.

After a sleepless night fortunately the day broke dry and clear and with a backlog of work we were all kept busy and I was able to put my fears behind me. There are many men alive today due to the fact that the Spitfire, especially near the stall, was a very forgiving aircraft; but there was a limit to what it could take.

23　The coming of the jets

Early in June 1944, it became evident that something was about to happen. The traffic through our local village of Amesbury built up to a crescendo of grinding and creaking tanks, all moving west by day and by night, making walking along our narrow pavements highly dangerous. Even the air became crowded. There happened to be heavy overcast skies with a base at about 1,500 feet forcing all the air traffic into a narrow band. Many squadrons spread out in ragged formation were criss-crossing Salisbury Plain, their leaders map reading to try to find strange airfields. Every type of combat aircraft seemed to be airborne and on the move.

After news of the invasion of Normandy and the difficulties of landing supplies on the exposed beachheads, the armies seemed to get bogged down as the Germans brought up their powerful mobile reserves. It was with relief that we heard of the American breakout and sweeping movement round to the south and east.

The RP-equipped Typhoons then came into their own. The German Panzer's escape route through the Falaise gap, flanked by the British to the north and the Americans to the south turned into an enormous traffic jam of tanks head to tail over miles of typical French 'routes nationales', that is to say, dead straight. A more perfect target for the new rockets would be hard to imagine — with enfilading fire, if the rocket missed one tank it clobbered the next in line. Furthermore, the armour of tanks was designed for deflecting a horizontal attack, not one coming at 30° from above, with the result that the rocket heads went clean through like a hot knife through butter. According to eye witnesses later, the shambling, bloody chaos had to be seen to be believed. With the teeth of their army knocked out, enemy resistance crumbled, allowing the allied armies to make a wild dash forward to Paris and as far as the Rhine, by-passing the Germans bottled up in the Channel ports where they had expected the invasion to be. Those rocket Typhoons were surely the right weapons at the right place at the right time.

On 15 March 1944 Brunner and I were ordered to fly over to the Gloster Aircraft Company's aerodrome at Moreton Valence to fly and report on the handling characteristics of the F9/40. We had expected a conventional aircraft and had no knowledge whatever of a gas turbine or even the existence of such an engine. We met Crosby Warren, the chief test pilot, who with a pencil and a sheet of foolscap explained how air was sucked in by a centrifugal blower, compressed and passed into a combustion chamber into which paraffin was sprayed and burned, finally passing on out through a turbine. The vastly increased speed of the mass of air exhaust-ing through the jet pipe gave a forward thrust acting according to Newton's law that action and reaction are equal and opposite. He explained how the fuel being pumped into the engine was controlled with a spill valve, although it was still called a throttle, and how gently one had to accelerate the engine to avoid over-heating the turbine. The starting procedure was different from a conventional engine although an electrical timing device made the various contacts in the correct sequence.

When Gloster designed their twin-engined jet-propelled fighter, the F9/40, the only engine available was the Whittle W.IIb. This engine, like other gas turbines, was sensitive to coarse movements of the throttle lever — the fuel had to be fed in gradually during acceleration to avoid over-heating. They therefore designed an unusual type of throttle control instead of the standard box with two sprouting levers. This comprised a long double slide with two knobs. By twisting one's wrist in the lateral plane it was possible to use one knob as a leverage point to move the other knob, thus avoiding any violent movement with a consequent sudden increase in fuel flow. One very quickly got used to it, although it was not ideal for formation flying.

The F9/40 was later named the Meteor and the prototype's two Whittle W.IIb engines gave 1,350 lbs of thrust each. Crosby Warren warned us of the long take-off run and poor angle of climb. Moreton Valence had a very long concrete runway, but even so it took a long time to gain flying speed. The aircraft's handling characteristics were normal except that at high speed in a dive it started 'snaking' or yawing from side to side combined with a rolling motion. The object of our visit was to assess this behaviour and report on its acceptability as a gun platform.

At any speed above 250 mph it was not possible to keep the aiming mark of the gunsight steady on a target as the period of the snaking was shorter than one's own reaction time to correct it with rudder. At higher speeds the period became progressively shorter so that the aircraft was at that stage unacceptable as a fighter. A series of modifications including the elimination of friction in the rudder circuit, skinning the rudder with metal instead of fabric, reducing the fin area and thickening the trailing edge of the rudder finally overcame the snaking. What had not been appreciated at the time of the Meteor's original design was the big damping effect a normal

The first production de Havilland Vampire seen at Boscombe Down in April 1944.

propeller has on directional stability, as the usual parameters of fin and rudder area in relation to the wing did not apply to a jet aircraft.

As an aircraft, it was a delight to fly, the impression being that of a glider with power. The cockpit was quiet, roomy, pressurised and, since there was no engine in front, had good forward visibility. It was, with the W.IIb, badly under-powered but, as the first British fighter with a tricycle under-carriage, very easy to fly.

The delivery of the prototype Meteor to Boscombe was followed in April by the arrival of Geoffrey de Havilland with the E6/41, code name Spider Crab, later to be familiarly known as the Vampire, with a single Halford Ib gas turbine. Both of these aircraft were A star top secret. Part of our hangar was screened off, other pilots from our own flight were not even allowed in, security guards maintained a 24-hour patrol and Brunner and I were forbidden to mention the aircraft in the mess. The inhabitants of Amesbury must have been aware of these strange aircraft because they made a totally different noise and obviously had no propellers. Imagine our surprise when, within a couple of months, one day every newspapers' front page was plastered with the news of this new British invention. Apparently the explanation for this sudden disclosure was that the Americans, to whom we had sent a couple of gas-turbine engines for evaluation were just about to announce their existence. Churchill got to hear of this and gave his consent to have the news released in the UK first. After the war we discovered that the Germans had actually flown their own jet-propelled aircraft shortly before we did.

The Vampire had a considerably better performance than the early Meteor and was comparable with contemporary fighters, largely due to the Halford engine which gave the aircraft a high thrust-to-weight ratio. The combustion chambers pointed aft and converged on the turbine whereas the Whittle combustion chambers reversed the air flow, thereby losing a lot of energy in the process. These early gas turbines were mechanically quite reliable, thanks largely to the simple centrifugal compressors and low compression; the Germans were more ambitious in choosing to go for higher efficiency by designing multi-stage axial compressors, and unfortunately for them these suffered badly from unreliability and burn-outs. Our main worry centred around fuel pumps which were of the gear type and had to be overhauled every five hours, the more sophisticated variable-output pumps coming as a later development. The other weakness was a tendency to get a 'wet' start. Anyone who has used a paraffin blow lamp will know what happens when the burner is not hot enough to vapourise the fuel: a jet of flaming liquid squirts out. This is exactly what a 'wet' start is, only the flames are much bigger and longer! On the twin-engined Meteor this did not matter much as the tail was well

clear, but the Vampire with the single engine had twin booms carrying the rudders, and the raised tailplane was only just out of the line of fire. When sitting in the pilot's seat and starting up a Vampire the only indication of a 'wet' start was a look of horror on the faces of bystanders! Orange flames at least 20 feet long would not infrequently shoot out.

On almost his first flight in the Vampire, Brunner had a wet start but shut off the high pressure cock immediately. Restarting, he taxied out to take-off and we noticed a wisp of smoke coming from the rear cone of the fuselage. Having no radio to warn him we rushed out onto the aerodrome with Verey pistols shooting off any cartridges which came to hand. Fortunately, he saw them and landed immediately rather irritated at being brought back. The bottom of the fuselage had already been partly burned away and was still burning. Obviously liquid paraffin had collected behind the ribs of the engine nacelle and been set alight by the heat of the jet pipe. Following this experience, we always tipped the aircraft back on its tricycle undercarriage to drain any surplus fuel away after a wet start.

De Havilland urgently wanted the aircraft back, so our early trials were limited to measuring speed and climb. A performance climb to altitude was normally preceded by partial climbs at varying speeds and altitudes to obtain the best climbing speed but I was sent off using my own judgement as to the best speed. The early jet engines had a fail safe overspeed governor which cut off the fuel above the maximum rpm, and another safety cut out device, activated by the jet pipe temperature, protected the turbine blades against excessive temperature. There was, however, no automatic control to maintain a constant rpm for a fixed throttle setting, and the pilot had to constantly close the throttle as altitude was gained because the rpm increased as the air became less dense. To my surprise, at high altitude the position of the throttle was only about one quarter open and on throttling back the fire would sometimes go out. I was told that this was due to the burners not spraying the limited quantity of fuel passing but that they merely dribbled. Whatever it was, the maintenance at high altitude of any steady rpm was most difficult, requiring constant attention.

I set off from Boscombe one evening in April in a north westerly direction. The Vampire seemed uncannily smooth and quiet; the sun was already low in the west shining on the waters of the Bristol Channel, with the outline of both the Welsh and North Devon coastlines showing clearly and, incidentally, giving a good navigational fix. I flew on and on in the rather dreamlike world, concentrating on recording what I hoped were some good figures and getting as high as possible. The climb above 35,000 feet was very flat but by keeping a good forward speed the engine, which had been running out of breath by then, seemed to take on new life and finally 40,000 feet came up. It was time to turn for home which was back down there somewhere in the murk while I cruised along in my own world in a strange way enjoying the sun and crystal clear atmosphere. Riding the quiet ripple free air in an aircraft whose engine was so smooth that the only indication of its turning was the rev counter, was a new experience and for me very thrilling. I realised at that moment that the advent of this new invention was by far the greatest advance in aviation during my lifetime.

The return to Boscombe was only a question of pointing in the right direction helped by the Bristol Channel and 30,000 odd feet of altitude, but I was short of fuel and it was important to hit the right spot and not have to search around in the dusk, because a jet engine uses a lot of fuel low down. All was well and the de Havilland engineers were glad to see their baby safely back after such a relatively long flight. Three weeks later, after the completion of the preliminary trials, I flew the aircraft back to Hatfield.

In June 1944, the first production line Meteor arrived at Boscombe Down. The main difference from the prototype was the installation of Rolls-Royce B37 engines. This engine had more thrust than the W.IIb and the combustion chambers converged on the turbine like those of the Halford engine in the Vampire, thus improving the internal air flow. One of the new engines gave trouble after a few hours due to a bearing failure. The early gas turbines had ball bearings throughout and these were lubricated on a 'total loss' system, rather similar to early motor cars with drip feed! Our new engines had a plain white metal bearing between the compressor and the turbine with a full oil circulation system. Presumably this was intended to dissipate some of the internal heat, but instead the heat melted the white metal of the bearing. This fault was soon rectified, but even the best engineers make mistakes sometimes! Eventually this basic engine, used as a gas generator to drive a turbo-prop and known as the Dart, powered most of the early gas turbine-driven civil airliners, achieving a life of 5,000 hours between overhauls, a very big forward step.

Apart from the 'snaking' troubles, the Meteor as an aircraft was very free of vices and, although not a great fighter, it was an excellent introduction for the Royal Air Force to this new form of propulsion.

As the first gas turbine aircraft to undergo full performance and handling trials at the A & AEE, the Meteor required new methods of measurement and techniques. Performance was more affected by the aircraft's weight and the ambient air temperature compared with a conventional piston-engined aircraft. On measuring speeds, for instance, instead of flying at 2,000 feet intervals at decreasing altitudes, the exact reverse was carried out. With the heavy fuel consumption, this practice compensated in some measure for the decrease in weight, due to the consumption of fuel. So far as take-off distance was concerned, we were aware of the effect of high air temperatures lengthening the unstick distance but, having no concrete runway, measurement was unsatisfactory.

One of the troubles encountered with gas turbines was a phenomenon known as 'surge'. The symptom occurred particularly when climbing at full power and consisted of a series of thuds or hesitations in the engine, very similar in feel to driving a car when the engine is cold and spits back into the carburettor. On throttling back a little, it would stop. The cause was not fully understood but was believed to be a stall in the compressor. No failures ever occurred on this account, but even a momentary hesitation in the main air flow through the combustion chambers was enough to enrich the fuel-to-air mixture and raise the temperature of the blades of the turbine. Jet pipe temperatures respond instantly to the fuel flow as opposed to the relatively slow rises in the oil and water temperature of a piston engine.

On the introduction of jet-propelled aircraft with their characteristic whine, it was interesting to note how quickly a new language or jargon came into use. Instead of 'start up' the new phrase became 'light up' or 'fire up'. 'Did you have a good flight' became 'did you have a good squirt' or, alternatively, 'did you enjoy a bit of curving'. Perhaps one reason for these new descriptions of flying a jet aircraft was that the usual practice of making a circuit of the aerodrome before landing was made at a much higher speed. In losing height, the aircraft, which had no air brakes, gained a lot of speed and, in addition, there was a considerable residual thrust from the engine even with the throttle fully closed so that to check on whether other aircraft were circling to land it was best to enter the circuit below 1,000 feet, use a lot of G in the turns and ultimately pull up to lose more momentum and speed before lowering the undercarriage. To be baulked on the approach to land was quite a serious matter as opening up and going round again might easily take 25 gallons, a margin which was not always available.

Another characteristic which I noticed was the much greater height required to recover from a loop. On going over the top at what would normally be a reasonable speed, the aircraft would gain speed from the inverted position very rapidly indeed making the pull out prolonged. The residual thrust when throttled back together with the lack of resistance of a propeller were obviously the cause, but it was disconcerting to the pilot and later resulted in some fatal crashes before it was realised what was happening.

Geoffrey de Havilland used to give a spectacular demonstration of the Vampire using a special technique of his own. On take-off he would go into an extremely low turn maintaining full throttle while circling the aerodrome and so build up to a high speed, then use the momentum to make a vertical climb to about 5,000 feet. To a pilot, high speed at ground level or plenty of altitude is like money in the bank, a comfortable feeling.

24 Hornets and Furies

Ever since a child, I have had a great love of engines, starting with a working model steamboat, then a 1914 Royal Enfield motor bike, followed by an ABC, a Red Indian, and many others which were all a tremendous source of interest in taking them apart and tuning them. While learning to fly at Brooklands, I saw many of the racing cars of the day being prepared by Thomson & Taylor — Delage, Talbot, Sunbeam, Bugatti, and the supercharged Alfa Romeo. I found the big aero engines even more exciting, the air-cooled Jaguar, American engines like the Pratt & Whitney Wasp and the Wright Whirlwind. Then the Rolls-Royce Merlin and Griffon, wonderful pieces of engineering built to technical perfection regardless of cost. Other engines such as the Bristol sleeve-valve family and the Napier Sabre had their admirers, but for me the gradual development of more and more power was always of intense interest.

I always enjoy seeing the engine of any ship in which I travel, be it paddle steamer or trans-Atlantic liner. The robust and ornate construction of some of the machinery of the Victorian engineers is greatly to be admired as are the massive cylinders, crankshaft and turbo-chargers of the modern big ship diesels. All these engines give me a thrill when seen in action or even when stationary. An engine is to an engineer what a sculpture is to an artist, every line, every curve and every shaft is suitably proportioned to take the load to which it is subjected; the good designer moulds the many functions into a three-dimensional whole.

An engine is one of the few material objects which becomes 'alive'. To fly a single-seater de Havilland Hornet with 4800 horsepower was to experience this eager animal called power to the *n*th degree. The gentlest pressure of the palm of one's hand was all that was required to release a burst of noise, a surge of thrust, a whole explosion of activity propelling one onwards and upwards to the sky. The jockey on a racehorse must experience the same sort of sensation at the start of a race. The thrill it gives a human being is not to be despised even if, as in my case, it is given by an engine.

I regard myself as unbelievably lucky in being sent to fly the early Gloster F9/40 or Meteor. This was not their first jet-propelled aircraft, which was the Gloster E/28, but was their first jet fighter. The two Whittle W.IIb engines were built by Rovers at Coventry before Rolls-Royce took over all the

A de Havilland Hornet F Mk I (Merlin 130/131 engines) at Boscombe Down in March 1945. A lot of power for one man but with controls to match its performance, the Hornet was the ultimate in piston-engined aircraft. The author nearly wrote off this aircraft on his first flight in it.

The Beech Traveller was a surprisingly efficient biplane with reverse stagger, good low speed characteristics and a good pilot's view. It was also known in civil guise as the Staggerwing. (The Aeroplane)

later development. These engines and de Havilland's Halford HIb were historic, in that they were the first to fly and prove the principle of jet propulsion in Great Britain. Early British gas turbines engines had the supreme merit of being simple and used centrifugal fans for compressing the air, the fundamentals of which were well understood. The Germans used axial fans which theoretically are more efficient, and ultimately became so, but which at the time proved most unreliable.

My job, as described earlier, was to investigate the flying characteristics of the Meteor and had nothing to do with the engines, although with my early background of engineering training and love of engines, I found it fascinating, and rather hogged the hours, enjoying every minute of it. Every single operation on these new engines, whether starting up, taxi-

ing, climbing or measuring speed, required a different technique and, still being in the experimental stage, at least sympathetic handling and a watchful eye. For me the change from piston engines to gas turbines was a transformation. Almost for the first time in my life, I felt relatively safe flying.

Nevertheless, the fact that even the Meteor was an unknown quantity was brought home to me in an abrupt and very unpleasant fashion. One morning Majergik, a Polish officer, took off to carry out the first spins. He was not in the mess at lunch. Later in the day we heard that an eyewitness had seen the Meteor spin into the ground. Presumably there was insufficient response from the rudder. It was to my knowledge the first time a jet had been spun and it caused much concern. It had not been appreciated that the lack of slipstream from a propeller in a jet might prove disastrous in spin recovery.

It took me many years to learn how conservative and slow people are in accepting any invention or new idea. I had seen how slow the Admiralty was in adopting the then highly secret airborne radar in 1940, and the Air Ministry's resis-

The Miles Messenger, flown by the author. It was a good light communication aircraft with retractable undercarriage and extendable flaps.

tance to monoplanes, variable-pitch propellers and retractable undercarriages in the 1930s; so also with the jet engine. To my surprise, very few of the fighter pilots or squadron commanders who flew these aircraft liked the early Meteors, as their fighting methods were not suited to these new jet engines. The jet has little thrust at low speed compared with a propeller and mixing it in a dog-fight showed the jet at its worst. There was little acceptance of the fact that this was something different, the first effort in a new field. Sir Charles Parsons had found the same with his steam-turbine-powered *Turbinia* years before.

Geoffrey de Havilland produced another interesting aircraft in the spring of 1945, the twin-engined Hornet. It had two of the latest versions of the Merlin which, using 150 grade fuel, were boosted to 25 lbs per square inch manifold pressure. The wing area was just adequate but was increased for landing by large extending flaps and also helped by the slipstream from two large diameter four-bladed propellers. The engines were handed and this led to some longitudinal instability until the respective directions of rotation were reversed when, with the change in the slipstream over the tail, the trouble disappeared. With 4,800 horsepower, the performance was staggering and it had the handling qualities to match. With the war in Europe drawing to a close, the Hornet was being considered for the Fleet Air Arm for operation in the Pacific. When it first came to us, the hook for deck-landing had already been fitted.

On arrival at Boscombe Down for a brief preliminary assessment, Geoffrey brought the prototype over. He explained that the aircraft had a thermostat controlling device on the radiator exit flaps which was opened and closed automatically to obtain an even engine temperature with minimum drag from the radiators. He also warned us that lowering the wing flaps gave a big nose down change of trim and that full flap could not be used. He had stuck a piece of white tape on the flap position indicator and marked with a pen the maximum to be used. Brunner flew the aircraft first and I took over while the engines were kept running. I noticed that the water temperature of the starboard engine was over 100°C so hurried to take-off and get a good airflow through the underwing radiators.

On crossing the boundary of the aerodrome I saw what appeared to be grey smoke pouring from the front of the bank of exhaust pipes on my side of the starboard engine. I thought it was about to burst into flames and throttled the engine back while still climbing away in a left hand turn on the port engine intending to land as soon as I was downwind of the aerodrome. Not being familiar with the layout of the cockpit and in a great hurry to get down I could not see the fire button immediately and did not feather the propeller as the engine was still idling and it could be of use in the approach to land. Having lined up for the landing, I dropped the undercarriage and selected flaps down forgetting about the limit on flap angle. The flaps went down all right but so did the nose. In fact, to hold any sort of reasonable approach angle of descent took most of the aft elevator travel but, worse still, reducing power made the attitude even steeper. Eventually I managed to fly parallel with the ground and by throttling back on the good engine and easing the stick forward touched the ground at about 130 miles an hour. The fuselage felt as if it was about horizontal, if anything nose down, but the flaps were creating a big ground effect. The wind was from the north east and the ground fortunately sloped slightly uphill so gradually the speed fell off and the tail dropped down out of my control. Immediately, the aircraft leapt into the air about six feet and landed on three points with a bump. By now I had about reached the perimeter road and finally came to rest on some rough ground near the outer fence. It was only then that I realised that it was steam and not smoke pouring from the engine.

Subsequent investigation showed that the 'inching' device on the radiator flap had an electrical fault, the effect of which was to close the outlet completely so that no cooling air could pass. All the rest was entirely my own fault and it taught me a number of lessons. I was just glad not to have wrecked the aircraft, an extremely valuable prototype.

As the intention was to operate the Hornet from aircraft carriers, Lieutenant Commander Brown, a test pilot from the Royal Aircraft Establishment, Farnborough, and I were sent to Hatfield, de Havilland's private aerodrome, to assess it for deck-landing qualities. The two big propellers sweeping their slipstream over the wing gave the necessary control over the lift at low speed, and my only criticism was of the throttles. They were fitted with large, clumsy knobs and the mechanism had a lot of friction and backlash. Considering the importance for deck landing of delicate control near the stall, and the rapid response from the fuel-injected engines, there was room for improvement. In the event, 'Winkle' Brown did the actual deck landing trials on HMS *Ocean* at the same time as I was doing them with the Sea Fury.

The 150 grade fuel used in the Merlins of the Hornet was something special. Ever since the Schneider Trophy days a great deal of research and development had been done in this field. Although the Merlin had not changed in its basic design, being 27 litres capacity, the power was increased from about 1,000 to 2,400 horsepower, and yet the maximum rpm of 3,000 was never altered. Rolls-Royce worked in collaboration with the fuel specialists and so was able constantly to increase the supercharge or boost pressure and obtain the power without increasing the piston speed, a wonderful achievement by both engine manufacturer and fuel chemists.

The problem of the so-called 'sound barrier' began to be of some importance towards the end of the war. The Royal Aircraft Establishment, Farnborough had been investigating this for some time but the A&AEE were also interested. A pilot at RAE was reputed to have reached a Mach number of .9, or 90 per cent of the speed of sound in a specially cleaned up version of a PR (Photographic Reconnaissance) Spitfire, which carried no guns and whose wings had no bulges or other excrescences to upset the airflow. Although the tips of the propeller are, of course, moving supersonically or at a much higher speed in relation to the air than the main body of the aircraft, they produce virtually no thrust travelling at Mach .9, but we were advised to use full engine rpm as the ejector type exhausts give considerable thrust at high engine speed, particularly at high altitude, in fact, a minor form of jet propulsion.

Flying our Welkin and a Spitfire Mk XXI, we started an investigation into compressibility with a series of high dives at increasing speeds. The Welkin was almost in trouble in level flight at 40,000 feet but the Spitfire could be dived at very steep angles without showing signs of loss of control. The procedure was to reach maximum speed at 40,000 feet in level flight and then dive at an angle of 30° until a terminal speed was reached. Gradually the angle was increased to about 80°, which feels very steep but I lacked the courage to invert the aircraft and dive vertically. The highest speed I recorded was Mach .8. One thing which I did notice was that buffeting occurred in the pull out under G, and the higher the speed, the lower the figure of G which could be pulled before buffeting occurred. By plotting the figure of G against speed it was fairly clear at what speed the buffeting or onset of compressibility would occur in steady flight i.e. 1G. One of the biggest mistakes made by our technical authorities was not to pursue these investigations postwar. Instead of continuing with manned flight experiments, presumably because it was thought to be too dangerous, it was decided to use models. The developing jet engine would have made these experiments easier as the thrust does not decrease with speed as with a propeller. Clearly, if one could have achieved supersonic speed in a climb as later became possible, any breakdown in control would have solved itself by the immediate loss of speed and resumption of subsonic flight on closing the throttle.

The relatively poor take-off characteristics of jet-propelled aircraft was an area which could not be properly investigated at Boscombe Down as no runway was yet in use, although one was being built. Our Commanding Officer, Air Commodore Boothman made a case for an extension of the A&AEE technical facilities by arranging for tests to be carried out in a hot climate. Whereas a propeller-driven aircraft can be pulled off the ground and into the air with insufficient flying speed, this is not so with a jet-propelled one. The drag of a wing at a big angle of incidence may exceed the thrust of the jet and the aircraft will then lose flying speed and perhaps never take-off. This tendency is increased in hot weather when the engine thrust is decreased and the wing lift

The Vickers Supermarine Spiteful prototype, NN664, at Boscombe Down in 1945. A new laminar flow wing rested on a basically Spitfire fuselage. The wing was later used on Supermarine's first Naval jet aircraft, the Attacker.

lowered so that a higher forward speed is required to lift off.

We set off on 16 April 1945 in a Liberator for Khartoum which is supposed to be one of the hottest places on earth. With due respect to my Commanding Officer, I think his experience of four-engined bombers was little more than mine, which was practically nil. After a nine-hour flight, we landed at Castel Benito, Tripoli and the following day flew to Cairo West where we were delayed overnight by engine trouble. Disembarking at Khartoum, the temperature was 110°F and with the wind blowing through the hot engine nacelles, it was so hot that one instinctively put an arm up to shield one's face from the searing heat. Having no previous experience and no one to turn to for advice, my own problem was to decide what a Naval Officer should wear in the Tropics 1,000 miles from the sea. I could not bring myself to wear white shorts so compromised on some light khaki trousers, a white shirt with epaulettes and my naval cap with a white cover. I doubt if Their Lordships would have approved even if they had known where I was.

Having completed the arrangements for tropical trials to be undertaken there, we set out for home. We landed at Cairo West again for petrol but were delayed a day while a magneto was changed. At least it gave me a chance to visit Mena House, the Pyramids and to buy my daughter Jane a toy leather camel and a bunch of bananas. This latter great wartime treat was not a success as she immediately spat her first bite out in disgust! We landed at Luqa in Malta the next evening, but although we touched down in good time and got busy on the brakes, backed up with full auxiliary brake power, I thought the runway was very short for a Liberator.

An unusual feature of this aircraft was the flexibility of the big span wings; from the cockpit the wingtips were out of sight when taxiing but in flight they appeared to be at least a couple of feet above the engine cowlings. En route back to England we passed over the Channel Islands which were still occupied by the Germans, although the Allied armies had already advanced almost to the Rhine. In spite of all the freedom of flying and of landing wherever we chose outside the UK we still had to clear HM Customs at Lyneham before returning to Boscombe.

Back at Boscombe Down the pressure to get results was easing off as the war in Europe was clearly drawing to a close. We became engaged on odd jobs such as the dropping of 'window'. This was the secret weapon consisting of stranded metal foil intended to confuse the enemy radar by causing an almost unlimited number of 'blips' on the screen. By releasing the 'window' in a kind of paper chase, the enemy could sometimes be misled into believing an alternative target to the true one was about to be attacked. For other trials we fitted fighters with containers carrying 900 lb of incendiaries, something which had previously always been dropped at night by the heavy bombers; other alternatives were extra external fuel tanks of every description, slipper, streamline, underwing, all intended to give longer range and to be dropped before combat.

In this connection I did a lot of measurement of longitud-

The Hawker Sea Fury, the last piston-engined fighter from a celebrated background of world beaters, was a real aristocrat with the sort of performance, handling and formidable weaponry expected from over thirty years' experience of building fighters.

inal stability in a Spitfire, taking the centre of gravity well aft of the acceptable range approved by Supermarine. It was intended to extend the range by adding extra internal fuel tanks, so that the aircraft could be used for long distance day bombing escort purposes. The delicate balance between accepting an unstable aircraft for a limited purpose against the peace of mind of the pilot in having fully adequate fuel to return to base, was a matter of opinion very difficult to assess. It could be perfectly safe at take-off when flown by an experienced pilot in good flying weather, but for an inexperienced pilot on a misty autumn day with a low sun, it was an entirely different matter, as it was highly dangerous to fly such an unstable aircraft on instruments.

On flying back from Farnborough one day in a Tempest Mk II, which had a Centaurus with fuel injection, the engine suddenly cut out at about 1,500 feet. However, on throttling back it picked up again and continued to run so long as the throttle was not opened beyond about one third, which just gave enough power to maintain height. It seemed a long drag back to Boscombe watching out for each possible landing field, rather like a game of musical chairs, but fortunately it kept going and I was able to go straight into a landing. Fuel injection was just being introduced on the latest engines, the mixture being controlled by a black box or computer which measured the engine rpm, the manifold pressure and temperature, and metered the correct amount of fuel. In the past all the vital functions of flight had been mechanically controlled by the pilot but the introduction of electronics seemed to have introduced a new element of risk; I was particularly conscious of this after the recent near shave with

the Hornet in which one engine overheated. Both of these incidents shook my confidence even more than total engine failure as they gave no prior warning or feedback of information.

Every new type or even variation of an existing type of aircraft that came to Boscombe was photographed for recognition purposes by the Observer Corps. Most people like to have their photograph taken and as the aircraft was invariably another new type to be added to one's log book these sorties were much sought after. The rear gunner's turret had been removed from a Hampden bomber in order to give the photographer a good all round view. There was a standard set of positions: astern, quarter, abreast, ahead on the quarter, taken from above, level and from below. If possible these were taken just above the clouds so that the reflected light shone on the lower surfaces and gave a good silhouette. At the time this routine exercise seemed of very minor importance as the Observer Corp was manned by a devoted band of older men who were well able to recognise British aircraft at a glance but the official historical record may be of considerable interest to later generations. Sadly, many of these historic photographs were destroyed while stored in a basement which flooded at Boscombe Down after the war.

With my previous association with Supermarines the arrival of their new Spiteful was of great interest. Carrying on their policy of only making one alteration at a time, the prototype Spiteful had a new laminar-flow low-drag wing but retained the Spitfire fuselage. The wing section was built to an accuracy of five thousandths of an inch and was very free of any roughness, such as rivet heads, to give it the desired airflow characteristics. Even dust was supposed to degrade its performance. For the same power the top speed increased by about 30 mph but so also did the landing speed. Later, the same wing was incorporated in another fuselage fitted with a turbojet engine; this was in use by the Royal Navy for many years and was called the Attacker.

25 Last days at Boscombe

At Boscombe Down we were fortunately spared visits from VIPs. Nearly everything there was top secret, but after the Germans had been driven back out of France, we did welcome a party of senior officers from the French Air Force, and later from some Russians, none of whom had seen a jet aircraft. The latter were treated to a fine display of aerobatics by Zurakowski in a Spitfire, but to his embarrassment, in making a show of its low speed manoeuvrability and landing a few yards in front of the party, he knocked the tail wheel off.

General Smuts, our old enemy of the Boer War, but now highly respected and, of course, our ally, was given a great reception, and for the first time in the two and a half years I had been at Boscombe Down, everyone turned out on parade. He was a great believer in an independent air force and the effectiveness of the strategic heavy bomber. He was obviously surprised to see a Naval officer on a Royal Air Force station, as he stopped on seeing Torrens-Spence and asked him questions. He could not have chosen a better man to state the Fleet Air Arm's case.

One visitor to Boscombe Down I got to know was MacLaren. He had invented a kind of swivelling undercarriage which allowed an aircraft with the then conventional landing gear to land with drift on. The object was to avoid building expensive runways by making use of a single strip only. This idea was not adopted, but years later, the US Air Force used the same principle for the multi-wheeled landing gear of their very big Globemaster. His knowledge and expertise in this particular field was applied to a baby's pushchair! Today practically every young mother one sees in the street has her child in one of MacLaren's chairs. It is very light, folds up simply without trapping one's fingers, and looks like a two handled walking stick easily carried on to a bus.

Another interesting visitor was Geoffrey Tyson, chief test pilot of Shorts, builders of the highly successful Sunderland flying boat. In his younger days he had been a great aerobatic pilot and used to tour the country with Cobham's Flying Circus, giving demonstrations of inverted flying at no height just to liven up the crowd. He was a very keen character, who took his test flying very seriously. He borrowed several aircraft from us, and on each occasion came back with his pad covered with figures and notes. In one single flight he would have taken the measure of its performance and handling qualities, a useful independent report to supplement our own assessment.

George Bulman, the highly respected chief test pilot of

Hawkers up to the launch and production of the Hurricane (which he handed over to Philip Lucas), was the doyen of the test pilots' world and represented their interests at the highest level. He had been responsible for the development and handling qualities of the much loved family of pre-war biplanes, of which the Fury was the last of the line. By the middle of the war when I first met Philip Lucas, he had picked up the torch, carrying on the tradition of Hawkers for building great fighters. The latest, the new Fury (and Sea Fury) was a real pilot's aeroplane, and the last to be powered by a piston engine. By then other test pilots were taking over including Bill Humble, and Richard Muspratt (from 'A' per T). Bill, always immaculately turned out, would step into a Tempest or a Fury, and give a demonstration which really shook those watching, squeezing every ounce of performance out of the aircraft and showing off its manoeuvrability to the spectacular limit. Taxiing in afterwards and throwing back the hood, he would emerge smiling without a hair out of place!

On the entry of the United States into the war, any qualified American test pilot was given official clearance to fly any of our aircraft, and some of them made the most of the opportunity. I remember particularly one who used to like doing aerobatics in the Typhoon, hurtling it round the sky. He thought it was terrific, but I thought *he* was, as it was no boy's toy, and not everyone's choice, weighing as it did about as much as a double decker bus.

On 1 June 1945, a new division was formed at the Aeroplane and Armament Experimental Establishment, 'C' Squadron. This was the first Naval test squadron and became responsible for the testing of Naval aircraft only. For administrative purposes it came under HMS *Daedalus* at Lee-on-Solent but was subject to the discipline of the Royal Air Force at Boscombe Down, our hosts. By this time I had had nearly three years test-flying experience but, in spite of my lack of experience of Naval administration or discipline, I was appointed to command the new squadron with the acting rank of Commander (A) RNVR. We were allotted some wooden huts near the officers' mess as our headquarters and dispersed our aircraft on the slope below the control tower. This was very convenient but it was, at times, very noisy. Just below our site there was a firing range for testing guns and beyond that, in a slight dip, was an open-air wind tunnel which had been used for investigating the behaviour of jettisoned hoods, tanks and other external stores.

In their advance across Northern France, the Army had captured some V-1 sites in France and these included some

The Stinson Reliant was a good steady plodder with a decade of pre-war development. This is the actual aircraft used by the author to fly to Paris to collect a French-built Storch in May 1945. (Richard Riding)

The Fieseler Fi-156 Storch (Argus engine) was a very low speed, short landing and take-off aircraft. This example was built by Morane-Saulnier in occupied France for the Germans. (Flight)

serviceable flying bombs. One at least found its way to Boscombe Down and was set up near us in the blast from the wind tunnel where measurements of the engine thrust, consumption and other data were collected. There was considerable excitement when the engine started for the first time but interest quickly died away due to the noise generated. It was unbelievable and literally shook one's whole body. Londoners on the other hand, took a different view of this noise as they just prayed that the engines would keep going and at least get over their own heads before cutting out. The engine's operating cycle was based on resonance and depended on a large number of light metal flaps which acted as a form of inlet valve in a very similar manner to the inlet valve of some outboard motors. Fortunately, the trials only lasted a couple of months, after which we in 'C' Squadron were able to settle down to a relatively peaceful routine.

Shortly after Paris was relieved by the US Army, Group Captain Wroath, my old flight commander but now returned to A&AEE as Officer Commanding Flying Wing, was asked to pick up a Fieseler Storch from Paris. I flew him over to Le Bourget together with an engineering officer in a Stinson Reliant, a six-seater American civilian aircraft which somehow had come our way. The Storch was not at Le Bourget as we had expected but at a very small grass aerodrome near the centre of Paris. It was too small for a Stinson Reliant to land in so we spent the night in the city. Apparently, the Storch had been built by the French and assembled at this aerodrome where the Germans had realised it would be safe from Allied bombers. Because of its very short take-off and landing characteristics, the Storch was an excellent aircraft and very easy to fly, but our own Auster fulfilled much the same role at a fraction of the cost.

Returning to England we flew in company following the

twisting course of the Seine to Le Havre where we had to land for fuel. Camped out round the aerodrome were hundreds of German prisoners, most of whom looked very young to me, only about sixteen to eighteen. They were being guarded by French colonial troops who did not look the types to argue with, guns at the ready and fingers on the trigger. Even our little party were rather nervous as, of course, one of our aircraft was German! I fear our combined effort to explain ourselves in French was not very convincing and it was a relief to depart for home without incident.

In the early autumn of 1945 Vice Admiral Boyd, KCB, CBE, DSC, the head of the Fleet Air Arm, decided to come over to Boscombe Down on an official visit of inspection of the Naval Test Squadron. 'C' Squadron had by then been in existence for three months and had settled down well, on what was basically a Royal Air Force station. Admiral Boyd, although not a pilot himself, was known and held in very high esteem by all the Armed Services as the victor over the Italian fleet. He had commanded HMS *Illustrious* and planned the night attack on the Italians at Taranto harbour and also defeated the remainder of their fleet at Matapan. The Taranto operations were carried out by Swordfish with torpedoes and virtually eliminated the Italian fleet in the Mediterranean. The night attack was brilliantly executed. Three aircraft dropped flares to the south of the anchored fleet, while the main force approached low down from the north. The attack came as a complete surprise to the enemy who fired wildly at the flare-dropping aircraft while the main attack met little resistance and found the ships clearly silhouetted against the light.

Wartime parades and inspections were not exactly up to the Guards standard, but we put on the best show we could and gave the Admiral lunch, when he also met all the senior boffins from the Technical Office. He had planned to return

Vice Admiral Sir Denis Boyd prepares for a flight as a passenger in a Meteor at Boscombe Down on 11 September 1945.

to his headquarters at Lee-on-Solent in his official car in the afternoon, but when I suggested that he should fly back in a two-seater Meteor he jumped at the idea; jet aircraft were very rare in 1945 and there was only one which had a passenger seat. For certain trials an observer was required and the ammunition tank and guns had been removed from the compartment immediately behind the pilot's cockpit. It was not pressurised, visibility through the perspex roof was very poor, there was no proper ventilation or heating, but as I expected, he was keen to have a go.

To give him some impression of the speed I dived down to about 200 feet along the West Solent, the ASI showing about 450 mph and approached Lee still travelling fairly fast. I knew the aerodrome well but made two circuits to lose speed and to ensure that other slower aircraft were clear of the approach. On landing and taxiing back to the Watch Tower a small delegation was there to meet us, but I was surprised as I had forgotten and had failed to send a signal notifying the Admiral's change of plan. I helped the Admiral out but to avoid the complication of having to restart the engines, kept them running and shortly afterwards made my departure.

It turned out later that the group of people by the Watch Tower were there to arrest me! Apparently I had broken the aerodrome rules, landing without prior notification, high speed in the circuit, landing without a green light and other crimes. However, when the Admiral appeared all was

Vice Admiral Sir Denis Boyd being strapped into the Meteor's modified ammunition tank for the flight to Lee-on-Solent on 11 September 1945, after inspecting 'C' Flight, A&AEE.

'Winkle' Brown making the first Sea Hornet carrier landing on HMS Ocean. The Sea Hornet was a big morale booster for the Royal Navy, who, in 1945, were getting priority for its use in the Pacific war.

quickly forgiven. I also heard a rumour later that the biggest ticking off was received by the Admiral himself from his wife, who said he had no right to go tearing round in jet aircraft at his age. As Flag Officer commanding the Fleet Air Arm, he was I believe, the first head of any flying service to fly in a jet aircraft.

The end of the war in Europe, V-E Day, 8 May 1945, was, of course, a day to celebrate and a day of relief. All flying ceased for three days. It seemed at first hard to believe that at last after six years it was over. Ella and I tried to explain to Jane, now aged three, what an important day it was, but she was too young to understand.

There was great rejoicing in the Officers' mess with Mr Noble, the chief steward and majordomo, at his very best, and drink flowed all day. 'B' Squadron celebrated by firing their cannon at odd moments which added to the general excitement.

The following evening all the officers and men, together with their wives and families, were invited to an enormous bonfire and firework party. An effigy of Hitler was put on the top of the bonfire, as well as a captured German flag which was attached to a wire strung between two tall poles. It was a clear dark night when Air Commodore Boothman put a match to the bonfire, which blazed quickly. The Hitler

dummy disappeared in the flames but much to everyone's surprise the swastika did not. The cloth was obviously made of some special asbestos material and it would not burn, so nearby aircraft were raided for their Verey pistols and cartridges. From then on we had a fine coloured display as these were used to shoot through the flag, but it was only brought down finally by cutting the guy wire off the poles.

Life slowed down considerably after VE-Day. On 10 August 1945, I was sent to do the first deck landing trials of the Sea Fury on HMS, *Ocean*, a light fleet carrier. I flew it up to Prestwick from Boscombe, where I met 'Winkle' Brown who was doing similar trials on the Sea Hornet. Waiting to join the ship, I was doing practice deck landings on the

The Sea Fury, with the author at the controls, makes its first landing on HMS Ocean, on 10 August 1945, the day the Japanese asked for an armistice.

The author in the Hawker Sea Fury making the first take-off from the light Fleet Carrier HMS Ocean *(Captain Casper John, RN) on 10 August 1945. Interestingly, this Sea Fury is in standard RAF day fighter camouflage.*

aerodrome, when, while in flight, a pressure gauge in the cockpit burst, and a jet of hot hydraulic fluid squirted into my face. Instinctively I put my hand over the gauge, and small chips of glass were driven into my hand. The stream of oil soon stopped and fortunately the undercarriage had already locked down. Overnight, the Hawker engineer blanked off the pipe, and I continued flying the next day. The hydraulic gauge had been installed in the prototype for test purposes only.

Eventually, Winkle and I were ordered to rendezvous with the ship off the Mull of Kintyre. She was doing sea trials when we reached her, so we circled round watching her. She was going full speed astern, and then applying full rudder — no mean test of a rudder! Finally, she headed into wind, and with a wind speed of thirty knots over the deck, I was given the 'Land on' signal. I caught a wire and landed safely and after shutting down, I made my way to the bridge to report to Captain Caspar John. I found the whole ship in an uproar

of excitement as it had just been announced that the atom bomb had been dropped on Japan and the Japanese had just asked for an armistice. The war was over. The night was spent at Lamlash Bay, but no one had much sleep. The next morning Winkle and I continued with the trials, and by the time we had completed the scheduled six landings, we were beginning to feel the effects of the previous night's celebrations. About three in the afternoon we had finished, and flew off as the ship made her way back to the Clyde. I had just one thought, to get home to my family, so poured on the power and headed south. An hour and five minutes later, I landed at Boscombe. I was home for tea by 4.30.

Epilogue

was released from the Navy early in December 1945, and Ella and I bought a house in Surrey about 20 miles from London within commuting distance of the City, and I returned to the Stock Exchange. We were fortunate as we were left and given furniture by relations to replace ours which had been lost in the blitz. After seventeen moves during the war, it was good to have a settled home again, and we lived there for 20 years.

There were many surplus aircraft for sale in the spring of 1946. I bought a Fairey Tipsy, which had been built by the Belgian subsidiary Company before the war. Richard Muspratt (a friend from 'A' per T, who was still a test pilot with Hawkers) and I entered the Tipsy for a race at Lympne, and though we came nowhere in the race, we had a good day, meeting friends and doing some low flying. In many

ways it was a delightful aircraft of very light construction, but the 60 hp of the Walter Mikron engine was not really powerful enough to make it a practical machine, so I sold it and bought a Percival Proctor.

The Proctor was nearly new, and was similar to those used by the Fleet Air Arm at Worthy Down to train wireless operators. I never liked it, and sold it shortly afterwards, but not before Ella and I flew to Deauville, when the French Aero Club had very kindly invited members of the Royal Aero Club to a weekend rally. We stayed at the Hotel Royale, which had been Goering's headquarters during the Battle of Britain. The receptions on both evenings were held in the restaurant of the Casino, Les Ambassadeurs. We were astonished to find such luxury after the war years. The dinners were real gourmets' dreams, seven courses with appropriate wines. The women were wearing most lovely clothes, obviously the latest Paris models, and laden with jewels. We were still very heavily rationed for clothes, in fact everything, so we just stared and wondered.

Fairey Tipsy at Heston in April 1946. Left to right: *Dixon, Fairey's Chief Test Pilot, the author, and McLaren, undercarriage designer.*

The author in his DH94 Moth Minor (Gipsy Minor) at the start of an air race in 1954. (Flight)

In 1950, a friend of mine, Jack Davis lent me his Hirtenberg to compete in the *Daily Express* Challenge Trophy, a race round the south coast. This was an open two-seater, high wing, braced monoplane, but built more as a military trainer than as a private aircraft, a pleasant aircraft to fly but slightly underpowered with the 120 hp Gipsy Major. Having had my appetite whetted again, I found and bought a Moth Minor for £160.

The de Havilland Company had built the Moth Minor in 1939 when it had been commandeered by the Government at the outbreak of war. De Havillands had intended phasing out the Tiger Moth, a fifteen-year-old biplane design and were concentrating on this new monoplane as a trainer. The start of the war, however, led to an immediate demand for large numbers of trainers and as the Moth Minor was still in an early stage of development, and also fitted with the Gipsy Minor, an entirely new 90 hp engine, it was decided to concentrate on the Tiger Moth, of which thousands were ultimately built.

I liked the Moth Minor, and kept it for nine years. It was a simple clean design, economical to run with a cruising speed of about 100 mph. As it was normally flown from the front seat, the cockpit was relatively free of draught, and quiet.

I entered several Air Races during 1953 and 1954. By making a number of minor modifications to the standard Moth Minor and by preparing the engine carefully I obtained an increase in speed of the order of 4 or 5 mph. Unfortunately, these modifications were noticed by the handicappers who promptly altered my starting time after estimating that the aircraft would be 7 or 8 mph faster. The following year I removed all the visible alterations but left in

place a non-standard bulkhead between the cockpits, and another at the front of the engine cowling which gave about an extra 3 mph by sealing off air leaks. The result was that I won the Grosvenor Challenge Cup Race, and was third in the King's Cup.

Another form of competition for private aircraft was an economy and navigation exercise. This seemed in many ways more sensible than air racing, and certainly had a more practical application for the private owner. I took a lot of trouble and enjoyed preparing the Moth Minor for an event of this kind which took place at Panshangar. I gave the engine a top overhaul during the winter, taking the cylinder heads home to my workshop for polishing, completing the final tuning of the carburettor by fitting short exhaust stubs and running it at night to get the right mixture for economy from the colour of the flames from the exhaust. Over the course, which extended to about 160 miles, the aircraft averaged 28 miles to a gallon which was good enough to win the first prize of £100. Its most economic cruising speed was, however, only about 70 mph.

One evening in the summer of 1955 I was flying from Redhill to take part in another navigation competition at Cranfield. At about 2,000 feet over Great Missenden and cruising along quietly the engine suddenly lost power. The engine ran all right at a fast idle speed but coughed and spluttered on opening the throttle. There was a fair-sized field to the east of the village, but the crop had recently been

The author flew a friend's Hirtenberg H.S.9A (DH Gipsy) G–AGAK in the 1950 Daily Express Challenge Trophy, finding it pleasant to fly.

harvested and it was covered haphazardly with bales of straw. I thought I could see a straight line through these but unfortunately the field sloped slightly downhill and at the end of my run the port wing trailing edge hit a bale.

I suspected a choked main jet, which in fact it proved to be, but I had hardly opened the engine cowling when three people appeared offering help. They introduced themselves as Roald Dahl, his wife Patricia Neal and Sir Matthew Smith. At the time their names meant little to me but it is not often that one can drop out of the sky, so to speak, to be greeted by a well-known author, a glamorous film star, and a celebrated portrait painter!

The author with his Moth Minor, entered in an air race. (Flight)

The author's Moth Minor. (Flight)

The author in the cockpit of a Hawker Sea Fury. He did the type's carrier qualification trials in August 1945. (Charles E. Brown)

As they had a car they very kindly drove me into Missenden to the local cobbler where I bought some thick thread and a needle to repair the wing fabric and then on to the local farmer for me to apologise for landing in his field. On arrival the door was opened by a butler who greeted me with the news that my host was changing and would be down in a few minutes but in the meantime would I like a drink. It turned out that there was to be a party that night and the butler had mistaken me for a guest. Altogether a forced landing to be remembered.

I had kept the Moth Minor at Redhill, and after it was sold, as a member of the Redhill Tiger Club, I continued flying the club aircraft and was able to keep my licence up-to-date. In 1970, however, my licence finally lapsed, when high blood pressure put an end to my flying. I was disappointed, but I had had a good run, as I had forty-two years of active flying and more than my share of luck and excitement.

One evening recently I was walking in the grounds of the Royal Hospital Chelsea, when I heard a roar of engines, and saw Concorde for the first time. That long white delta shape of her wings, and typical nose up attitude on the approach to London Airport, filled me with pride at seeing such a beautiful aircraft, the culmination of man's efforts in my lifetime.

Appendix — Aircraft Types Flown

Date	Aircraft	Engine	Comments	Date	Aircraft	Engine	Comments
9.8.28	Avro 548	Renault 80	V-8 air-cooled	15.8.40	V-S Spitfire	R-R Merlin	Marks: IA, IIB, VA, VB, VI, VII, VIII, VIIIC, IX, IXC
9.8.28	Avro 504	Anzani	10-cylinder Radial				
6.12.28	DH Moth	Cirrus					
17.7.28	Fairchild FC1	Wright Whirlwind	Engineer	1.8.40	DH Leopard Moth	DH Gipsy	
2.8.29	Vickers Vedette		Dual	12.12.40	Fairey Battle	R-R Merlin	
24.8.29	Fairchild FC2-W2	P&W Wasp	Engineer	26.2.41	Hawker Hurricane	R-R Merlin	
6.9.29	Curtiss HS2L	Liberty	Dual	28.2.41	Grumman Martlet	Wright Cyclone	RN F4F Wildcat
10.10.29	Ireland Amphibian		Dual	26.6.41	Curtiss Mohawk	Wright Cyclone	RAF P-36
8.12.29	Lockheed Vega	P&W Wasp	Engineer	17.8.41	Fiat C.R.42	Fiat	
6.1.30	Bellanca CH300	Wright Whirlwind	Skis	5.9.41	Bristol Blenheim	Bristol Mercury	
8.2.30	Bellanca Pacemaker	Wright Whirlwind	Skis	22.11.41	Messerschmitt Bf 109E-3	Daimler-Benz DB 601Aa	
13.5.30	Bellanca Pacemaker	Wright Whirlwind	Floatplane				
9.6.34	Klemm	Salmson		8.7.42	Miles Falcon	DH Gipsy	
6.7.35	Desoutter	DH Cirrus		8.7.42	Hawker Tomtit	A.S. Mongoose	
25.7.36	DH Hornet Moth	DH Gipsy		9.7.42	Monospar	Pobjoy	
18.2.39	DH Tiger Moth	DH Gipsy		20.7.42	V-S Seafire	R-R Merlin	Marks: IB, IIC, III
28.8.39	DH Moth Minor	DH Gipsy Minor		20.7.42	V-S Seafire	R-R Griffon	Marks: XV, XVII
20.9.39	Miles Magister	DH Gipsy		6.8.42	V-S Spitfire	R-R Merlin	Pressure Cabin, Mark VI
25.9.39	Hawker Osprey	R-R Kestrel					
28.9.39	Fairey Seal	A.S. Panther		2.9.42	V-S Spitfire	R-R Griffon	Marks: XIV, XIX, XXI
3.10.39	Hawker Nimrod	R-R Kestrel					
4.10.39	Percival Vega Gull	DH Gipsy 6		6.9.42	Airspeed Oxford	A.S. Cheetah	
11.10.39	Blackburn Shark	A.S. Tiger		19.9.42	NA Mustang	R-R Merlin	RAF P-51
11.1.40	Fairey Sea Fox	Napier Dagger I	Floatplane	13.10.42	V-S Spitfire	R-R Merlin	Floatplane
19.1.40	Percival Proctor	DH Gipsy 6		17.10.42	Hawker Tornado	R-R Vulture	Contra-Propeller
20.1.40	Fairey Swordfish	Bristol Pegasus		22.11.42	V-S Spitfire	R-R Merlin	Marks: PRs X, XI
22.1.40	Blackburn Skua	Bristol Perseus		23.11.42	V-S Sea Otter	Bristol Mercury	Amphibian
8.2.40	Supermarine Walrus	Bristol Pegasus	Amphibian	15.3.43	Supermarine S24/37	R-R Merlin	
				28.4.43	Hawker Typhoon	Napier Sabre	
9.3.40	Fairey Albacore	Bristol Taurus		28.4.43	Fairey Firefly	R-R Griffon	
11.4.40	Blackburn Roc	Bristol Perseus		30.4.43	Westland Welkin	R-R Merlin	
6.5.40	Blackburn Roc	Bristol Perseus	Floatplane	4.5.43	Miles Mentor	DH Gipsy 6	
21.5.40	Fairey Fulmar	R-R Merlin		5.5.43	Curtiss Kittyhawk	Allison	RAF P-40
24.6.40	Gloster Gladiator	Bristol Pegasus		11.5.43	Republic Thunderbolt	P&W Double Wasp	RAF P-47

Date	Aircraft	Engine	Comments	Date	Aircraft	Engine	Comments
1.6.43	Fairey Barracuda	R-R Merlin 32		14.9.44	Miles Monarch	DH Gipsy Major	
13.6.43	Boeing B-17 Flying Fortress	Wright Cyclone		23.10.44	Hawker F2/43	Bristol Centaurus	Fury
14.6.43	Handley Page Halifax	R-R Merlin		30.10.44	Bristol Beaufighter	Bristol Hercules	
15.6.43	Curtiss Seamew	Ranger		19.1.45	Douglas Boston Mk IIIA	Wright Cyclone	
27.6.43	Avro Anson	A.S. Cheetah		20.1.45	Beech Traveller	P&W Wasp	
5.7.43	Boulton & Paul P.92	DH Gipsy	Turret Gun	27.2.45	Miles Messenger	DH Gipsy	
5.7.43	Grumman F6F Hellcat	Wright Cyclone		28.2.45	Grumman F7F Tiger Cat	P&W Double Wasp	
28.7.43	Stinson Reliant	Lycoming		1.3.45	DH Hornet	R-R Merlin	
5.8.43	Blackburn Firebrand	Napier Sabre III		3.3.45	Douglas Skymaster	P&W Double Wasp	
7.8.43	Vought Corsair	P&W Double Wasp	RN F4U	20.3.45	Lockheed Hudson	P&W Wasp	
27.10.43	Hawker Tempest Mk II	Bristol Centaurus		1.5.45	GAL Cygnet	Cirrus	
12.12.43	Short Stirling. Model	Pobjoy	Half-scale	17.5.45	Fieseler Fi-156 Storch	Argus	
1.1.44	Auster	Lycoming		25.5.45	Hawker Sea Fury	Bristol Centaurus	
8.1.44	DH Mosquito Mk IX	R-R Merlin 72		12.6.45	V-S Spiteful	R-R Griffon	
9.3.44	Blackburn Firebrand Mk IV	Bristol Centaurus		21.6.45	Grumman F4F Wildcat	P&W Double Wasp	
15.3.44	Gloster F.9/40	Whittle WIIb	Meteor	20.7.45	Fairey Barracuda Mk V	R-R Griffon	
26.3.44	NA Harvard	P&W Wasp		27.8.45	Grumman TBF Avenger	Wright Cyclone	
26.3.44	Handley Page Hampden	Bristol Pegasus		20.9.45	Consolidated B-24 Liberator	P&W Wasp	
22.4.44	DH E6/41	DH Halford HIb	Vampire	29.9.45	DH Dominie	DH Gipsy 6	
6.6.44	Gloster Meteor Mk III	R-R B/37		4.4.46	Fairey Tipsy	Walter Mikron	
5.7.44	Miles M.17	Gipsy		21.8.50	Hirtenberg H.S.9.A	DH Gipsy	
6.7.44	Beechcraft	P&W Wasp		11.7.62	Jodel 1050	Continental	
15.8.44	Douglas SBD Dauntless	Wright Cyclone		6.3.63	DH Puss Moth	DH Gipsy	
27.8.44	NA Mustang Mk V	Packard Merlin	RAF P-51H	10.7.63	Condor	DH Gipsy	
				12.10.63	Turbulent	Volkswagen	
				29.5.64	Jodel 150 Muscaret	Continental	
				1.6.66	Britten Norman Islander	Lycoming	
				9.2.69	Piper Tripacer	Lycoming	

Index